THE MIN

CARDIGA

**Metalliferous and Associated Minerals 1845-1913**

*Roger Burt*

*Peter Waite*

*Ray Burnley*

Published by

The Department of Economic History

University of Exeter

in association with

The Northern Mine Research Society

Other publications in this series

*The Derbyshire Mineral Statistics 1845 - 1913*

*The Yorkshire Mineral Statistics 1845 - 1913*

*The Cumberland Mineral Statistics 1845 - 1913*

*The Lancashire and Wetsmorland Mineral Statistics with the Isle of Man 1845 - 1913*

*The Durham and Northumberland Mineral Statistics 1845 - 1913*

*Devon and Somerset Mines 1845 - 1913*

ISBN 0 9507624 5 8

*Printed in Great Britain by A. Wheaton & Co. Ltd, Exeter*

# CONTENTS

# PREFACE

This is the eighth volume in our continuing series of county studies of metalliferous mining in the United Kingdom, from the mid-nineteenth century to the First World War and the first on the old counties of Wales. The series arises from a project, funded by the Social Science Research Council in the Department of Economic History at Exeter, to create a computer based data bank of material originally published in the annual volumes of *The Mineral Statistics of the United Kingdom*. We have used the facility of the computer to re-arrange this material in a mine-by-mine format and this book, like the earlier volumes for the North Pennines and the South West, has been reproduced directly from the output of a high quality printer. The data is stored in a form permitting flexible programming for the internal and cross analysis of the production, ownership, management and employment series, and readers wishing to make use of the data bank, through terminals in Exeter or elsewhere on the network, should write to the Department of Economic History, University of Exeter.

The material presented here is in a very similar form to that which appeared in the original returns, *with a minimum of editorial adjustment*. Accordingly, mine names have been adopted and spelt in the same way as they most commonly occurred in the returns made to the Mining Record Office by the original owners of the mines; information under the different headings starts and stops just as it did in the first annual publications; and no attempt has been made to merge material where the same mine was worked under different names. This latter problem is discussed in more detail in the *Introduction*. Problems caused by multiple entries for mines of the same name *but with no clear and readily apparent connection*, have been resolved by recording them as separate numbered entries in these listings, eg. Loveden Nos.1 & 2. The only important changes and new information that we have introduced relate to locations. Following the precedent first set in the Yorkshire volume, we have changed the locations given in the original returns to more appropriate current usage and have added Ordnance Survey Grid References where known. In general, however, the original data for Cardiganshire was more straightforward and easily usable than that for the northern counties and posed fewer problems of interpretation. Nevertheless, the authors would be very pleased to hear of any errors that may have crept in during these editorial adjustments or of any other major improvements that might be made so that the data bank can be amended. We would like to thank S.J.S.Hughes for his help and advice in the preparation of this volume and for supplying the Bibliography.

# INTRODUCTION

## I

## *The Mineral Statistics*

The official government collection and publication of details of the output of the British mineral industry was instituted in the 1840s under the auspices of the Geological Survey and Museum, directed by Sir Henry de la Beche. We have discussed the development of the ensuing series of annual publications, which have continued down to the present day, at some length elsewhere.[1] It is useful, however, to outline the main stages of that development. The work was conducted by the Mining Record Office, which was initially part of the Geological Survey and Museum, and was effectively the responsibility of Robert Hunt, Keeper of the Mining Records. The first published series, relating to the output of copper and lead, principally in the years 1845 to 1847, appeared in *Memoirs of the Geological Survey of Great Britain and the Museum of Practical Geology in London* Vols. I and II, (H.M.S.O. 1845 and 1847). This was regarded at the time as a limited exercise and no commitment was made for the publication of further annual series. In 1853, however, Hunt took the opportunity to update and extend these earlier series in a volume published by the Geological Survey, under his name, entitled *Records of the School of Mines and of Science Applied to the Arts,* Vol. I Pt IV. In that same year a Treasury Committee inquiring into the working of the Geological Survey and Museum reported favourably on the activities of the Mining Record Office and recommended that its activities should be placed, "on a more regular footing". This signalled the beginning of the regular collection and publication of a widening range of data relating to mineral extraction and related manufacturing and transportation.

The first of the new annual series, published under the title *Memoirs of the Geological Survey of Great Britain and of the Museum of Practical Geology: Mining Records: The Mineral Statistics of the United Kingdom of Great Britain and Ireland,* appeared in 1855 and was for the year 1853, so continuing an unbroken run for some production data, eg. lead and copper, from 1845. Thereafter the volumes were published by the Geological Survey in unbroken series until 1882, usually appearing in the autumn of the year following the record year. Robert Hunt retired following the preparation of the 1881 volume and the opportunity was taken to reorganise and consolidate the now considerably expanded range of data collection. This was done by transferring the Mining Record Office from the Museum of Practical Geology to the Home Office, where the Mine Inspectors, established by the *Coal Mine Inspection Act* of 1850, had for many years been publishing a similar range of output data in their annual reports. In particular, the *Coal* and *Metalliferous Mines Regulation Acts* of 1872 had required all active mines in the country to furnish the Mines Inspectorate with details of their output and employment and it was thought wasteful to continue the collection of voluntary returns and computations of the Mining Record Office alongside these.

The first of the new series, which was prepared by Hunt's old staff and closely followed the format of the earlier publications, appeared in 1884 under the title *The Mining and Mineral Statistics of the United Kingdom of Great Britain and Ireland for 1882* and was produced, unlike its earlier counterparts, as a Parliamentary Paper. The following year the title changed again to *Summaries of the Reports of the Inspectors of Mines to Her Majesty's Secretary of State, and the Mineral Statistics of the United Kingdom of Great Britain and Ireland, including Lists of Mines and Mineral Works* and for the years 1884 to 1887 inclusive they appeared annually as *The Mineral and Mining Statistics of The United Kingdom of Great Britain and Ireland, including Lists of Mines and Minerals Worked.* During these years the volumes included returns of a) the quantity and value of all minerals wrought b) the numbers of people employed in and about the mines and open works c) the number of fatal accidents in the mines d) a list of the mine owners, managers and agents e) a list of the recorded plans of abandoned mines that had been deposited at the Home Office f) an appendix showing the production of minerals in the British colonies and possessions.

From 1888 to 1896 the returns appeared as *The Mineral Statistics of the United Kingdom of Great Britain and Ireland with the Isle of Man* and this time the change in title was accompanied by important changes in the content. The details of accidents in the mines, previously held over from the early annual reports of the Inspectors of Mines, were dropped for separate publication, as was *The List of Mines,* a regular appendix of the names of the mine owners, agents, managers and numbers employed, which had been included at the back of *The Mineral Statistics* since 1853 for coal mines, 1859 for most metalliferous mines and 1863 for iron mines. Finally in 1897 the title and content of the annual returns were changed to a format that they were to keep through to the First World War. For that year the volume appeared under the general title *Mines and Quarries: General Report and Statistics.* It was divided into four separate sections, Part III containing details of output and being subtitled *General Report and Statistics Relating to the Output and Value of the Minerals Raised in the United Kingdom, the Amount and Value of the Metals Produced and the Exports and Imports of Minerals.*

It is notable that until 1897 the "Clerks of the Mineral Statistics", who had responsibility for preparing the publications, were still largely the same men that had worked with Robert Hunt from the earliest days of the Mining Record Office. This provided a strong element of continuity and an unparalleled wealth of experience in collecting and editing the material. Following Hunt's retirement in 1882, the new Home Office department had been jointly run by Richard Meade and James B.Jordan. Meade had originally been appointed by Hunt as early as 1841 and had been joined by Jordan in 1858. Meade retired from the Home Office in 1889 but Jordan continued until 1897, so consolidating a period of more than half a century's data gathering under three close associates.

# II

## Cardiganshire Mineral Production

Metal mining in Central Wales was heavily dominated by the production of lead and silver. In Cardiganshire, these were the only minerals produced in significant quantities until the last quarter of the nineteenth century. At that point, the mining of zinc briefly acquired some importance. The first great period of lead/silver production in the district was during the early years of the eighteenth century, under the auspices of the Mine Adventurers. Cardiganshire was in the forefront of British mining during these years and helped to lead the industry into the modern era of large-scale organisation and finance.[2] From the middle of the century, however, the mines went into decline and generally stagnated through to the second quarter of the nineteenth century. They then began a rapid revival to a second period of comparative prosperity in the fifty years from the 1830's to the 1880's. This renewed activity was based heavily on the revival of English - particularly Cornish - interest in the district and an increased inflow of capital, enterprise and technical skill.

When regularly recorded production data first began to be collected in the mid-1840's, annual *lead* output from Cardiganshire mines was around 6,000 tons of ore per annum. There was some significant but brief fall-off in the late 1840's but output generally continued to increase steadily to over 7,000 tons per annum in the early 1850's and to nearly 10,000 tons in the middle of that decade. These levels of production were comparable to those achieved in Yorkshire and Derbyshire during the same period and slightly higher than those for Cumberland during the mid-1850's. These were peak years for both the Cardiganshire and the national industry, never to be repeated. Production fell off slightly in the late 1850's but generally remained remarkably steady on a high plateau of 7-8,000 tons per annum through to the early 1870's. See Table 1. There was then a sudden major downward shift to a new lower plateau of 5-6,000 tons per annum for the remainder of that decade. It was the 1880's, however, that saw the beginnings of the real slide into extinction for the centuries-old industry. Lead ore production slumped from 6,405 tons in 1880 to just 1,666 tons in 1890 and continued ever downwards to just a few hundred tons per annum in 1900. There was then some slight recovery during the first years of the new century but output seldom amounted to even an eighth of its peak mid-century level.

Through most of the years of the mid-nineteenth century, Cardiganshire mines clearly reflected trends similar to those in the national industry as a whole. Its share of total U.K. production remained reasonably steady at between seven and nine per cent from the 1840's through to the 1880's. The smallest contribution that Cardiganshire made to national output during those years was just less than six per cent in 1847 and the highest, just over ten per cent, in 1857. This was slightly higher than the contribution from Derbyshire and Cumberland during the 1860's and 1870's and very similar to that of Yorkshire. After the early 1880's, however, Cardiganshire mines declined more sharply than the average. The county's share of output fell to less than one per cent in 1894 and never rose above two per cent until the slight revival of the mines in the new century. Even then, however, it failed to regain its earlier position as Cardiganshire mines, now largely deserted by the London mining interest, failed to respond to the new conditions with the same vigour as mines in other parts of the country - eg. Cumberland.

Notwithstanding its numerous mines - almost two hundred produced lead and silver during the second half of the nineteenth century - and the now much celebrated status of some of the larger producers, Cardiganshire never saw any of the very large-scale operations which dominated many other districts. For example, there was no Cardiganshire equivalent of Van mine in neighbouring Montgomeryshire, Mill Close in Derbyshire, Wiregill in Durham, Greenside in Westmorland, or Foxdale in the Isle of Man. During the period from the mid-nineteenth century, Frongoch was the largest single lead producer in the county, with a total output of around 35,000 tons of lead and silver ore between 1852 and 1901. This compared with something over 32,000 tons of ore from Cwmystwyth 1845 to 1913 and almost 25,000 tons from East Darren 1859 to 1901. No other mines produced more than 20,000 tons of lead ore during the period and only three - Goginan, East Logylas and Cwmerfin - had a total output of much in excess of 10,000 tons. In a national context, all were essentially moderate sized ventures. Instead of the usual picture of the output of the district being dominated by a handful of very large producers, marginally supported by an army of very small-scale operations - as in Derbyshire and the Isle of Man, for example - in Cardiganshire there was a far more widely based distribution of production. The five largest mines in the county were together responsible for considerably less than 50 per cent of the county's total output, compared with the 90 per cent domination achieved by Foxdale and Laxey in the Isle of Man and Greenside mine in Westmorland. In Cardiganshire, the 40 or so medium sized mines, producing a total of between 500 and 10,000 tons of lead ore each, were responsible for over a third of the county's output, giving a breadth of production rarely paralleled in the Pennine mining districts.

One of the main reasons for the strength of medium and small-scale mining in Cardiganshire is probably to be found in the relatively shallow mineralisation of the district and the facility which the heavily broken terrain offered for low cost/low capital horizontal adit mining. The main lodes could be easily opened and worked for most of their length by simple horizontal "drift" type operations, generally requiring relatively little expensive dead work or deep pumping operations.[3] There were accordingly few direct technical insentives for consolidation and large-scale operations. The returns to scale were smaller than in mines working many of the richer deposits of the other districts. This is partly illustrated by the productivity of labour. For example, the 45 men employed at the relatively small Bronfloyd mine near Penrhyncoch in 1880 achieved an annual output of ore valued at £43.50 each, which was closely similar to the £42.60 achieved at Frongoch during the same year, with a total labour force of 294 men. These figures compare well with the £37.70 per miner at Old Gang mine in Yorkshire in 1880 - a mine of similar size and depth - but fall far below the £90.30 achieved at the much larger Greenside mine in Cumberland in that year and the £98.40 at Foxdale in the Isle of Man.

With little to be gained from the technical or physical integration of workings, the best route to large-scale mining operations was through the combined holding of a number of independent ventures. This was common in several of the north Pennine districts, where the London Lead Company and the Blackett-Beaumonts, among others, owned and operated a large number of separate enterprises under a central consolidated management. In Cardiganshire this was achieved on the Lisburne estates, where a number of the county's largest mines were centrally managed for many years. The largest of these mines were Frongoch, the Logylas, Glogfach and Glogfawr, which together were responsible for over one third of Cardiganshire's total lead output during the period. Much of their success was no doubt due to the astute management of the internationally famous John Taylor and Sons partnership, which had control of them for many years around the mid-century.

During the first period of prosperity in the early eighteenth century, Cardiganshire lead mines enjoyed a great reputation for their very high *silver* content. It had been the struggles of Sir Carbery Pryse to retain control of the silver-rich deposits on his Gogerddan estates that lead to the end of the pre-emptive "Terror of the Mines Royal" in the 1690's and mines like Esgair Hir and Esgair Ffraith became popularly known as the Welsh Potosi.[4] However, by the mid-nineteenth century, though still producing tens of thousands of ounces of silver per year, the most argentiferous ores appear to have been exhausted. For most of the period through to the First World War, Cardiganshire's share of total U.K. silver production was closely similar to its share of total lead output, suggesting a very "average" performance. Indeed, through to the early 1870's, the county's share of national silver production was marginally lower than its share of lead output. It performed slightly better during the remainder of the early 1880's but this was more the result of a rapid falling-off in production elsewhere than any great revival of its own fortunes. From the early 1890's, silver production in the county slumped with falling lead output and rose significantly above 10,000 oz per annum only in the two years 1909 and 1910. See Table 2. Silver production had undoubtedly been an important supplement to the major mineral, lead, in the overall economics of Cardiganshire mining but it failed to be found in sufficiently large quantities to check the decline of mining during the last decades of the century.

What silver could not do for the ailing mining industry, *zinc* production almost did. The production of zinc had become of importance in Cardiganshire as early as the mid-century. At that time almost a dozen lead and silver mines supplemented their income with an output of zinc ore which, in one year, amounted to almost a fifth of total national output. However, buoyant lead and silver prices did not strongly encourage interest in this secondary mineral and when the output from the two largest producers - Nantycreiau and Rheidol United - fell off, zinc production in the county dwindled into insignificance for most of the 1860's and 1870's. This situation was sharply reversed from the early 1880's. Rapidly falling lead prices now focused attention on every possible source of income and an increasingly large number of mines began to extract whatever zinc ores they could find. The county's total output had reached nearly 4,500 tons of zinc ore per annum by 1888 and it again ranked as a major British supplier - far more important than it had ever been as a lead/silver producer. See Table 3. The two largest lead/silver mines - Frongoch and Cwmystwyth - also emerged as the main zinc producers, closely supported in most years by Brynyrafr. Frongoch was easily the largest single zinc mine, with a total output of around 50,000 tons of ore, valued at almost £170,000, 44 per cent of total Cardiganshire production and made it one of the largest zinc mines in the country. Cwmystwyth came only a distant second, with something over 18,000 tons of ore, valued at around £20,000. In both cases, however, zinc production was essential to the survival of these major lead/silver mines from the late 1870's. In terms of value of product, Frongoch was clearly primarily a zinc mine after 1880 and Cwmystwyth after 1884. In 1890, when these two mines were still responsible for more than 20 per cent of Cardiganshire lead/silver output, Frongoch drew 86 per cent of its total income from the sale of zinc ore and Cwmystwyth over 64 per cent.

Although zinc production undoubtedly played a major role in slowing the rapid slide in Cardiganshire lead and silver production during the 1880's, it proved unable to continue this role through the 1890's and the early years of the new century. Those mines that had no commercially viable zinc deposits generally closed down and the remainder concentrated increasingly on zinc at the expense of other ores. There was some consequent loss of zinc output with the failure of the marginal lead/zinc producers but output generally remained high. In 1903, zinc production in the county stood at almost the same peak level as that achieved in 1888, supplying nearly 18 per cent of total U.K. output. New producers, such as Ystumtuen, Castell and a revived Cwmystwyth, replaced some of the earlier leaders and the county continued as a major zinc mining area up to the end of the first decade of the new century. At that point the few remaining mines began to reduce their ouput sharply and the county's total production plummeted to just a few hundred tons in the years immediately preceeding the First World War.

The production of *copper* in Cardiganshire seldom achieved any real commercial significance. Although the mineral was widely occuring in the county - over 30 mines sold ore at some point during the period - total output never amounted to more than a few hundred tons per annum. The county certainly never rivalled the major producers in the South West of England and like other marginal areas - such as Yorkshire, Cumberland and the Isle of Man - it had no appreciable effect on total market supply. The most important mines in the county were Cambrian and South Darren, which were responsible for nearly three quarters of total output. Cambrian was primarily a copper mine during the late 1870's and early 1880's, with some minor lead/silver production, while South Darren was predominantly a lead producer throughout. Copper made a very important contribution to South Darren's total income during the 1860's and 1870's, however, and as late as the early 1880's it was still responsible for around 20 per cent of the mine's ore sales. Only three other mines sold copper in any quantity - Cardigan Consols, Esgair Ffraith and Ystrad Einion - and they all derived most of their income from this mineral during the period.

# III

## *The Mine Tables*

The information which appears in the following tables is the same as that published in the annual editions of the *Mineral Statistics*, now re-arranged in a mine-by-mine format. Some editorial judgement has been exercised in re-compiling the material, in order to link returns together and provide for necessary cross-referencing, but wherever possible the mine names, production record, ownership, management, employment and even comments are given just as they appeared in the original. If any category of information is missing under a mine name, or if the series cover only a few years, or indeed if an entire entry is not included, it is because there were no returns in the *Mineral Statistics*.

A problem that has occured in earlier volumes in this series and which has also been apparent here, is that of the random transfer of returns for some mines between neighbouring counties. The original *Mineral Statistics* may have incorrectly located some of the production returns for up to 44 mines in Cardiganshire. Almost certainly 11 mines listed under Cardiganshire were Montgomeryshire mines, five were Flintshire mines, three Caernarvonshire's, one Radnorshire's and one Pembrokeshire's. At least 23 other workings mentioned in the original returns have no known location in Cardiganshire and may in fact be located in other counties. Equally, it is to be expected that some of the returns for Cardiganshire mines were mistakenly entered under other counties, particularly neighbouring Montgomeryshire. In some early volumes we tried to correct these problems by transferring the relevant material between counties but here, in the interests of the faithful reproduction of the original and acknowledging the possibility of our own error, we have left them unchanged. We have, however, attempted to indicate the relevant entries in the text and they are as follows:

Montgomeryshire mines incorrectly located in the Cardiganshire returns

| | |
|---|---|
| Bryntail | Cwmfron |
| Brynyfedwen | Foel Fawr |
| Caelan | Nanty |
| Caelan, North | Severn |
| Caelan, South | Snow Brook |
| Craigymwn | |

Cardiganshire mines incorrectly located in the Montgomeryshire returns

| | |
|---|---|
| Llawrcwmbach | Penycefn |
| Pantmawr | Van, Great West |

Flintshire mines incorrectly located in the Cardiganshire returns

| | |
|---|---|
| Bryngwiog | Pantygo, West |
| Chwarel Las | Penrhynwddu |
| Fronfawnog | |

Cardiganshire mines incorrectly located in the Flintshire returns

| | |
|---|---|
| Clara | Level Newydd |

Caernarvonshire mines incorrectly located in the Cardiganshire returns

| | |
|---|---|
| Coedmawrpool | Tanybwlch |
| Penrhyngwn | |

Pembrokeshire and Radnorshire mines incorrectly located in the Cardiganshire returns

| | |
|---|---|
| Dalrhiw | Llanfyrnach |

It is hoped that on completion of this series it will be possible to publish a full calendar of mislocated returns and to adjust the county totals tables accordingly. Not all entries for all of these mines were wrongly located. Some of the returns were under the correct county.

The only new material that has been added to the *Mine Tables* is some additional cross-referencing information, the adjustment of some locations for current usage, and Ordnance Survey Grid Reference figures. We are particularly grateful to Simon Hughes for his considerable help and advice in this respect. He has also kindly provided us with a wide range of editorial suggestions for re-arranging the Mine Tables. Unfortunately, we have not felt able to embody them in the text because of our policy of staying as close as possible to the original format. These suggestions are published in full, however, in the Appendix to this Introduction.

Four principal categories of information are included in the Mine Tables. *Production* data is given by type of mineral produced and often includes ore output, metal content, and value - the latter sometimes being calculated by assay and average market price. The absence of detailed production returns under a particular mine name should not necessarily be taken to imply that the mine was not working in those years, since its output might be disguised in the county aggregate figures, sundries or joint returns listed under other mines. Wherever possible we have tried to indicate such listings through cross references in the *Comment* section. Similarly, it has sometimes been possible to use the copper production comment section to indicate the method of sale of that ore; the sales being at the Swansea ticketings (S), or by private contract (P). The returns for the production of the different minerals on a mine-by-mine basis began to appear from different dates: lead from 1845; copper from 1845; silver from 1852; and zinc from 1854. In the early years there was undoubtedly some under-recording and the number of the mines included in the annual listings usually increased noticeably during the first few years of recording.[5]

*Ownership* and *Management* returns often give a good indication of the years of activity at a mine. Drawn from *The List of Mines*, appended to the back of the early *Mineral Statistics*, they are not available for non-ferrous mines before 1859 or for iron mines before 1863. These annual *Lists* were said to include the names and addresses of the owners and agents of all mines that were working during the year. However, careful examination of them reveals that major revisions were periodically conducted when unusually large numbers of mines suddenly disappeared. This suggests that they were not carefully edited for every edition and that they therefore continued to include some mines long after they had been abandoned. The *Employment* returns were also drawn from the *List of Mines* and provide a further check on the periods, level and type of activity at the mines. For example, a mine that was prospecting or developing might show significant levels of employment even though there was little or no production or sales of ore.

Similarly, a changing distribution of workers between underground and surface operations can give an idea of when ventures began to run down their mining operations and concentrate only on the redressing of spoil heaps. It should be remembered that many of the smaller mines at best provided only part-time employment for their labour force and that the same miners may have been counted several times over at different workings. The decision to publish detailed employment returns appears to have been left to the discretion of the local Mine Inspectors and started at different times for different districts. For most Cardiganshire mines, however, this was at the relatively early date of 1877.

## Footnotes

[1] See R.Burt and P.Waite, "An Introduction to the Mineral Statistics of the United Kingdom" Northern Mine Research Society, *British Mining* No.23 (1983) 40-58

[2] W.J.Lewis, *Lead Mining in Wales* (Cardiff,1967)

[3] S.J.S.Hughes, *The Cwmystwyth Mines* (Northern Mine Research Society, British Mining No.17, 1981)

[4] M.Palmer, *The Richest in all Wales: The Welsh Potosi or Esgair Hir and Esgair Ffraith Lead and Copper Mines of Cardiganshire* (Northern Mine Research Society, British Mining No.22, 1983)

[5] See R.Burt, "The Mineral Statistics of the United Kingdom: An Analysis of the Accuracy of the Copper and Tin Returns for Cornwall and Devon" *Journal of the Trevithick Society* No.8 (1981) 31-46

# APPENDIX

*Mines working similar or closely associated sites and synonyms for the same site*
(Communicated by S.J.S.Hughes - Mining Services).


Abbey Consols and Bronberllan, Florida, Strata Florida.
Aberystwyth and Bwlchgwyn, Llwynteify, Nanteos, Nanteos Consols,
    Penrhiw, Temple, Tynyfron & Ystumtuen.
Alltycrib and Blaencaelan, Cardigan, North, Talybont & Cwm Leri.
Alltycrib, North, Ty Hen & Cwm Leri.
Alltycrib, West and Tanyrallt.
Blaencaelan and Alltycrib, Cardigan, North & Talybont.
Blaendyffryn and Nantyrarian, Silver Brook & Silver Stream.
Bodcoll and Gertrude.
Bog and Craignant Bach, Darren, & Gogerddan Mines.
Bog, New and Bog, South, Llancynfelin, Llanganfelin, Ynys & Cardigan
    Old Bog.
Bog, South and Bog, New, Llancynfelin, Llanganfelin, Ynys & Cardigan
    Old Bog.
Bronberllan and Abbey Consols, Florida & Strata Florida.
Bronfloyd and Llechwydden.
Brongwyn and Bronmwyn.
Bronmwyn and Brongwyn.
Brynarian and Cardigan Bay Consols, Silver Bank, Silver Mountain &
    Taliesin.
Brynyrafr, North and Camdwrbach, Cambrian, New & Cambrian, South.
Brynystwyth and Grogwinion.
Bwlch Consols and Bwlch United & Bwlchcwmerfin.
Bwlch United and Bwlch Consols & Bwlchcwmerfin.
Bwlchcwmerfin and Bwlch Consols & Bwlch United.
Bwlchgwyn and Aberystwyth, Llwynteify, Nanteos, Nanteos Consols,
    Penrhiw, Temple, Tynyfron & Ystumtuen.
Caegynon and Glanrheidol United & Gogerddan Mines.
Cambrian and Esgair Ffraith.
Cambrian, New and Brynyrafr, North, Cambrian, South & Camdwrbach.
Cambrian, South and Brynyrafr, North, Cambrian, New & Camdwrbach.
Camdwrbach and Brynyrafr, North, Cambrian, New & Cambrian, South.
Cardigan Bay Consols and Brynarian, Silver Bank, Silver Mountain &
    Taliesin.
Cardigan Consols and Esgair Hir & Welsh Potosi.
Cardigan Old Bog and Bog, South, Bog, New, Llancynfelin, Llanganfelin &
    Ynys.
Cardigan, North and Alltycrib, Blaencaelan & Talybont.

Castell and Castell, Dyffryn & Glan Castell.
Castell, Dyffryn and Castell & Glan Castell.
Cefngwirion and Ynys Tudor.
Clara and Llywernog United, Ponterwyd & Powell.
Court Grange and Penycefn.
Craignant Bach and Bog, Darren & Gogerddan Mines.
Cwmerfin, West and Goginan, West, Melindwr & Bronllangwrda.
Cwmsebon and Darren, South & Thomas United.
Cwmsymlog and Darren, East.
Cwmsymlog, West and Gwaithyrafon.
Cwmystwyth and Kingside & May.
Cwmystwyth, South and Ystwyth.
Darren and Bog, Craignant Bach, & Gogerddan Mines.
Darren, East and Cwmsymlog.
Darren, South and Cwmsebon & Thomas United.
Ddu and Esgair Ddu.
De Broke and Dolwen, Mynach Vale & Tygwyn.
Devil's Bridge and Ella, Hendre, Hendrefelen & Lisburne, West.
Dolclettwr and Llainhir.
Dolgoch and Penforrddgoch & Ystrad Einion.
Dolwen and De Broke, Mynach Vale & Tygwyn.
Drisgol and Royal Mines.
Ella and Devil's Bridge, Hendre, Hendrefelen & Lisburne, West.
Erglodd and Penpompren, Penybontpren, Penny Bank & Loveden No.1.
Erwtoman and Foxpath, Gwaithcoch, Pantmawr, Penclayen & Rheidol
    United.
Esgair Ddu and Ddu.
Esgair Ffraith and Cambrian.
Esgair Hir and Cardigan Consols & Welsh Potosi.
Esgair Lle, West and Van Great, West.
Florida and Abbey Consols, Strata Florida & Bronberllan.
Foxpath and Erwtoman, Gwaithcoch, Pantmawr, Penclayen & Rheidol
    United.
Frongoch, West and Wemys.
Gertrude and Bodcoll.
Glan Castell and Castell & Castell, Dyffryn.
Glandovey and Loveden No.2 & Penrhyn Gerwen.
Glanrheidol United and Caegynon & Gogerddan Mines.
Gogerddan Mines and Bog, Caegynon, Craignant Bach, Darren &
    Glanrheidol United.
Goginan, West and Cwmerfin, West, Melindwr & Bronllangwrda.
Graigcoch and Red Rock.
Grogwinion and Brynystwyth.
Grogwinion, North and Pantanhirion.
Gwaithcoch and Erwtoman, Foxpath, Pantmawr, Penclayen & Rheidol
    United.

Gwaithyrafon and Cwmsymlog, West.

Havan and Henfwlch.

Hendre and Devil's Bridge, Ella, Hendrefelen & Lisburne, West.

Hendrefelen and Devil's Bridge, Ella, Hendre & Lisburne, West.

Henfwlch and Havan.

Kingside and Cwmystwyth & May.

Leri Valley and Lerry, Pendinas & Pendmas.

Lerry and Leri Valley, Pendinas & Pendmas.

Lisburne, New and Lisburne, South.

Lisburne, South and Lisburne, New.

Lisburne, West and Devil's Bridge, Ella, Hendre & Hendrefelen.

Llainhir and Dolclettwr.

Llancynfelin and Bog, New, Bog, South, Cardigan Old Bog, Llanganfelin &
   Ynys.

Llanganfelin and Bog, New, Bog, South, Cardigan Old Bog, Llancynfelin &
   Ynys.

Llechwedhelig and Willow Bank.

Llechwydden and Bronfloyd.

Llettyhen and Vaughan.

Llwynmalees and Swyddffynon.

Llwynteify and Aberystwyth, Bwlchgwyn, Nanteos, Nanteos Consols,
   Penrhiw, Temple, Tynyfron & Ystumtuen.

Llywernog United and Clara, Ponterwyd & Powell.

Loveden No.1 and Penny Bank, Penpompren, Penybontpren & Erglodd.

Loveden No.2 and Penrhyn Gerwen & Glandovey.

May and Cwmystwyth & Kingside.

Melindwr and Bronllangwrda, Cwmerfin, West & Goginan, West.

Mynach Vale and De Broke & Dolwen & Tygwyn.

Nanteos and Aberystwyth, Bwlchgwyn, Llwynteify, Nanteos Consols,
   Penrhiw, Temple, Tynyfron & Ystumtuen.

Nanteos Consols and Aberystwyth, Bwlchgwyn, Llwynteify, Nanteos,
   Penrhiw, Temple, Tynyfron & Ystumtuen.

Nantyrarian and Blaendyffryn, Silver Brook & Silver Stream.

Pantanhirion and Grogwinion, North.

Pantmawr and Erwtoman, Foxpath, Gwaithcoch, Penclayen & Rheidol
   United.

Penclayen and Erwtoman, Foxpath, Gwaithcoch, Pantmawr & Rheidol
   United.

Pendinas and Leri Valley, Lerry & Pendmas.

Pendmas and Leri Valley, Lerry & Pendinas.

Penforrddgoch and Dolgoch & Ystrad Einon.

Penny Bank and Loveden No.1, Penpompren, Penybontpren, Erglodd.

Penpompren and Penybontpren, Erglodd & Penny Bank.

Penrhiw and Aberystwyth, Bwlchgwyn, Llwynteify, Nanteos, Nanteos
   Consols, Temple, Tynyfron & Ystumtuen.

Penrhyn Gerwen and Loveden No.2 & Glandovey.

Penybontpren and Penpompren, Erglodd, Penny Bank & Loveden No.1.
Penycefn and Court Grange.
Ponterwyd and Clara, Llywernog United & Powell.
Powell and Clara, Llywernog United & Ponterwyd.
Red Rock and Graigcoch.
Rheidol United and Erwtoman, Foxpath, Gwaithcoch, Pantmawr & Penclayen.
Royal Mines and Drisgol.
Silver Bank and Brynarian, Cardigan Bay Consols, Silver Mountain & Taliesin.
Silver Brook and Blaendyffryn, Nantyrarian & Silver Stream.
Silver Mountain and Brynarian, Cardigan Bay Consols, Silver Bank & Taliesin.
Silver Stream and Blaendyffryn, Nantyrarian & Silver Brook.
Strata Florida and Abbey Consols, Bronberllan & Florida.
Swyddffynon and Llwynmalees.
Taliesin and Brynarian, Cardigan Bay Consols, Silver Bank & Silver Mountain.
Talybont and Alltycrib, Blaencaelan & Cardigan, North.
Tanyrallt and Alltycrib, West.
Temple and Aberystwyth, Bwlchgwyn, Llwynteify, Nanteos, Nanteos Consols, Penrhiw, Tynyfron & Ystumtuen.
Thomas United and Cwmsebon & Darren, South.
Tygwyn and Dolwen, DeBroke & Mynach Vale.
Tynyfron and Aberystwyth, Bwlchgwyn, Llwynteify, Nanteos, Nanteos Consols, Penrhiw, Temple & Ystumtuen.
Ty Hen and Alltycrib, North.
Van, Great West and Esgair Lle, West.
Vaughan and Llettyhen.
Welsh Potosi and Cardigan Consols & Esgair Hir.
Wemys and Frongoch, West.
Willow Bank and Llechwedhelig.
Ynys and Bog, New, Bog, South, Cardigan Old Bog, Llancynfelin & Llanganfelin.
Ynys Tudor and Cefngwirion.
Ystrad Einon and Dolgoch & Penforrddgoch.
Ystumtuen and Aberystwyth, Bwlchgwyn, Llwynteify, Nanteos, Nanteos Consols, Penrhiw, Temple & Tynyfron.
Ystwyth and Cwmystwyth, South.

# Table 1

## Cardiganshire lead ore production and its share of total U.K. output 1845 to 1913

| Year | Card'n Ore(ton) | U.K. Ore(ton) | %UK Ore | Year | Card'n Ore(ton) | U.K. Ore(ton) | %UK Ore |
|------|------|------|------|------|------|------|------|
| 1845 | 5,726 | 78,267 | 7.32 | 1880 | 6,405 | 72,245 | 8.87 |
| 1846 | 5,719 | 74,551 | 7.67 | 1881 | 4,598 | 64,702 | 7.11 |
| 1847 | 4,899 | 83,747 | 5.85 | 1882 | 4,037 | 65,002 | 6.21 |
| 1848 | 4,882 | 78,944 | 6.18 | 1883 | 2,979 | 50,980 | 5.84 |
| 1849 | 5,989 | 86,823 | 6.90 | 1884 | 2,293 | 54,485 | 4.21 |
| 1850 | 6,698 | 92,958 | 7.21 | 1885 | 2,072 | 51,302 | 4.04 |
| 1851 | 7,183 | 92,312 | 7.78 | 1886 | 1,744 | 53,420 | 3.26 |
| 1852 | 7,370 | 91,198 | 8.08 | 1887 | 2,123 | 51,563 | 4.12 |
| 1853 | 6,553 | 85,043 | 7.71 | 1888 | 1,974 | 51,259 | 3.85 |
| 1854 | 7,034 | 90,554 | 7.77 | 1889 | 1,862 | 48,465 | 3.84 |
| 1855 | 7,043 | 92,038 | 7.65 | 1890 | 1,666 | 45,651 | 3.65 |
| 1856 | 8,560 | 101,998 | 8.39 | 1891 | 2,150 | 43,859 | 4.90 |
| 1857 | 9,914 | 96,820 | 10.24 | 1892 | 1,345 | 40,024 | 3.36 |
| 1858 | 7,087 | 95,856 | 7.39 | 1893 | 843 | 40,808 | 2.07 |
| 1859 | 7,467 | 91,382 | 8.17 | 1894 | 323 | 40,599 | 0.80 |
| 1860 | 7,355 | 88,791 | 8.28 | 1895 | 700 | 38,412 | 1.82 |
| 1861 | 7,755 | 90,666 | 8.55 | 1896 | 553 | 41,069 | 1.35 |
| 1862 | 8,300 | 95,312 | 8.71 | 1897 | 422 | 35,338 | 1.19 |
| 1863 | 7,132 | 91,283 | 7.81 | 1898 | 625 | 32,985 | 1.89 |
| 1864 | 7,464 | 94,463 | 7.90 | 1899 | 598 | 30,999 | 1.93 |
| 1865 | 7,835 | 90,452 | 8.66 | 1900 | 584 | 32,010 | 1.82 |
| 1866 | 7,700 | 91,048 | 8.46 | 1901 | 1,090 | 27,976 | 3.90 |
| 1867 | 7,839 | 93,432 | 8.39 | 1902 | 1,314 | 24,606 | 5.34 |
| 1868 | 7,231 | 95,236 | 7.59 | 1903 | 1,823 | 26,567 | 6.86 |
| 1869 | 8,180 | 96,866 | 8.44 | 1904 | 911 | 26,374 | 3.45 |
| 1870 | 7,307 | 98,177 | 7.44 | 1905 | 1,062 | 27,649 | 3.84 |
| 1871 | 7,553 | 93,965 | 8.04 | 1906 | 1,021 | 30,795 | 3.32 |
| 1872 | 6,764 | 81,619 | 8.29 | 1907 | 987 | 32,533 | 3.03 |
| 1873 | 5,373 | 73,500 | 7.31 | 1908 | 891 | 29,249 | 3.05 |
| 1874 | 5,423 | 76,202 | 7.12 | 1909 | 1,273 | 29,744 | 4.28 |
| 1875 | 5,835 | 77,746 | 7.51 | 1910 | 1,736 | 28,534 | 6.08 |
| 1876 | 5,962 | 79,096 | 7.54 | 1911 | 1,368 | 23,910 | 5.72 |
| 1877 | 5,850 | 80,850 | 7.24 | 1912 | 998 | 25,409 | 3.93 |
| 1878 | 6,801 | 77,351 | 8.79 | 1913 | 1,335 | 24,282 | 5.50 |
| 1879 | 5,080 | 66,877 | 7.60 | | | | |
| | | | | Total | 296,568 | 4,408,228 | 6.73 |

# Table 2

## Cardiganshire silver ore production and its share of total U.K. output 1851 to 1913

| Year | Card'n Ore (ozs) | U.K. Ore (ozs) | %UK Ore | Year | Card'n Ore (ozs) | U.K. Ore (ozs) | %UK Ore |
|------|------|------|------|------|------|------|------|
| 1851 | 52,380 | 674,458 | 7.77 | 1883 | 30,615 | 344,053 | 8.90 |
| 1852 | 91,680 | 818,325 | 11.20 | 1884 | 22,551 | 325,718 | 6.92 |
| 1853 | 60,000 | 700,000 | 8.57 | 1885 | 19,954 | 320,520 | 6.23 |
| 1854 | 33,418 | 562,659 | 5.94 | 1886 | 13,966 | 325,427 | 4.29 |
| 1855 | 28,079 | 561,906 | 5.00 | 1887 | 11,694 | 320,345 | 3.65 |
| 1856 | 38,751 | 614,188 | 6.31 | 1888 | 11,064 | 321,425 | 3.44 |
| 1857 | 37,097 | 532,866 | 6.96 | 1889 | 10,263 | 306,149 | 3.35 |
| 1858 | 41,100 | 569,345 | 7.22 | 1890 | 9,739 | 291,724 | 3.34 |
| 1859 | 37,787 | 576,027 | 6.56 | 1891 | 14,731 | 279,792 | 5.26 |
| 1860 | 44,807 | 549,720 | 8.15 | 1892 | 12,662 | 271,259 | 4.67 |
| 1861 | 54,989 | 569,530 | 9.66 | 1893 | 4,250 | 274,100 | 1.55 |
| 1862 | 62,678 | 686,123 | 9.14 | 1894 | 63 | 275,696 | 0.02 |
| 1863 | 58,846 | 634,004 | 9.28 | 1895 | 3,737 | 280,434 | 1.33 |
| 1864 | 46,486 | 641,088 | 7.25 | 1896 | 4,202 | 283,826 | 1.48 |
| 1865 | 54,617 | 724,856 | 7.53 | 1897 | 635 | 249,156 | 0.25 |
| 1866 | 61,455 | 636,688 | 9.65 | 1898 | 3,199 | 211,403 | 1.51 |
| 1867 | 63,113 | 805,394 | 7.84 | 1899 | 1,496 | 191,927 | 0.78 |
| 1868 | 67,502 | 841,328 | 8.02 | 1900 | 1,440 | 187,842 | 0.77 |
| 1869 | 66,145 | 831,891 | 7.95 | 1901 | 2,862 | 178,324 | 1.60 |
| 1870 | 56,553 | 784,562 | 7.21 | 1902 | 3,904 | 145,873 | 2.68 |
| 1871 | 46,980 | 761,490 | 6.17 | 1903 | 7,921 | 152,855 | 5.18 |
| 1872 | 41,690 | 628,920 | 6.63 | 1904 | 6,150 | 141,592 | 4.34 |
| 1873 | 39,869 | 524,307 | 7.60 | 1905 | 9,236 | 163,399 | 5.65 |
| 1874 | 41,047 | 509,277 | 8.06 | 1906 | 10,272 | 147,647 | 6.96 |
| 1875 | 46,624 | 487,358 | 9.57 | 1907 | 9,299 | 150,521 | 6.18 |
| 1876 | 45,418 | 483,422 | 9.40 | 1908 | 9,934 | 135,154 | 7.35 |
| 1877 | 47,284 | 497,375 | 9.51 | 1909 | 15,389 | 142,006 | 10.84 |
| 1878 | 49,028 | 397,471 | 12.33 | 1910 | 17,579 | 136,192 | 12.91 |
| 1879 | 42,770 | 333,674 | 12.82 | 1911 | 10,672 | 118,395 | 9.01 |
| 1880 | 49,445 | 295,518 | 16.73 | 1912 | 6,076 | 118,540 | 5.13 |
| 1881 | 28,755 | 308,398 | 9.32 | 1913 | 11,544 | 128,154 | 9.01 |
| 1882 | 29,626 | 372,449 | 7.95 | | | | |
| | | | | Total | 1,863,118 | 25,834,065 | 7.21 |

The Cardiganshire county silver production figures for the years 1851 to 1853 included the output of mines in Caernarvonshire and Carmarthenshire.

# Table 3

## Cardiganshire zinc ore production and its share of total U.K. output 1856 to 1913

| Year | Card'n Ore(ton) | U.K. Ore(ton) | %UK Ore | Year | Card'n Ore(ton) | U.K. Ore(ton) | %UK Ore |
|------|------|------|------|------|------|------|------|
| 1856 | 1,097 | 9,004 | 12.18 | 1885 | 3,273 | 24,668 | 13.27 |
| 1857 | 1,371 | 9,290 | 14.76 | 1886 | 3,423 | 23,156 | 14.78 |
| 1858 | 1,612 | 11,556 | 13.95 | 1887 | 3,460 | 25,445 | 13.60 |
| 1859 | 2,590 | 13,039 | 19.86 | 1888 | 4,492 | 26,408 | 17.01 |
| 1860 | 2,231 | 15,553 | 14.34 | 1889 | 3,787 | 23,202 | 16.32 |
| 1861 | 1,808 | 15,770 | 11.46 | 1890 | 3,734 | 22,041 | 16.94 |
| 1862 | 336 | 7,498 | 4.48 | 1891 | 3,741 | 22,216 | 16.84 |
| 1863 | 757 | 13,699 | 5.53 | 1892 | 2,442 | 23,880 | 10.23 |
| 1864 | 794 | 15,232 | 5.21 | 1893 | 2,688 | 23,754 | 11.32 |
| 1865 | 715 | 17,843 | 4.01 | 1894 | 3,033 | 21,821 | 13.90 |
| 1866 | 116 | 12,770 | 0.91 | 1895 | 2,562 | 17,478 | 14.66 |
| 1867 | 223 | 13,489 | 1.65 | 1896 | 2,246 | 19,319 | 11.63 |
| 1868 | 77 | 12,782 | 0.60 | 1897 | 1,844 | 19,278 | 9.57 |
| 1869 | 70 | 15,533 | 0.45 | 1898 | 3,328 | 23,552 | 14.13 |
| 1870 | 212 | 13,586 | 1.56 | 1899 | 1,819 | 23,135 | 7.86 |
| 1871 | 630 | 17,736 | 3.55 | 1900 | 1,718 | 24,675 | 6.96 |
| 1872 | 1,604 | 18,543 | 8.65 | 1901 | 2,596 | 23,752 | 10.93 |
| 1873 | 431 | 15,969 | 2.70 | 1902 | 3,618 | 25,060 | 14.44 |
| 1874 | 326 | 16,830 | 1.94 | 1903 | 4,425 | 24,888 | 17.78 |
| 1875 | 50 | 23,978 | 0.21 | 1904 | 3,644 | 27,655 | 13.18 |
| 1876 | 263 | 23,613 | 1.11 | 1905 | 3,810 | 23,909 | 15.94 |
| 1877 | 588 | 24,406 | 2.41 | 1906 | 2,772 | 22,824 | 12.15 |
| 1878 | 505 | 25,438 | 1.99 | 1907 | 2,316 | 20,082 | 11.53 |
| 1879 | 526 | 22,200 | 2.37 | 1908 | 2,491 | 15,225 | 16.36 |
| 1880 | 2,630 | 27,548 | 9.55 | 1909 | 1,395 | 9,902 | 14.09 |
| 1881 | 3,453 | 35,527 | 9.72 | 1910 | 952 | 11,238 | 8.47 |
| 1882 | 3,543 | 32,539 | 10.89 | 1911 | 1,116 | 17,652 | 6.32 |
| 1883 | 3,546 | 29,728 | 11.93 | 1912 | 778 | 17,704 | 4.39 |
| 1884 | 3,712 | 25,563 | 14.52 | 1913 | 678 | 17,294 | 3.92 |
| | | | | Total | 113,997 | 1,157,475 | 9.85 |

# Table 4

## Cardiganshire copper ore production and its share of total U.K. output 1845 to 1904

| Year | Card'n Ore(ton) | U.K. Ore(ton) | %UK Ore | Year | Card'n Ore(ton) | U.K. Ore(ton) | %UK Ore |
|---|---|---|---|---|---|---|---|
| 1845 | 26 | 184,740 | 0.01 | 1875 | 79 | 71,528 | 0.11 |
| 1846 | 35 | 169,568 | 0.02 | 1876 | 42 | 79,252 | 0.05 |
| 1847 | 12 | 171,104 | 0.01 | 1877 | 127 | 73,141 | 0.17 |
| 1848 | - | 147,701 | 0.00 | 1878 | 306 | 56,094 | 0.55 |
| 1849 | - | 155,025 | 0.00 | 1879 | 474 | 51,032 | 0.93 |
| 1850 | - | 150,380 | 0.00 | 1880 | 617 | 52,128 | 1.18 |
| 1851 | - | 165,593 | 0.00 | 1881 | 287 | 52,556 | 0.55 |
| 1852 | - | 181,944 | 0.00 | 1882 | 494 | 52,237 | 0.95 |
| 1853 | - | 186,007 | 0.00 | 1883 | 465 | 46,820 | 0.99 |
| 1854 | - | 186,008 | 0.00 | 1884 | 100 | 42,149 | 0.24 |
| 1855 | 95 | 207,770 | 0.05 | 1885 | 81 | 36,379 | 0.22 |
| 1856 | 67 | 260,669 | 0.03 | 1886 | 62 | 18,617 | 0.33 |
| 1857 | 155 | 218,689 | 0.07 | 1887 | 22 | 9,359 | 0.24 |
| 1858 | 46 | 226,852 | 0.02 | 1888 | 29 | 15,550 | 0.19 |
| 1859 | 35 | 236,789 | 0.01 | 1889 | 20 | 9,310 | 0.21 |
| 1860 | 76 | 236,696 | 0.03 | 1890 | 33 | 12,481 | 0.26 |
| 1861 | 68 | 231,487 | 0.03 | 1891 | 5 | 9,158 | 0.05 |
| 1862 | 185 | 224,171 | 0.08 | 1892 | 19 | 6,265 | 0.30 |
| 1863 | 266 | 210,947 | 0.13 | 1893 | 5 | 5,576 | 0.09 |
| 1864 | 300 | 214,604 | 0.14 | 1894 | - | 5,994 | 0.00 |
| 1865 | 300 | 198,298 | 0.15 | 1895 | - | 7,791 | 0.00 |
| 1866 | 223 | 180,378 | 0.12 | 1896 | 20 | 9,168 | 0.22 |
| 1867 | 155 | 158,544 | 0.10 | 1897 | 20 | 7,352 | 0.27 |
| 1868 | 123 | 157,335 | 0.08 | 1898 | - | 9,131 | 0.00 |
| 1869 | 132 | 129,953 | 0.10 | 1899 | - | 8,319 | 0.00 |
| 1870 | 117 | 106,698 | 0.11 | 1900 | 20 | 9,488 | 0.21 |
| 1871 | 114 | 97,129 | 0.12 | 1901 | 46 | 6,792 | 0.68 |
| 1872 | 17 | 91,893 | 0.02 | 1902 | 65 | 6,112 | 1.06 |
| 1873 | 71 | 80,189 | 0.09 | 1903 | 49 | 6,867 | 0.71 |
| 1874 | 93 | 78,521 | 0.12 | 1904 | 21 | 5,465 | 0.38 |
| | | | | Total | 6,219 | 6,027,793 | 0.10 |

The figures for 1878 to 1881 do not take account of the sales of ore at Swansea.

# BIBLIOGRAPHY

## I *Books*

Adams, D. 1970 *Survey of Llaymynech Ogo Mine.* Shropshire Mining Club

Agricola, G. 1556 *De Re Metallica.*

Arundell, W. 1864 *Law relating to Mines in Great Britain.*

Bevan, CWL. 1980 *Ogofau Gold Mine.* University of Wales.

Bevan-Evans, M. 1960 *Royal Mines in North Wales.* Flints. Hist. Soc. Vol.18
   No.19.

Bick, DE. 1978 *Old Metals Mines of Mid Wales.* 5 Vols. Private.

Bick, DE. 1975 *Dylife.* Private.

Bird, RH. 1974 *Britains Old Metal Mines.* Barton.

Bird, RH. 1977 *Yesterday's Golcondas.* Moorland.

Bonner, DE. 1909 *Gweithfeydd Mwyn Ceredigon.* Cymru Vol.36.

Bushell, T. 1642 *A Just & True Remonstrance Etc.* Thos Barker.

Bushell, T. 1649 *The Case of Thomas Bushell.*

Camden, W. 1586 *Brittania.*

Carpenter, K. 1923 *Cardiganshire Lead Mines.* Aber. Studies. Vol.5.

Cocks & Walters. 1968 *Zinc Smelting Industry in Britain.* Private.

Collins, HF. 1900 *The Metallurgy of Lead.* Griffin.

Collins, HF. 1922 *The Metallurgy of Silver.* Griffin.

Crawford, H. 1979 *Subterranean Britain.* Baker.

Darlington & Phillips. 1857 *Records of Mining & Metallurgy.*

Davies, DC. 1892 *Earthy Minerals & Mining.* Crosby Lockwood.

Davies, DC. 1887 *Slate & Slate Quarrying.* Crosby Lockwood.

Davies, DC. 1880 *Metalliferous Minerals & Mining.* Crosby Lockwood.

Davies, EH. 1892 *Machinery for Metalliferous Mines.* Crosby Lockwood.

Davies, G. 1964 *Minera.* Private.

Davies, JH. 1906 *The Morris Letters.* Oxford.

Davies, O. 1935 *Roman Mines in Europe.* Oxford.

Davies, W. 1815 *Agriculture of South Wales.* Agriculture Board. 2 Vols.

Davies, W. 1810 *The Agriculture of North Wales.* Agriculture Board.

Davies, WJK. 1964 *The Vale of Rheidol Light Railway.* Ian Allan.

Edwards, IO. 1929 *The Star Chamber Proceedings Relating to Wales.*

Foster, C. 1879 *The Van Mine.* Trans. Royal. Geol. Soc. of Cornwall. Vol.10 p33
   1887.

Francis, A. 1874 *History of the Cardiganshire Mines.* Morgan.

Glynn, J. 1870 *The Power of Water.*

Guy, J. 1976 *History of Rudry.* Private.

Hamer, E. 1873 *Parochial Account of Llanidloes.* Private.

Healy, JF. 1978 *Mining & Metallurgy in the Greek & Roman World.* Thames &
   Hudson.

Hughes, SJS. 1976 *Cardiganshire: Its Mines & Miners*. Private.
Hughes, SJS. 1981 *Cwmystwyth Mines*. NMRS. BM 17
Hunt, R. 1848 *Notices of the History of the Mines of Cardiganshire*. Geol. Survey.

Hunt, R. 1884 *British Mining*. Crosby Lockwood.
Institution of Mining and Metallurgy. 1959 *The Future of Non Ferrous Mining*. IMM.
Jones, EW. 1963 *Ar Llethrau Ffair Rhos*. Cambrian News.
Jones, JA & Moreton N. 1977 *Mines & Minerals of Mid Wales*. Private
Jones, OT. 1921 *Lead & Zinc*. HMSO. Special Reports on Mineral Resources. Vol.XX.
Le Neve Foster, C. 1901 *Ore & Stone Mining*. Griffin.
Lewis, S. 1833 *A Topographical Atlas of Wales*.
Lewis, WJ. 1967 *Lead Mining In Wales*. University of Wales.
Leyland, J. 1536 *Itinerary in Wales*.
Liscombe, A. 1880 *Mines of Cardiganshire, Montgomeryshire & Shropshire*.
Mackworth, H. 1710 *Book of Vouchers*. Parts 1 & 2. Private.
Mackworth, H. 1698 *The Mine Adventure*. Private.
Mackworth, H. 1700 *A Familiar Discourse*. Private.
Mackworth, H. 1701 *State of the Mines at Esgairhir*. Private.
Mackworth, H. 1704 *Affidavits in the Mine Adventure*. Private.
Mackworth, H. 1705 *The Case of Humphrey Mackworth*. Private.
Mackworth, H. 1706 *The Case of Humphrey Mackworth & the Adventure*. Private.
Mackworth, H. 1710 *State of the Case of the Mine Adventure*. Private.
Metcalfe, JE. 1969 *British Mining Fields*. Institution of Mining and Metallurgy.
Meyrick, SR. 1808 *History of Cardiganshire*. Private.
North, FJ. 1962 *Mining For Metals in Wales*. National Museum of Wales.
Percy, J. 1861 *The Art of Extracting Metals from their Ores*.
Percy, J. 1865 *The Metallurgy of Lead*.
Pettus, J. 1670 *Fodinae Regales*. Private.
Pettus, J. 1683 *Fleta Minor*.
Raistrick, A. 1967 *The Hatchet Diary*. Barton.
Ray, J. 1662 *Itinerary to Ray's Proverbs*.
Rees, DM. 1969 *Mines Mills & Furnaces*. HMSO.
Rees, W. 1968 *Industry before the Revolution*. University of Wales. 2 Vols.
Richardson, JB. 1974 *Metal Mining*. Allen-Lane.
Saer, DJ. 1910 *Cardiganshire*.
Smythe, WW. 1848 *Mining District of Cardiganshire & Montgomeryshire*. Geol Survey.
Spargo, T. 1870 *Mines of Wales*. Private.
Stringer, M. 1699 *English & Welsh Mines & Minerals*.
Stringer, M. 1713 *Opera Mineralia Explicata*.
Thomas, TM. 1961 *Mineral Wealth of Wales & Its Exploitation*.
Tylecote, RF. 1962 *Metallurgy in Archaeology*.
Wade, EA. 1976 *The Plynlimon & Hafan Tramway*. Gemini.

Waller, W. 1698 *An Account of the Cardiganshire Mines*. Private.
Waller, W. 1710 *Answer to Mr Hawkins's Report*. Private.
Waller, W. 1698 *An Essay on the Value of the Mines*.
Waller, W. 1700 *The Present State of the Mines*.
Waller, W. 1699 *Some Account of Mines*.
Waller, W. 1709 *Mines of Esgairhir*.
Waller, W. 1714 *The Case of William Waller*.
Waller, W. 1699 *Maps & Accounts of Mines in Cardiganshire*.
Waller, W. 1700 *A Familiar Discourse re the Mine Adventure*.
Williams, CJ. 1980 *Metal Mines of North Wales*. Charter Press.
Williams, JG. 1866 *Account of British Camps in Cardiganshire*. Private.
Wren, WJ. 1968 *The Tannat Valley*. David & Charles.

## II *Articles and Short Publications*

Anon. 1975 Bryndyfi Mine. *Shropshire Mining Club.*
Anon. 1859 Darren Mine. *Arch Camb.* ff.349.
Anon. 1866 Darren Mine. *Arch Camb.* ff.544.
Anon. 1857 Dylife Mine. *Arch Camb.* ff.171.
Anon. 1873 Roman Mining Roads. *Arch Camb.* ff.121.
Anwyl. 1906 Mining. *Arch Camb.* ff.93.
Benjamin, EA. 1981 Cwmrheidol. *Ceredigion.* Vol.9 No.2 ff.128.
Bick, DE. 1978 Remnants of Mining. *Ceredigion.* Vol.8 No.3 ff.355.
Boon & Williams. 1966 Dolaucothi Drainage Wheel. *J Roman Studies.*
Boynes, RE. 1977 Bryndyfi Mine. *Ceredigion.* Vol.8 No.2 ff.210.
Boynes, T. 1976 Mines of Llywernog. *National Library of Wales Jour.* Vol.19 No.4 ff.430.
Brown, M. 1969 Methodism in Aberystwyth. *Cambrian News.*
Collins, RS. 1975 *Min. Res. Cons. Com.* Gold. HMSO.
Collins, RS. 1972 *Min. Res. Cons. Com.* Barytes. HMSO.
Davies, O. 1947 Cwmystwyth Mines. *Arch Camb.* ff.57.
Davies, O. 1936 Prehistoric Mining in Wales. *Journal of the British Association.*
Davies, W. 1933 Aberystwyth Conference. *National Union of Teachers.*
Davies, WH 1961. Romans in Cardiganshire. *Ceredigion.* Vol.4 No.2 ff.85.
Foster Smith, J. 1977 Mines of Anglesey & Caernarvon. *NMRS.* BM 4.
Foster Smith, J. 1977 Mines of Meirioneth. *NMRS.* BM 6.
Foster Smith, J. 1978 Mines of Radnorshire & Montgomeryshire. *NMRS.* BM 10.
Foster Smith, J. 1978 Mines of Cardiganshire. *NMRS.* BM 12.
Foster Smith, J. 1981 Mines of South Wales. *NMRS.* BM 18.
Hall, GW. 1971 Metal Mines of South Wales. *Private.*
Hall, GW. 1972 Decline of Mining. *Ceredigion.* Vol.7 No.1 ff.85.
Hall, GW. 1975 Goldmining in Meirioneth. *Private.*
Holman, BW. 1911 Gold at Dolaucothi. *Mining Magazine.* ff.374.

Hughes, SJS. 1979 The Kehrrad. *Industrial Archaeology.* Vol.13 No.3. ff.196.
Hughes, SJS. 1980 Pumping Engines. *Industrial Archaeology.* Vol.15 No.3 ff.236.
Hughes, SJS. 1981 Mines of Talybont Part I. *Industrial Archaeology.* Vol.16 No.3 ff.199.
Hughes, SJS. 1982 Mines of Talybont Part II. *Industrial Archaeology.* Vol.16 No.4 ff.290.
Hughes, SJS. 1981 Bwlchglas Mines. *Industrial Archaeology.* Vol.16 No.2 ff.126.
Hughes, SJS. 1979 Mining at Cwmystwyth. *Ceredigion.* Vol.8 No.4.
Hughes, SJS. 1971 Mid Wales Mines. *Journal Brit. Spel. Assoc.* Vol.6 No.46 ff.23.

Jenkins, R. 1932 Thompson's Tour of the Mines. *Trans. Newcomen Soc.*
Jones & Lewis. 1971 Dolaucothi Gold Mines. *Carmarthenshire Co.* Museum. Pub No.1.
Lewis, ET. 1972 Llanfyrnach. *Private.*
Lewis, MTJ. 1970 Early Wooden Railways. *RK&P.*
Lewis, WJ. 1951 Some Aspects of Mining. *Ceredigion.* Vol.1 No.2 ff.176.
Morrision, TA. 1971 Van Mines. *Industrial Archaeology.*
Morrison, TA. 1976 Mining Settlements. *Industrial Archaeology.* Vol.10 No.2. D&C.
Morrison, TA 1975 Goldmining. Merion. *Hist. Res. Soc.*
Nelson, TRH. 1944 Gold Mining in South Wales. *Mine & Quarry Engineering.*
Palmer, M. 1983 Richest in all Wales. *NMRS.* BM 22.
Ridgeway, JM. 1983 *Min. Res. Cons. Com.* Silver. HMSO.
Sayce. 1921 Celtic & Goidelic Mining. *Trans. Hon. Soc. Cymrodorion.*
Shaw & Critchley. 1978 Caegynon & Rheidol Utd. Mines. *PDMHS Bull.* Vol.7 No.2.
Various. 1967 *Shrops. Min. Club. Yearbook.*
Various. 1978 A Glimpse of the Past. *Wales Tourist Board.*
Williams, CJ. 1979 Llandudno Copper Mines. *NMRS.* BM 9.
Williams, CJ. 1972 Llandudno Copper Mines. *Caernarvon. Hist. Soc. Trans.*
Wright, FS. 1920 Celtic & Goidelic Mining. *Aberystwyth Studies.* Vol.2.

NMRS = Northern Mine Research Society.
PDMHS = Peak District Mines Historical Society.

# Tables of Mine

# Production

# Ownership

# Management

# and Employment

ABBEY CONSOLS  STRATA FLORIDA  SN 744662 0001

Production: Lead & Silver

| | Ore(tons) | Lead(tons) | Silver(ozs) | Value(£) |
|---|---|---|---|---|
| 1856 | 121.90 | 81.00 | 0.00 | 0.00 |
| 1857 | 97.60 | 76.00 | 426.00 | 0.00 |
| 1858 | 84.00 | 66.60 | 175.00 | 0.00 |
| 1859 | 95.50 | 66.00 | 74.00 | 0.00 |
| 1860 | 47.20 | 32.50 | 58.00 | 0.00 |
| 1861 | 20.00 | 14.00 | 112.00 | 0.00 |
| 1908 | 24.00 | 18.00 | 0.00 | 161.00 |
| 1909 | 76.00 | 51.00 | 304.00 | 526.00 |

Zinc

| | Ore(tons) | Metal(tons) | Value(£) |
|---|---|---|---|
| 1857 | 14.20 | 0.00 | 42.30 |
| 1908 | 10.00 | 3.00 | 40.00 |
| 1909 | 17.00 | 5.00 | 70.00 |

Ownership: 1859–1865 WM.BATTYE & CO.; 1907–1911 ST.JAMES' SYNDICATE
LTD.; 1912–1913 CAMBRIAN LEAD & ZINC MINING CO.LTD.
Comment 1863–1865 SUSPENDED
Management: Chief Agent 1859–1862 NICH.BRAY; 1907–1913 THOS.EDWARDS
Employment:

| | Underground | Surface | Total |
|---|---|---|---|
| 1908 | 17 | 15 | 32 |
| 1909 | 22 | 11 | 33 |
| 1910 | 10 | 2 | 12 |
| 1911 | 5 | 1 | 6 |
| 1912 | | 2 | 2 |
| 1913 | | 1 | 1 |


ABERNANT  RHEIDOL VALLEY  SN 685786 0002

Production: Lead No detailed return
Ownership: 1861–1865 ABERNANT MINING CO.
Comment 1864–1865 SUSPENDED
Management: Chief Agent 1861–1865 RICH.WILLIAMS


ABERYFFRWYDD  RHEIDOL VALLEY  SN 689787 0003

Production: Lead & Silver

| | Ore(tons) | Lead(tons) | Silver(ozs) | Value(£) |
|---|---|---|---|---|
| 1850 | 11.00 | 8.40 | 0.00 | 0.00 |
| 1851–1852 No detailed return | | | | |
| 1854 | 20.00 | 15.20 | 0.00 | 0.00 |
| 1855 | 66.00 | 44.00 | 200.00 | 0.00 |
| 1856 | 40.60 | 26.20 | 120.00 | 0.00 |
| 1857 | 60.00 | 45.50 | 0.00 | 0.00 |
| 1858 | 39.00 | 29.10 | 0.00 | 0.00 |
| 1859–1861 No detailed return | | | | |

Copper

| | Ore(tons) | Metal(tons) | Value(£) |
|---|---|---|---|
| 1857 | 5.10 | 0.00 | 0.00 |

Comment 1857 (P) ABERFFROOD
Ownership: 1859–1860 KING STEPHENS
Comment 1859–1860 ABERYFFRWD
Management: Chief Agent 1859–1860 GEO.GREEN


ABERYSTWYTH  PONTERWYD  SN 736787 0004

Production: Lead & Silver

| | Ore(tons) | Lead(tons) | Silver(ozs) | Value(£) |
|---|---|---|---|---|
| 1848 | 20.00 | 10.00 | 0.00 | 0.00 |
| 1849 | 31.00 | 20.00 | 0.00 | 0.00 |
| 1850 | 5.50 | 3.50 | 0.00 | 0.00 |
| 1872 | No detailed return | | | |
| 1873 | 50.00 | 39.50 | 0.00 | 0.00 |
| 1874 | 50.30 | 36.00 | 186.00 | 0.00 |
| 1875 | 30.00 | 22.00 | 120.00 | 0.00 |

| Lead & Silver | Ore(tons) | Lead(tons) | Silver(ozs) | Value(£) |
|---|---|---|---|---|
| 1877 | 16.40 | 11.50 | 0.00 | 205.00 |
| 1878 | 30.00 | 21.70 | 0.00 | 270.00 |
| 1879 | 14.00 | 9.60 | 0.00 | 143.70 |
| 1880 | 25.90 | 19.50 | 0.00 | 250.00 |
| 1881 | 40.00 | 30.00 | 0.00 | 380.50 |
| 1882 | 15.00 | 12.00 | 0.00 | 105.00 |

Comment 1848–1850 SMALL MINES

| Zinc | Ore(tons) | Metal(tons) | Value(£) |
|---|---|---|---|
| 1882 | 8.00 | 3.50 | 19.00 |

Ownership: 1875–1884 ABERYSTWYTH MINING CO.
Comment 1884 SUSPENDED
Management: Manager 1875–1876 JOHN TREVETHAN
Chief Agent 1877–1884 JOHN H.CROUCHER
Secretary 1882 ? BUCKLAND

| Employment: | Underground | Surface | Total |
|---|---|---|---|
| 1877 | 13 | 4 | 17 |
| 1878 | 6 | 4 | 10 |
| 1879 | 9 | 2 | 11 |
| 1880 | 8 | 5 | 13 |
| 1881 | 5 | 6 | 11 |
| 1882 | 4 | 3 | 7 |
| 1883 | 2 | | 2 |

ALLTYCRIB                    TALYBONT                    SN 650895 0005

| Production: Lead & Silver | Ore(tons) | Lead(tons) | Silver(ozs) | Value(£) |
|---|---|---|---|---|
| 1851 | 166.90 | 218.00 | 0.00 | 0.00 |
| 1852 | 64.00 | 42.50 | 0.00 | 0.00 |
| 1853–1854 No detailed return | | | | |
| 1858 | 11.70 | 8.50 | 0.00 | 0.00 |
| 1859 | No detailed return | | | |
| 1860 | 77.40 | 49.50 | 304.00 | 0.00 |
| 1861 | 64.00 | 50.00 | 400.00 | 0.00 |
| 1862 | 30.20 | 22.00 | 200.00 | 0.00 |
| 1863 | 44.50 | 33.30 | 0.00 | 0.00 |
| 1864 | 9.60 | 7.20 | 0.00 | 0.00 |
| 1865 | 9.60 | 7.20 | 0.00 | 0.00 |
| 1866 | No detailed return | | | |
| 1870 | 60.00 | 43.00 | 500.00 | 0.00 |
| 1871 | 20.00 | 14.00 | 143.00 | 0.00 |
| 1872 | 173.60 | 157.20 | 1605.00 | 0.00 |
| 1873 | 60.00 | 43.50 | 450.00 | 0.00 |
| 1907 | 1.00 | 1.00 | 36.00 | 12.00 |
| 1911 | 5.00 | 3.00 | 33.00 | 39.00 |
| 1912 | 10.00 | 7.00 | 65.00 | 79.00 |
| 1913 | 32.00 | 21.00 | 225.00 | 357.00 |

Comment 1911 LEAD EST

| Zinc | Ore(tons) | Metal(tons) | Value(£) |
|---|---|---|---|
| 1873 | 10.00 | 0.00 | 25.00 |

Comment 1873 ALTY CRIB
Ownership: 1859–1865 J.H.MURCHISON & CO.; 1868–1877 ALLTYCRIB CO.; 1881
NORTH CARDIGANSHIRE LEAD MINING CO.LTD; 1899 ALLTYCRIB MINING
CO.; 1900–1904 JAS. & ED.EVANS; 1907–1909 DAVID WILLIAMS;
1910 TALYBONT LEAD MINES; 1911–1913 TALYBONT LEAD MINES LTD.
Comment 1881 FORMERLY TALYBONT; 1882 SEE NORTH CARDIGAN;
1886–1890 SEE TALYBONT; 1897–1898 SEE TALYBONT; 1903–1904 NOT
WORKED
Management: Chief Agent 1859–1865 JOHN HUGHES; 1868–1871 GEO.GREEN;
1872–1877 JAS.LEEDHAM; 1881 JNO.PELL; 1899–1904 ED.EVANS

| Employment: | Underground | Surface | Total |
|---|---|---|---|
| 1881 | 22 | 9 | 31 |

ALLTYCRIB                         TALYBONT                        Continued

|           | Underground | Surface | Total |
|-----------|-------------|---------|-------|
| 1899      | 4           |         | 4     |
| 1900—1902 | 2           |         | 2     |
| 1907      | 2           |         | 2     |
| 1908      | 6           | 2       | 8     |
| 1909      | 2           |         | 2     |
| 1910      | 6           |         | 6     |
| 1911      | 12          | 3       | 15    |
| 1912      | 16          | 2       | 18    |
| 1913      | 25          |         | 25    |

ALLTYCRIB,NORTH                   TALYBONT                        SN 645895 0006

| Production: Lead & Silver | Ore(tons) | Lead(tons) | Silver(ozs) | Value(£) |
|---------------------------|-----------|------------|-------------|----------|
| 1871                      | 10.00     | 7.50       | 88.00       | 0.00     |
| 1872                      | 140.00    | 102.00     | 1155.00     | 0.00     |

Management: Chief Agent 1870—1871 CHAS.WILLIAMS


ALLTYCRIB,WEST                    TALYBONT                        SN 652902 0007

Production: Lead No detailed return
Ownership:  Comment 1873—1877 SEE TANYRALLT


ALLT FEDW                        LLANFIHANGEL                               0008

| Production: Zinc | Ore(tons) | Metal(tons) | Value(£) |
|------------------|-----------|-------------|----------|
| 1884             | No detailed return |    |          |

Comment 1884 ALT FEOW, SEE BLAENCENNANT


ALLT GOCH                         TALYBONT                        SN 639883 0009

Production: Lead No detailed return
Ownership:  1880 RICH.GILBERTSON; 1881 C.HERB.STOKES
            Comment 1881 INC.FRONGOCH
Management: Manager 1881 C.HERB.STOKES
            Chief Agent 1880 JOHN HUGHES

| Employment: | Underground | Surface | Total |
|-------------|-------------|---------|-------|
| 1880        | 2           |         | 2     |
| 1881        | 4           |         | 4     |


BARAMORE                                                                   0010

| Production: Lead | Ore(tons) | Metal(tons) | Value(£) |
|------------------|-----------|-------------|----------|
| 1851             | 38.00     | 28.00       | 0.00     |


BLAEN                                                                      0011

| Production: Lead | Ore(tons) | Metal(tons) | Value(£) |
|------------------|-----------|-------------|----------|
| 1871             | 277.00    | 207.70      | 0.00     |
| 1872             | No detailed return |    |          |


BLAENCAELAN                       TALYBONT                        SN 715905 0012

| Production: Lead | Ore(tons) | Metal(tons) | Value(£) |
|------------------|-----------|-------------|----------|
| 1855             | 1.50      | 1.00        | 0.00     |
| 1856—1857        | No detailed return |   |          |

MC—C

| Lead | Ore(tons) | Metal(tons) | Value(£) |
|---|---|---|---|
| 1865 | 7.60 | 5.70 | 0.00 |
| 1866 | No detailed return | | |
| 1871 | 250.00 | 185.00 | 0.00 |
| 1872 | 80.00 | 55.00 | 0.00 |
| 1873 | No detailed return | | |
| 1879 | 24.00 | 18.00 | 247.00 |
| 1880 | 41.00 | 30.80 | 395.00 |
| 1881 | 27.10 | 21.60 | 234.00 |
| 1882 | 7.30 | 5.30 | 59.00 |

Comment 1855–1857 BLAENCILAN; 1865–1866 OR WELSH POTOSI; 1882 BLAEN CAELAN UNITED

| Copper | Ore(tons) | Metal(tons) | Value(£) |
|---|---|---|---|
| 1865 | 9.30 | 0.20 | 60.20 |
| 1881 | 7.00 | 0.50 | 24.50 |
| 1882 | 2.30 | 0.10 | 2.00 |

Comment 1865 (P) BLAENCILLAN–COPPER EST.; 1881 (P); 1882 (P) BLAENCAELAN UNITED

Ownership: 1863–1866 GEO.PELL & CO.; 1868 BLAENCAELAN CO.; 1869 GEO.PELL & J.B.BALCOMBE; 1870–1871 BLAENCAELAN CO.; 1873 BLAENCAELAN CO.; 1878 BLAENCAELAN MINING CO.LTD.; 1880–1885 BLAENCAELAN UNITED LEAD MINING CO.LTD.; 1886–1887 C.O.ROGERS
Comment 1863–1866 OR WELSH POTOSI; 1868 OR WELSH POTOSI; 1871 BLAENCAELAN CONSOLIDATED; 1884 STOPPED JULY 1884; 1885–1887 SUSPENDED

Management: Manager 1870–1871 J.B.BALCOMBE; 1873 J.B.BALCOMBE; 1881 JNO.PELL
Chief Agent 1863–1866 HY.TYACK; 1868–1869 JAS.WILLIAMS; 1870 JOHN EVANS; 1871 THOS.KEMP; 1873 JAS.DUNKIN; 1878 JNO.GILL; 1880 JNO.PELL; 1881 RICH.JONES; 1882–1883 JNO.PELL; 1884 RICH.JONES
Secretary 1881 A.W.SNELLING (S)

Employment:

| | Underground | Surface | Total |
|---|---|---|---|
| 1878 | 12 | 4 | 16 |
| 1879 | 16 | 8 | 24 |
| 1880 | 19 | 10 | 29 |
| 1881 | 8 | 6 | 14 |
| 1882 | 6 | 6 | 12 |
| 1883 | 6 | | 6 |
| 1884 | 4 | 2 | 6 |


BLAENCENNANT           LLANFIHANGEL           SN 690770 0013

Production:

| Lead | Ore(tons) | Metal(tons) | Value(£) |
|---|---|---|---|
| 1870 | 27.00 | 19.50 | 0.00 |
| 1871 | 10.00 | 7.00 | 0.00 |
| 1872 | 11.50 | 8.60 | 0.00 |
| 1873 | 8.00 | 6.00 | 0.00 |
| 1876 | 9.00 | 6.70 | 117.00 |
| 1877 | 7.00 | 5.20 | 87.50 |

| Zinc | Ore(tons) | Metal(tons) | Value(£) |
|---|---|---|---|
| 1871 | 10.00 | 0.00 | 37.50 |
| 1873 | 5.00 | 0.00 | 12.50 |
| 1874 | No detailed return | | |
| 1876 | 34.00 | 0.00 | 170.00 |
| 1884 | 10.00 | 0.00 | 30.00 |
| 1885 | 3.00 | 1.00 | 6.00 |

Comment 1873 BLAENCANANT; 1884 INC.ALLT FEDW; 1885 BLAEN UNITED

Ownership: 1872 BLAENCENNANT CO.; 1875–1881 ROBT.SMITH; 1884–1887 BLAEN UNITED MINING CO.LTD.
Comment 1872 BLAENCAENANT; 1885–1887 BLAEN UNITED :

BLAENCENNANT             LLANFIHANGEL            Continued

SUSPENDED
Management: Manager 1872 J.B.BALCOMBE
Chief Agent 1872 JAS.DUNKIN; 1875—1881 GEO.WRIGHT; 1884—1887
HUGH J.JONES

Employment:

| | Underground | Surface | Total |
|---|---|---|---|
| 1877 | 2 | 3 | 5 |
| 1884 | 9 | 10 | 19 |

BLAENDYFFRYN             GOGINAN            0014

Production: Lead No detailed return
Ownership: 1863—1867 ROBT.NORTHEY & CO.; 1868—1875 BLAENDYFFRYN MINING
CO.LTD.
Management: Manager 1868—1871 WM.BATTYE; 1872—1874 ROBT.NORTHEY
Chief Agent 1863—1871 ROBT.NORTHEY; 1875 NICH.BRAY

BODCOLL             DEVIL'S BRIDGE        SN 757768 0015

Production:

| Lead | Ore(tons) | Metal(tons) | Value(£) |
|---|---|---|---|
| 1870 | 10.00 | 7.00 | 0.00 |
| 1874 | No detailed return | | |

Comment 1870 BODCOTE; 1874 SEE GERTRUDE
Ownership: 1870—1871 ROBT.GIRDWOOD & CO.; 1890—1892 CARDIGAN
CONSOLIDATED LEAD MINING CO.; 1893 THOS.W.WARD
Comment 1872 SEE GERTRUDE; 1876 SEE GERTRUDE; 1890 STARTED
OCT.1890; 1892—1893 SUSPENDED
Management: Manager 1870—1871 ROBT.NORTHEY
Chief Agent 1870—1871 GEO.GREEN; 1890—1892 WM.MITCHELL

Employment:

| | Underground | Surface | Total |
|---|---|---|---|
| 1890 | | 2 | 2 |
| 1891 | 2 | | 2 |

BOG             PONTERWYD            SN 739815 0017

Production:

| Lead | Ore(tons) | Metal(tons) | Value(£) |
|---|---|---|---|
| 1847 | No detailed return | | |
| 1849 | No detailed return | | |
| 1853 | 5.00 | 3.70 | 0.00 |
| 1858 | 68.00 | 50.00 | 0.00 |
| 1871 | 120.00 | 92.00 | 0.00 |
| 1872 | 155.00 | 120.00 | 0.00 |
| 1873 | 250.00 | 193.00 | 0.00 |

Comment 1847 SEE GOGERDDAN MINES

| Zinc | Ore(tons) | Metal(tons) | Value(£) |
|---|---|---|---|
| 1857 | 12.50 | 0.00 | 40.00 |
| 1871 | 130.00 | 0.00 | 452.50 |
| 1872 | 560.00 | 0.00 | 2826.00 |

Comment 1857 NORTH WALES; 1871—1872 ORE & WASTE TOTALLED

BOG,NEW             TRERDDOL            SN 650920 0018

Production:

| Lead | Ore(tons) | Metal(tons) | Value(£) |
|---|---|---|---|
| 1887 | 5.75 | 4.00 | 43.00 |
| 1888 | 0.25 | 0.00 | 2.00 |
| Zinc | Ore(tons) | Metal(tons) | Value(£) |
| 1887 | 5.00 | 2.00 | 15.00 |
| 1888 | 1.00 | 0.30 | 1.50 |

Ownership: 1887—1888 DOLCLETTWR & LLAINHIR MINING CO.LTD.
Management: Chief Agent 1887—1888 J.H.CLINT

BOG,NEW                         TRERDDOL                    Continued

Employment:              Underground      Surface      Total
              1887            7              7           14
              1888            6              2            8


BOG,SOUTH                       TRERDDOL                              0019

Production: Lead No detailed return
Ownership:  1859—1860 J.HANMER & CO.
Management: Chief Agent 1859—1860 JAS.KEMP


BRONBERLLAN                  PONTRHYDFENDIGAID              SN 733670 0020

Production: Lead              Ore(tons) Metal(tons)    Value(£)
              1848              15.00       7.00         0.00
              1849       No detailed return
              1852               4.20       3.10         0.00
              1853—1854 No detailed return


BRONFLOYD                     PENRHYNCOCH                  SN 660835 0021

Production: Lead & Silver     Ore(tons)  Lead(tons) Silver(ozs)    Value(£)
              1851              12.00      11.00        0.00          0.00
              1852              10.00       7.50       70.00          0.00
              1853—1854 No detailed return
              1855               5.40       1.80        0.00          0.00
              1856               1.20       0.30        0.00          0.00
              1857              10.60       9.20       93.00          0.00
              1858             115.00      83.50      800.00          0.00
              1859             202.00     152.00     1520.00          0.00
              1860             115.00      88.00      880.00          0.00
              1861              55.00      41.00      410.00          0.00
              1862             235.00     182.00     1460.00          0.00
              1863             355.00     287.50     2152.00          0.00
              1864             337.30     253.30     1518.00          0.00
              1865             411.70     288.00     1644.00          0.00
              1866             334.30     247.40        0.00          0.00
              1867             374.00     279.90        0.00       4900.60
              1868             482.00     326.40      500.00       6024.50
              1869             533.00     362.00     1086.00          0.00
              1870             549.30     411.50     5490.00          0.00
              1871             550.00     412.00     1236.00          0.00
              1872             170.00     127.50     1785.00          0.00
              1873       No detailed return
              1874             184.00     125.00     1750.00       2810.40
              1875             100.00      75.00     1394.00          0.00
              1876             286.00     177.00     3292.00          0.00
              1877             240.00     180.00     3240.00       3240.00
              1878             150.00     117.70     1995.00       1762.40
              1879              45.00      33.00      462.00        470.40
              1880             140.00     109.50     1365.00       1960.00
              1881             135.00     102.00     1250.00       1478.50
              1882              43.00      34.40      515.00        473.00
              1883              80.00      64.00     1200.00        931.00
              1884               4.00       0.00        0.00         29.00
              1886              36.00      27.00      353.00        340.00
              1887              33.00      25.00      289.00        309.00
              1888              24.00      18.00      260.00        223.00
              1891              21.00      15.00        0.00        167.00
              1892              14.00      11.00      123.00         90.00
       Comment 1866—1867 LEAD EST.; CORRECTED FIGURES; 1877—1881 NEW
                                  6

BRONFLOYD
| Copper | Ore(tons) | Metal(tons) | Value(£) |
|---|---|---|---|
| 1865 | 23.20 | 2.70 | 60.30 |

Comment 1865 (P) COPPER EST.

Ownership:   1859-1872 J.B.BALCOMBE & CO.; 1873 BRONFLOYD CO.; 1874-1877
BRONFLOYD CO.LTD.; 1878-1881 NEW BRONFLOYD CO.LTD.; 1882
BRONFLOYD MINING CO.; 1883-1885 JOHN JENKINS & CO.; 1886-1904
JOHN JENKINS,PETER JONES & GRIF.JONES
Comment 1877-1881 NEW BRONFLOYD; 1893-1899 SUSPENDED;
1903-1904 NOT WORKED

Management:  Manager 1870 THOS.KEMP; 1871-1875 JOHN DAVIS
Chief Agent 1859-1860 M.BARBERY; 1861-1863 JAS.LESTER;
1864-1865 JAS.KEMP; 1866-1869 THOS.KEMP; 1876-1881 THOS.KEMP;
1882-1904 PETER JONES
Secretary 1873 J.B.BALCOMBE (S); 1874-1878 C.E.SHEA (S);
1879-1881 W.F.TARN

Employment:
| | Underground | Surface | Total |
|---|---|---|---|
| 1877 | 59 | 20 | 79 |
| 1878 | 46 | 16 | 62 |
| 1879 | 18 | 6 | 24 |
| 1880 | 32 | 13 | 45 |
| 1881 | 28 | 12 | 40 |
| 1882 | 22 | 7 | 29 |
| 1883 | 16 | 9 | 25 |
| 1884 | 2 | 2 | 4 |
| 1885 | 2 | | 2 |
| 1886 | 12 | | 12 |
| 1887 | 6 | | 6 |
| 1888 | 6 | 3 | 9 |
| 1889 | 2 | | 2 |
| 1890 | 4 | 2 | 6 |
| 1891 | 4 | 3 | 7 |
| 1892 | 4 | | 4 |
| 1900-1902 | 2 | | 2 |

BRONFLOYD,EAST              PENRHYNCOCH                    SN 665836 0022

Production: Lead No detailed return
Ownership:  1863-1865 W.H.PUNCHARD & CO.
Comment 1864-1865 SUSPENDED
Management: Chief Agent 1863 AND.WILLIAMS

BRONGWYN                                                              0023

Production: Lead & Silver
| | Ore(tons) | Lead(tons) | Silver(ozs) | Value(£) |
|---|---|---|---|---|
| 1854 | 179.20 | 140.00 | 420.00 | 0.00 |
| 1855 | 33.50 | 26.00 | 72.00 | 0.00 |
| 1856 | 31.70 | 24.00 | 66.00 | 0.00 |

BRONLLANGWRDA               GOGINAN                        SN 668807 0024

Production: Lead No detailed return
Ownership:  1863-1865 ATWOOD & CO.
Management: Chief Agent 1863-1865 W.TREGONING

BRONMWYN                    PONTRHYDFENDIGAID              SN 723652 0025

Production: Lead No detailed return
Ownership:  1870-1875 BRONMWYN CO.; 1876-1877 THOS.GUNDRY & WM.GUNDRY

BRONMWYN                    PONTRHYDFENDIGAID              Continued

Management: Chief Agent 1870–1875 JOHN WILLIAMS; 1876–1877 THOS.WILLIAMS


BRUSINPIANS                                                          0026

Production: Lead             Ore(tons) Metal(tons)    Value(£)
            1862              20.00        15.00        0.00


BRYNAMBOR                   LLANDDEWI BREFI            SN 744508 0027

Production: Lead             Ore(tons) Metal(tons)    Value(£)
            1862              10.00         7.50        0.00
Ownership:  1861–1867 BRYNAMBOR MINING CO.
Management: Chief Agent 1861–1862 ED.WILLIAMS; 1863–1867 EVAN GRIFFITHS


BRYNARIAN                      TALIESIN               SN 664916 0028

Production: Lead & Silver    Ore(tons)  Lead(tons) Silver(ozs)   Value(£)
            1849              40.00       28.00       0.00         0.00
            1850              60.00       48.00       0.00         0.00
            1851              95.00       76.00       0.00         0.00
            1852              31.00       23.50       0.00         0.00
            1853–1854 No detailed return
            1861              40.00       31.00      248.00        0.00
            1862        No detailed return
            1871              20.00       15.00       0.00         0.00
            1874               8.00        6.00       48.00        0.00
            Comment 1871 INC.PENSARN.LATE CRDGN BAY CLS; 1874
            INC.PENSARN
            Zinc             Ore(tons) Metal(tons)    Value(£)
            1871              23.00        0.00        86.30
            1872              20.00        0.00        75.00
            1874               5.00        0.00        12.50
            1875               3.00        0.00        12.50
            Comment 1872 INC.PENSARN; 1874–1875 INC.PENSARN
            Copper No detailed return
Ownership:  1860–1862 GLEDHILL & CO.; 1872–1874 R.S.SADLER; 1875–1877
            ED.BENNETT; 1881–1885 CWM DWYFOR & BRYNARIAN MINING CO.LTD.;
            1886 ED.BENNETT; 1887 CWM DWYFOR & BRYNARIAN MINING CO.LTD.
            Comment 1863–1865 SUSPENDED; 1872–1877 INC.PENSARN; 1884
            STOPPED OCT.1884
Management: Chief Agent 1860–1862 CHAS.WILLIAMS; 1872–1877 JOHN RIDGE;
            1881–1887 GEO.J.GRAY
Employment:                  Underground     Surface       Total
            1881–1885             4                           4
            1886–1887             2                           2


BRYNDYFI                      GLANDOVEY              SN 683934 0029

Production: Lead & Silver    Ore(tons)  Lead(tons) Silver(ozs)   Value(£)
            1882              24.00       19.00      210.00        0.00
Ownership:  1880–1883 BRYNDYFI MINING CO.LTD.; 1884–1887 EVAN REESE; 1888
            J.M.FLINT; 1889–1890 BRYNDYFI MINING CO.
            Comment 1884–1888 SUSPENDED; 1889 STOPPED OCT.1889; 1890
            SUSPENDED
Management: Chief Agent 1880–1881 THOS.WILLIAMS; 1882–1887 EVAN REESE;
            1889–1890 W.STAINTON
            Secretary 1881 D.C.DAVIES & SON
Employment:                  Underground     Surface       Total
            1880                 18             12            30

                                    8

BRYNDYFI                    GLANDOVEY                    Continued

|      | Underground | Surface | Total |
|------|-------------|---------|-------|
| 1881 | 32          | 33      | 65    |
| 1882 | 16          | 7       | 23    |
| 1883 | 10          | 2       | 12    |
| 1889 | 6           | 3       | 9     |

BRYNGLAS                    PONTERWYD                    SN 760817 0030

Production: Lead

|      | Ore(tons) | Metal(tons) | Value(£) |
|------|-----------|-------------|----------|
| 1845 | 10.00     | 6.50        | 0.00     |
| 1860 | 31.70     | 0.00        | 0.00     |
| 1861 | No detailed return | | |

Ownership:  1859-1865 DAVID LLOYD & CO.
            Comment 1864-1865 SUSPENDED
Management: Chief Agent 1859-1863 O.OWEN

BRYNGWIOG                   HALKYN, FLINTSHIRE                      0031

Production: Lead & Silver

|      | Ore(tons) | Lead(tons) | Silver(ozs) | Value(£) |
|------|-----------|------------|-------------|----------|
| 1854 | 108.00    | 85.00      | 300.00      | 0.00     |
| 1855 | 51.00     | 39.00      | 132.00      | 0.00     |
| 1856-1857 | No detailed return | | | |

BRYNHOPE                                                           0032

Production: Lead & Silver

|      | Ore(tons) | Lead(tons) | Silver(ozs) | Value(£) |
|------|-----------|------------|-------------|----------|
| 1862 | 25.00     | 19.00      | 100.00      | 0.00     |

BRYNTAIL                    LLANIDLOES, MONTGOMERY       SN 914869 0033

Production: Lead & Silver

|      | Ore(tons) | Lead(tons) | Silver(ozs) | Value(£) |
|------|-----------|------------|-------------|----------|
| 1852 | 63.00     | 44.00      | 120.00      | 0.00     |
| 1854 | 10.00     | 7.50       | 0.00        | 0.00     |
| 1855 | 52.00     | 38.00      | 150.00      | 0.00     |
| 1856 | No detailed return | | | |

Ownership:  1860 BRYNTAIL MINING CO.
Management: Chief Agent 1860 JAS.ROACH

BRYNYFEDWEN                 PENEGOES, MONTGOMERY         SN 858972 0034

Production: Lead & Silver

|      | Ore(tons) | Lead(tons) | Silver(ozs) | Value(£) |
|------|-----------|------------|-------------|----------|
| 1857 | 151.70    | 105.60     | 525.00      | 0.00     |

BRYNYRAFR                   PONTERWYD                    SN 745878 0035

Production: Lead & Silver

|      | Ore(tons) | Lead(tons) | Silver(ozs) | Value(£) |
|------|-----------|------------|-------------|----------|
| 1881 | 120.00    | 90.00      | 0.00        | 1063.00  |
| 1882 | 100.00    | 75.00      | 0.00        | 882.00   |
| 1883 | 54.20     | 40.10      | 0.00        | 394.00   |
| 1884 | 128.00    | 96.00      | 0.00        | 817.00   |
| 1885 | 175.00    | 126.00     | 0.00        | 1244.00  |
| 1886 | 172.00    | 127.00     | 0.00        | 1494.00  |
| 1887 | 263.00    | 192.00     | 724.00      | 2141.00  |
| 1888 | 263.00    | 194.00     | 740.00      | 2234.00  |
| 1889 | 359.00    | 273.00     | 1000.00     | 3090.00  |
| 1890 | 316.00    | 240.00     | 888.00      | 2658.00  |
| 1891 | 312.00    | 238.00     | 877.00      | 2338.00  |

| Lead & Silver | Ore(tons) | Lead(tons) | Silver(ozs) | Value(£) |
|---|---|---|---|---|
| 1892 | 181.00 | 138.00 | 0.00 | 1180.00 |
| 1893 | 97.00 | 74.00 | 0.00 | 591.00 |
| 1894 | 80.00 | 61.00 | 0.00 | 488.00 |
| 1895 | 301.00 | 232.00 | 0.00 | 1952.00 |
| 1896 | 208.00 | 160.00 | 0.00 | 1361.00 |
| 1897 | 199.00 | 151.00 | 0.00 | 1570.00 |
| 1898 | 225.00 | 171.00 | 2657.00 | 1821.00 |
| 1899 | 205.00 | 158.00 | 0.00 | 2069.00 |
| 1900 | 237.00 | 182.00 | 0.00 | 2576.00 |
| 1901 | 265.00 | 204.00 | 0.00 | 2071.00 |
| 1902 | 246.00 | 189.00 | 0.00 | 1684.00 |
| 1903 | 152.00 | 117.00 | 0.00 | 1083.00 |
| 1904 | 75.00 | 57.00 | 0.00 | 500.00 |
| 1905 | 50.00 | 38.00 | 0.00 | 380.00 |
| 1906 | 67.00 | 51.00 | 0.00 | 728.00 |
| 1907 | 48.00 | 36.00 | 0.00 | 626.00 |
| 1908 | 20.00 | 15.00 | 0.00 | 137.00 |
| 1910 | 1.00 | 1.00 | 0.00 | 8.00 |
| 1911 | 18.00 | 14.00 | 0.00 | 135.00 |
| 1912 | 15.00 | 11.00 | 0.00 | 150.00 |

Comment 1881 BRUN YR AFR; 1910 LEAD EST

| Zinc | Ore(tons) | Metal(tons) | Value(£) |
|---|---|---|---|
| 1881 | 173.00 | 104.00 | 642.80 |
| 1882 | 95.10 | 49.40 | 333.00 |
| 1883 | 85.00 | 42.50 | 240.00 |
| 1884 | 169.00 | 0.00 | 517.00 |
| 1885 | 212.00 | 83.00 | 696.00 |
| 1886 | 287.00 | 96.00 | 634.00 |
| 1887 | 319.00 | 117.00 | 1024.00 |
| 1888 | 384.00 | 137.00 | 1383.00 |
| 1889 | 545.00 | 186.00 | 1878.00 |
| 1890 | 505.00 | 177.00 | 1787.00 |
| 1891 | 294.00 | 93.00 | 740.00 |
| 1892 | 78.00 | 27.00 | 181.00 |
| 1893 | 99.00 | 36.00 | 174.00 |
| 1894 | 77.00 | 28.00 | 179.00 |
| 1895 | 232.00 | 85.00 | 597.00 |
| 1896 | 437.00 | 135.50 | 933.00 |
| 1897 | 328.00 | 115.00 | 1110.00 |
| 1898 | 730.00 | 273.00 | 3636.00 |
| 1899 | 315.00 | 225.00 | 3691.00 |
| 1900 | 376.00 | 132.00 | 1351.00 |
| 1901 | 377.00 | 129.00 | 969.00 |
| 1902 | 342.00 | 120.00 | 1214.00 |
| 1903 | 369.00 | 129.00 | 1388.00 |
| 1904 | 455.00 | 148.00 | 1850.00 |
| 1905 | 132.00 | 39.00 | 470.00 |
| 1906 | 90.00 | 33.00 | 548.00 |
| 1907 | 137.00 | 48.00 | 505.00 |
| 1908 | 36.00 | 10.00 | 123.00 |
| 1910 | 5.00 | 2.00 | 25.00 |
| 1911 | 79.00 | 28.00 | 392.00 |
| 1912 | 54.00 | 20.00 | 327.00 |

Comment 1910 ZINC & VALUE EST.

Ownership: 1880—1893 BRYNYRAFR MINE CO.LTD.; 1894—1895 NICH.BRAY & JOHN MITCHELL; 1896—1902 MID—WALES MINES LTD.; 1903—1906 JOHN MITCHELL; 1896—1906 JOHN MITCHELL; 1908 CARDIGAN MINES LTD.; 1909 LONG MINING CO.LTD.; 1910—1912 HAVAN MINING CO.LTD.; 1913 HAFNA MINING CO.LTD. Comment 1908 IDLE

Management: Chief Agent 1880—1891 JAS.PHILLIPS; 1892—1895 NICH.BRAY; 1896—1906 JOHN MITCHELL; 1908 JAS.MITCHELL; 1911—1913 F.H.AHIER

Employment:

| | Underground | Surface | Total |
|---|---|---|---|
| 1880 | 12 | 10 | 22 |
| 1881 | 21 | 13 | 34 |
| 1882 | 14 | 15 | 29 |
| 1883 | 12 | 20 | 22 |
| 1884 | 17 | 16 | 33 |
| 1885 | 16 | 19 | 35 |
| 1886 | 23 | 27 | 50 |
| 1887 | 21 | 25 | 46 |
| 1888 | 34 | 41 | 75 |
| 1889 | 36 | 33 | 69 |
| 1890 | 29 | 36 | 65 |
| 1891 | 22 | 31 | 53 |
| 1892 | 10 | 23 | 33 |
| 1893 | 10 | 18 | 28 |
| 1894 | 24 | 12 | 36 |
| 1895 | 30 | 15 | 45 |
| 1896 | 32 | 18 | 50 |
| 1897 | 35 | 33 | 68 |
| 1898 | 38 | 44 | 82 |
| 1899 | 55 | 40 | 95 |
| 1900 | 45 | 39 | 84 |
| 1901 | 26 | 24 | 50 |
| 1902 | 27 | 21 | 48 |
| 1903 | 20 | 19 | 39 |
| 1904 | 15 | 17 | 32 |
| 1905 | 6 | 7 | 13 |
| 1906 | 12 | 4 | 16 |
| 1907 | 10 | 8 | 18 |
| 1909 | 11 | 9 | 20 |
| 1910 | 27 | 43 | 70 |
| 1911 | 53 | 27 | 80 |
| 1912 | 22 | 16 | 38 |
| 1913 | 32 | 22 | 54 |

BRYNYRAFR,NORTH                     PONTERWYD                                    0036

Ownership:   1898 WM.BOUNDY; 1899-1901 JOHN JAMES
             Comment 1898-1900 INC.CAMDWRBACH; 1901 INC.CAMDWRBACH:NOT
             WORKED IN 1901
Management:  Chief Agent 1898 J.C.JAMES; 1899-1901 JOHN JAMES
Employment:

| | Underground | Surface | Total |
|---|---|---|---|
| 1898 | 10 | | 10 |
| 1899 | 4 | | 4 |
| 1900 | 2 | | 2 |

Comment 1898-1900 INC.CAMDWRBACH

BRYNYSTWYTH                         PONTRHYDYGROES                    SN 715721 0037

Production: Lead

| | Ore(tons) | Metal(tons) | Value(£) |
|---|---|---|---|
| 1870 | 95.00 | 70.00 | 0.00 |
| 1871 | 140.00 | 110.00 | 0.00 |
| 1872 | No detailed return | | |

            Comment 1872 SEE GROGWINION
Ownership:  1868-1875 BRYNYSTWYTH CO.
Management: Manager 1871-1875 JOHN KITTO
            Chief Agent 1868-1870 J.TREGONING

BWADRAIN                    RHEIDOL VALLEY                    SN 713797 0038

Production: Lead & Silver    Ore(tons)  Lead(tons) Silver(ozs)    Value(£)
            1867                85.00       64.50       0.00          0.00
            1868               244.00      186.50       0.00          0.00
            1869               364.00      278.00       0.00          0.00
            1870               250.00      192.00       0.00          0.00
            1871               175.00      133.00    2815.00          0.00
            1872               220.00      160.00    3386.00          0.00
            1873               190.00      146.00    3066.00          0.00
            1874               134.00      100.00     400.00       1667.00
            1875                65.00       49.50     235.00          0.00
            1876                17.00       13.00      52.00          0.00
            Comment 1875 BWADRAIN CONSOLS
            Zinc             Ore(tons)  Metal(tons)     Value(£)
            1873                 5.00        0.00       15.00
Ownership:  1867 ROBT.NORTHEY & CO.; 1868—1875 BWADRAIN MINING CO.LTD.
Management: Manager 1867—1871 ROBT.NORTHEY; 1872—1873 WM.BATTYE
            Chief Agent 1868—1871 WM.BATTYE; 1872—1873 ROBT.NORTHEY;
            1874—1875 NICH.BRAY


BWADRAIN,SOUTH               RHEIDOL VALLEY                    SN 713787 0039

Production: Zinc             Ore(tons)  Metal(tons)     Value(£)
            1876                 3.00        0.00       10.50
Ownership:  1876 ABS.FRANCIS
Management: Manager 1876 ABS.FRANCIS


BWLCH CONSOLS                   GOGINAN                        SN 703824 0040

Production: Lead & Silver    Ore(tons)  Lead(tons) Silver(ozs)    Value(£)
            1847          No detailed return
            1848               289.00      192.00       0.00          0.00
            1849               635.00      425.00       0.00          0.00
            1850               460.00      345.00       0.00          0.00
            1851               445.00      367.00       0.00          0.00
            1852               205.00      157.50    3925.00          0.00
            1853               165.10       97.50    1258.00          0.00
            1854                20.00       14.00     160.00          0.00
            1855               302.00      220.00    2684.00          0.00
            1856               372.00      299.00    5580.00          0.00
            1857               248.90      180.50    3360.00          0.00
            1858               226.00      168.00       0.00          0.00
            1859               244.00      186.00    2405.00          0.00
            1860               168.00       92.50    1526.00          0.00
            1861               250.00      192.00    3840.00          0.00
            1862               172.00      131.00    3160.00          0.00
            1863               210.00      168.00    4032.00          0.00
            1864               246.50      185.40    3885.00          0.00
            1865               280.00      213.00    4256.00          0.00
            1866               280.00      213.00    4480.00          0.00
            1867               378.00      293.00    5670.00          0.00
            1868               413.00      312.00    4592.00          0.00
            1869               558.00      427.00    6959.00          0.00
            1870               380.00      292.50    4770.00          0.00
            1871               190.00      143.50    2718.00          0.00
            1872               140.00      105.00    2154.00          0.00
            1873                44.00       33.00     665.00          0.00
            1874                36.00       27.00     162.00        542.80
            1875                32.00       24.00     430.00          0.00
            Comment 1847 SEE BWLCHCWMERFIN
Ownership:  1859—1862 WM.BATTYE & CO.; 1863—1867 PRICE & CO.; 1868—1875
            BWLCH CONSOLS CO.LTD.

                                    12

BWLCH CONSOLS        GOGINAN        Continued

Management: Chief Agent 1859-1874 ROBT.NORTHEY; 1875 NICH.BRAY

BWLCH UNITED        GOGINAN        SN 703824 0041

Production: Lead & Silver

| | Ore(tons) | Lead(tons) | Silver(ozs) | Value(£) |
|---|---|---|---|---|
| 1880 | 20.00 | 16.00 | 0.00 | 193.00 |
| 1881 | 55.00 | 39.00 | 0.00 | 650.40 |
| 1882 | 105.00 | 86.10 | 1550.00 | 1210.00 |
| 1883 | 35.00 | 28.00 | 630.00 | 370.00 |
| 1885 | 8.00 | 6.00 | 133.00 | 64.00 |

Zinc

| | Ore(tons) | Metal(tons) | Value(£) |
|---|---|---|---|
| 1881 | 6.80 | 4.00 | 25.40 |

Ownership: 1878 BWLCH UNITED CO.; 1879-1884 BWLCH UNITED MINING CO.LTD.;
1885-1890 JAS.MCILQUHAN & CO.
Comment 1884 STOPPED APR.1884; 1885 INC.PENCRAIGDDU &
CAENANT; 1886-1890 INC.PENCRAIGDDU & CAENANT:SUSPENDED
Management: Manager 1881 J.DARREN
Chief Agent 1878-1880 NICH.BRAY; 1881-1890 WM.NORTHEY
Secretary 1881 WM.BATTYE

Employment:

| | Underground | Surface | Total |
|---|---|---|---|
| 1878 | 16 | 2 | 18 |
| 1879 | 30 | 6 | 36 |
| 1880 | 25 | 10 | 35 |
| 1881 | 24 | 14 | 38 |
| 1882 | 40 | 22 | 62 |
| 1883 | 2 | 1 | 3 |
| 1884 | 4 | 1 | 5 |
| 1885 | 2 | 4 | 6 |
| 1887 | | 1 | 1 |

Comment 1885 INC.PENCRAIGDDU & CAENANT; 1887 INC.PENCRAIGDDU
& CAENANT

BWLCHCWMERFIN        GOGINAN        0042

Production: Lead

| | Ore(tons) | Metal(tons) | Value(£) |
|---|---|---|---|
| 1845 | 23.00 | 15.00 | 0.00 |
| 1846 | 20.00 | 13.00 | 0.00 |
| 1847 | 45.00 | 30.00 | 0.00 |
| 1848 | 40.00 | 26.00 | 0.00 |
| 1849 | 18.00 | 12.00 | 0.00 |

Comment 1847 INC BWLCH CONSOLS

BWLCHGLAS        TALYBONT        SN 710878 0043

Production: Lead & Silver

| | Ore(tons) | Lead(tons) | Silver(ozs) | Value(£) |
|---|---|---|---|---|
| 1892 | 23.00 | 17.00 | 191.00 | 144.00 |
| 1897 | 50.00 | 26.00 | 194.00 | 275.00 |
| 1899 | 6.00 | 4.00 | 0.00 | 42.00 |
| 1909 | 87.50 | 63.00 | 464.00 | 709.00 |
| 1910 | 208.00 | 154.00 | 1248.00 | 1664.00 |
| 1911 | 67.00 | 49.00 | 0.00 | 520.00 |
| 1913 | 25.00 | 18.00 | 126.00 | 276.00 |

Comment 1910 VALUE EST

Zinc

| | Ore(tons) | Metal(tons) | Value(£) |
|---|---|---|---|
| 1910 | 36.00 | 10.00 | 123.00 |
| 1911 | 43.00 | 14.00 | 123.00 |
| 1913 | 6.00 | 2.00 | 18.00 |

Comment 1910 VALUE EST.
Ownership: 1888 ED.EVANS; 1889 BWLCHGLAS PROSPECTING SYNDICATE LTD.;
1890-1893 BWLCHGLAS MINING CO.LTD.; 1894 P.S.BOULT; 1896-1898

PLYNLIMON & HAVAN CO.LTD.; 1899—1904 RICH.ROBERTS; 1908—1910
SCOTTISH CARDIGAN LEAD MINES LTD.; 1911—1913 CARDIGAN MINING
CO.LTD.
Comment 1900 SUSPENDED; 1901 NOT WORKED IN 1901; 1902—1904
NOT WORKED

Management: Chief Agent 1888—1890 ED.EVANS; 1891—1892 R.ART.THOMAS; 1893
THOS.GARLAND; 1896 FRED.WILLIAMS; 1897—1898 H.W.FRANCIS;
1899—1904 F.M.SIMMS; 1908 THOS.E.HARDY; 1909 K.FERGUSON;
1910—1913 J.MCKENDRICK

Employment:

| | Underground | Surface | Total |
|---|---|---|---|
| 1888 | | 2 | 2 |
| 1889 | 6 | | 6 |
| 1890 | 17 | | 17 |
| 1891 | 20 | 2 | 22 |
| 1892 | 16 | 10 | 26 |
| 1893 | 7 | 13 | 20 |
| 1894 | 12 | 4 | 16 |
| 1896 | 5 | | 5 |
| 1897 | 14 | 4 | 18 |
| 1898 | 4 | 5 | 9 |
| 1899 | 6 | | 6 |
| 1908 | 12 | 3 | 15 |
| 1909 | 32 | 23 | 55 |
| 1910 | 135 | 169 | 304 |
| 1911 | 95 | 57 | 152 |
| 1912 | 49 | 21 | 70 |
| 1913 | 48 | 34 | 82 |

BWLCHGWYN                PONTERWYD                    SN 744789 0044

Production: 

| Lead | Ore(tons) | Metal(tons) | Value(£) |
|---|---|---|---|
| 1880 | 1.00 | 0.70 | 9.60 |
| 1887 | 10.00 | 7.00 | 70.00 |
| 1891 | 8.00 | 6.00 | 59.00 |

Ownership: 1869 NANTEOS CONSOLS; 1886—1888 CARDIGAN UNITED MINES LTD.;
1890—1891 BWLCHGWYN MINE CO.; 1892 NICH.BRAY
Comment 1869 INC.PENRHIW; 1886—1888 INC.LLWYNTEIFY; 1889
INC.LLWYNTEIFY:SUSPENDED; 1890 STARTED JUNE 1890

Management: Chief Agent 1869 J.P.THOMAS; 1886—1887 AND.WILLIAMS; 1888
A.H.JENKS; 1890—1892 NICH.BRAY

Employment:

| | Underground | Surface | Total |
|---|---|---|---|
| 1886 | 4 | 5 | 9 |
| 1887 | 12 | 8 | 20 |
| 1888 | 1 | 1 | 2 |
| 1890 | 2 | 3 | 5 |
| 1891 | | 4 | 4 |
| 1892 | | 1 | 1 |

Comment 1886—1888 INC.LLWYNTEIFY

BWLCHSTYLLAN            TALYBONT                    SN 732863 0045

Production: Lead No detailed return
Ownership: 1863—1864 PRICE & CO.; 1866—1867 PRICE & CO.; 1868—1875
BWLCHSTYLLAN MINING CO.LTD.
Comment 1863 BWLCHCETYLLYN; 1864 BWLCHSTELLAN; 1866—1867
BWLCHSTELLAN
Management: Chief Agent 1863—1864 ROBT.NORTHEY; 1866—1873 ROBT.NORTHEY;
1875 NICH.BRAY
Secretary 1868—1871 WM.BATTYE; 1872—1874 ROBT.NORTHEY

Production: Lead

| | Ore(tons) | Metal(tons) | Value(£) |
|---|---|---|---|
| 1845 | 30.00 | 20.00 | 0.00 |

CAEGYNON           RHEIDOL VALLEY           SN 717784 0047

Production: Lead & Silver

| | Ore(tons) | Lead(tons) | Silver(ozs) | Value(£) |
|---|---|---|---|---|
| 1853 | 23.90 | 19.50 | 0.00 | 0.00 |
| 1854 | 52.00 | 37.00 | 0.00 | 0.00 |
| 1855 | 45.00 | 40.00 | 0.00 | 0.00 |
| 1856 | 38.00 | 28.30 | 0.00 | 0.00 |
| 1857 | No detailed return | | | |
| 1858 | 56.00 | 39.00 | 0.00 | 0.00 |
| 1859 | 10.50 | 7.50 | 0.00 | 0.00 |
| 1860–1861 | No detailed return | | | |
| 1871 | 55.00 | 40.00 | 0.00 | 0.00 |
| 1872 | 42.90 | 31.50 | 0.00 | 0.00 |
| 1873 | No detailed return | | | |
| 1874 | 35.00 | 25.50 | 0.00 | 455.00 |
| 1875 | 12.60 | 9.40 | 0.00 | 0.00 |

Comment 1857–1858 CAEGYON; 1874 FOR SILVER SEE CWMYSTWYTH

Zinc

| | Ore(tons) | Metal(tons) | Value(£) |
|---|---|---|---|
| 1854 | 33.10 | 0.00 | 0.00 |
| 1855 | 9.50 | 0.00 | 0.00 |
| 1858 | 10.00 | 0.00 | 27.50 |
| 1859–1861 | No detailed return | | |
| 1870 | 25.00 | 0.00 | 75.00 |
| 1871 | 134.00 | 0.00 | 402.00 |
| 1872 | 322.00 | 0.00 | 1416.00 |
| 1873 | 60.00 | 0.00 | 264.00 |
| 1874 | 127.80 | 0.00 | 370.00 |
| 1875 | 6.20 | 0.00 | 18.50 |

Comment 1854 CAE GIRON

Ownership: 1863–1865 W.H.PUNCHARD & CO.; 1866–1868 CARDIGAN CONSOLIDATED MINING CO.; 1869–1870 CAEGYNON CO.; 1871–1877 CAEGYNON LEAD MINING CO.; 1897–1898 H.R.MERTON & CO.; 1911–1912 LERI MINING CO.LTD.; 1913 LERY MINING CO.LTD.
Comment 1859–1860 ABANDONED; 1864–1865 SUSPENDED; 1866–1877 OR GLANRHEIDOL UNITED; 1912–1913 IDLE

Management: Chief Agent 1863 GEO.WILLIAMS; 1866–1867 S.PEARCE; 1868–1869 E.PEARCE; 1870–1877 THOS.HODGE; 1897 JOHN OWEN
Secretary 1871–1877 F.REED WILSON

Employment:

| | Underground | Surface | Total |
|---|---|---|---|
| 1897 | 1 | | 1 |
| 1898 | 20 | 5 | 25 |
| 1911 | 10 | | 10 |
| 1912 | | 1 | 1 |

CAELAN           MACHYNLLETH, MONTGOMERY           SN 863975 0048

Production: Lead & Silver

| | Ore(tons) | Lead(tons) | Silver(ozs) | Value(£) |
|---|---|---|---|---|
| 1880 | 15.00 | 12.00 | 120.00 | 220.00 |

CAELAN,NORTH           MACHYNLLETH, MONTGOMERY           SN 864977 0049

Production: Lead & Silver

| | Ore(tons) | Lead(tons) | Silver(ozs) | Value(£) |
|---|---|---|---|---|
| 1870 | 14.00 | 10.50 | 22.00 | 0.00 |

CAELAN,SOUTH       MACHYNLLETH, MONTGOMERY       SN 863972 0050

Production: 
| | Lead & Silver | Ore(tons) | Lead(tons) | Silver(ozs) | Value(£) |
|---|---|---|---|---|---|
| | 1870 | 8.00 | 6.00 | 108.00 | 0.00 |

CAENANT       GOGINAN       SN 708826 0051

Production: 
| | Lead & Silver | Ore(tons) | Lead(tons) | Silver(ozs) | Value(£) |
|---|---|---|---|---|---|
| | 1845 | 10.00 | 6.50 | 0.00 | 0.00 |
| | 1853 | 4.70 | 3.50 | 0.00 | 0.00 |
| | 1875 | 7.20 | 5.20 | 66.00 | 0.00 |

Ownership: 1861–1872 C.E.HAYWARD & CO.; 1873–1884 C.E.HAYWARD
Comment 1876–1883 INC.PENCRAIGDDU; 1884
INC.PENCRAIGDDU:SUSPENDED; 1885–1890 SEE BWLCH UNITED
Management: Manager 1873–1881 JAS.PHILLIPS
Chief Agent 1861–1865 S.TREGONING; 1866–1867 E.TREGONING;
1868 W.H.TREGONING; 1869–1871 JAS.LESTER; 1872 JAS.PHILLIPS;
1882–1883 JAS.PHILLIPS

Employment: 
| | Underground | Surface | Total |
|---|---|---|---|
| 1877–1878 | 4 | | 4 |
| 1879 | 6 | | 6 |
| 1880–1882 | 4 | | 4 |
| 1883 | 2 | | 2 |
| 1885 | | | |
| 1887 | | | |

Comment 1878–1883 INC.PENCRAIGDDU; 1885 SEE BWLCH UNITED;
1887 SEE BWLCH UNITED

CAMBRIAN       TALYBONT       SN 740912 0052

Production: 
| | Lead & Silver | Ore(tons) | Lead(tons) | Silver(ozs) | Value(£) |
|---|---|---|---|---|---|
| | 1851 | 40.00 | 26.00 | 0.00 | 0.00 |
| | 1852 | No detailed return | | | |
| | 1854 | No detailed return | | | |
| | 1878 | 20.00 | 15.00 | 0.00 | 180.50 |
| | 1879 | 21.00 | 15.70 | 0.00 | 210.00 |
| | 1886 | 29.00 | 20.00 | 0.00 | 275.00 |

Comment 1886 OR ESGAIR FFRAITH

| Copper | Ore(tons) | Metal(tons) | Value(£) |
|---|---|---|---|
| 1877 | 100.00 | 6.20 | 485.50 |
| 1878 | 377.00 | 56.10 | 3880.70 |
| 1879 | 559.00 | 81.50 | 4109.60 |
| 1880 | 704.00 | 84.20 | 4167.50 |
| 1881 | 136.50 | 15.30 | 1057.60 |
| 1882 | 294.00 | 44.10 | 2638.00 |

Comment 1877 (P); 1878–1880 (P)(S); 1881 (P)(S)NEW CAMBRIAN;
1882 NEW CAMBRIAN

Ownership: 1877–1878 CAMBRIAN MINING CO.; 1879–1880 CAMBRIAN MINING
CO.LTD.; 1881–1882 NEW CAMBRIAN MINING & SMELTING CO.LTD.;
1884 CAMBRIAN MINING CO.LTD.
Comment 1881–1882 NEW CAMBRIAN; 1883 SEE ESGAIR FFRAITH;
1885–1888 SEE ESGAIR FFRAITH
Management: Chief Agent 1877–1880 THOS.GLANVILLE; 1881 JOHN MORRIS; 1882
BEN.WILLIAMS; 1884 HY.JAMES
Secretary 1881 A.E.BROWN (P)

Employment: 
| | Underground | Surface | Total |
|---|---|---|---|
| 1877 | 23 | 22 | 45 |
| 1878 | 27 | 14 | 41 |
| 1879 | 39 | 20 | 59 |
| 1880 | 27 | 11 | 38 |
| 1881 | 29 | 13 | 42 |
| 1882 | 35 | 24 | 59 |
| 1884 | 23 | 10 | 33 |

CAMBRIAN,NEW                    PONTERWYD                         SN 743887 0053

Production: Lead & Silver    Ore(tons)  Lead(tons) Silver(ozs)    Value(£)
            1881               8.00        5.50       68.00         76.00


CAMBRIAN,SOUTH                  PONTERWYD                                   0054

Production: Lead             Ore(tons) Metal(tons)    Value(£)
            1880               2.00       1.30          18.00
Ownership:  1879-1881 SOUTH CAMBRIAN MINING CO.LTD.
Management: Chief Agent 1879-1881 AND.WILLIAMS
            Secretary 1881 A.J.W.STRINGER (S)
Employment:                Underground    Surface      Total
            1879                6            3            9
            1880               10           13           23


CAMDDWR MAWR                    PONTERWYD                         SN 751878 0055

Production: Lead             Ore(tons) Metal(tons)    Value(£)
            1856               4.70       3.10          0.00
            1857     No detailed return
            Copper           Ore(tons) Metal(tons)    Value(£)
            1855              22.20       0.00          0.00
            Comment 1855 CAMDWR MAWR
            Manganese        Ore(tons) Metal(tons)    Value(£)
            1874     No detailed return
            Comment 1874 CAMDURMAWR SEE ROYAL MINES
Ownership:  1863 PRICE & CO.; 1864-1865 W.H.PUNCHARD & CO.; 1880-1881
            GREAT CWMDWR MINING CO.; 1882-1884 C.HERB.STOKES
            Comment 1874-1877 SEE ROYAL MINES; 1882 SUSPENDED; 1883-1884
            GREAT CAMDWR. SUSPENDED
Management: Manager 1881 JOHN DAVIES
            Chief Agent 1863-1865 ROBT.NORTHEY; 1880-1884 C.HERB.STOKES
            Secretary 1880-1881 C.HERB.STOKES
Employment:                Underground    Surface      Total
            1880                8            1            9


CAMDWRBACH                      PONTERWYD                         SN 744887 0056

Production: Zinc             Ore(tons) Metal(tons)    Value(£)
            1904              21.00       8.00          96.00
            1905               5.00       2.00          15.00
Ownership:  1903-1906 CAMDWRBACH MINING CO.LTD.
            Comment 1898-1901 SEE NORTH BRYNYRAFR; 1905-1906 NOT WORKED
Management: Chief Agent 1903-1906 E.W.BROACKERS
Employment:                Underground    Surface      Total
            1898-1900
            1903                8            12           20
            1904               15                        15
            Comment 1898-1900 SEE NORTH BRYNYRAFR


CARADOCK                                                                    0057

Production: Copper           Ore(tons) Metal(tons)    Value(£)
            1860              14.00       1.00          0.00
            Comment 1860 (P) SUNDRIES-COPPER EST.


                                    17

Production: Lead　　　　　　　Ore(tons) Metal(tons)　　Value(£)
　　　　　　1868　　　　　　40.00　　　30.50　　　　0.00
　　　　　　1869-1870 No detailed return
　　　　　　Zinc　　　　　　Ore(tons) Metal(tons)　　Value(£)
　　　　　　1871　　　　　　5.00　　　　0.00　　　　18.80


CARDIGAN BAY CONSOLS　　　　　　TALIESIN　　　　　　　　SN 664916 0059

Production: Lead & Silver　　Ore(tons)　Lead(tons) Silver(ozs)　Value(£)
　　　　　　1871　　　No detailed return
　　　　　　Comment 1871 SEE BRYNARIAN
Management: Chief Agent 1870-1871 CHAS.WILLIAMS


CARDIGAN CONSOLS　　　　　　　TALYBONT　　　　　　　　SN 735913 0060

Production: Lead & Silver　　Ore(tons)　Lead(tons) Silver(ozs)　Value(£)
　　　　　　1858　　　　40.20　　　30.10　　179.00　　　0.00
　　　　　　1859　　　No detailed return
　　　　　　1860　　　　92.00　　　70.00　　　0.00　　　0.00
　　　　　　1861　　　　69.00　　　48.30　　　0.00　　　0.00
　　　　　　1862　　　　13.30　　　7.50　　　70.00　　　0.00
　　　　　　1863　　　　8.60　　　　6.40　　　0.00　　　0.00
　　　　　　1864　　　　3.30　　　　2.20　　　0.00　　　0.00
　　　　　　1865-1866 No detailed return
　　　　　　Comment 1858 LATE WELSH POTOSI; 1862 LATE ESGAIR HIR
　　　　　　Copper　　　　　Ore(tons) Metal(tons)　　Value(£)
　　　　　　1860　　　　24.00　　　1.70　　　321.70
　　　　　　1861　　　　41.00　　　3.40　　　485.00
　　　　　　1862　　　　158.50　　　13.70　　2474.50
　　　　　　1863　　　　226.00　　　18.50　　　0.00
　　　　　　1864　　　　168.30　　　16.70　　1707.90
　　　　　　1865　　　　64.90　　　6.50　　　943.00
　　　　　　1866　　　　51.10　　　4.30　　　0.00
　　　　　　Comment 1860-1865 (P) COPPER EST.
Ownership: 1859-1868 J.H.MURCHISON & CO.
Management: Chief Agent 1859-1862 J.SAUNDERS; 1863-1865 S.SAUNDERS;
　　　　　　1866-1868 HY.BOUNDY


CARDIGAN OLD BOG　　　　　　PONTERWYD　　　　　　　SN 739815 0061

Production: Lead No detailed return
Ownership: 1872-1877 CARDIGANSHIRE OLD BOG MINING CO.
Management: Manager 1872-1877 JAS.OVERTON


CARDIGAN,NORTH　　　　　　　TALYBONT　　　　　　　　　0062

Production: Lead & Silver　　Ore(tons)　Lead(tons) Silver(ozs)　Value(£)
　　　　　　1882　　　　45.00　　　36.40　　365.00　　455.00
　　　　　　Zinc　　　　　　Ore(tons) Metal(tons)　　Value(£)
　　　　　　1881　　　　28.00　　　12.10　　　84.00
Ownership: 1881 NORTH CARDIGAN MINE CO.; 1882-1883 NORTH CARDIGAN LEAD
　　　　　　MINING CO.LTD.
　　　　　　Comment 1882 FORMERLY ALLTYCRIB:IN LIQUIDATION; 1883 IN
　　　　　　LIQUIDATION; 1886-1890 SEE TALYBONT
Management: Manager 1881 JNO.PELL
　　　　　　Chief Agent 1882-1883 JNO.PELL
Employment:　　　　　　　　Underground　　Surface　　　Total
　　　　　　1882　　　　　18　　　　　8　　　　　26

MARKET SQUARE,
NEWENT,
GLOS., GL18 1PS.
Telephone: Newent 820650

N⁰ 003703

# THE POUND HOUSE

Mʳ K. Abernow

16.1 19 86

| Quantity | Titles | @ | £ | p |
|---|---|---|---|---|
| 1 | Mines of Cards + R.P. | | 4 | 40 |
| | Pd with thanks | | | |

Yes, we know of the old homes,
Hope to see you in Anglesey.
Thanks for your kind remarks
re The Pound House & WMS
— I do it because I enjoy
it — nothing altruistic
about it!

DB

+ Not sure this is the right word.

Payment due one month from invoice date

CARDIGAN,ROYAL                                                        0063

Production: Zinc          Ore(tons) Metal(tons)      Value(£)
            1877            20.00       0.00           75.00


CARON                         PONTRHYDFENDIGAID                       0064

Production: Lead          Ore(tons) Metal(tons)      Value(£)
            1878            30.00      23.70           257.20
            1879            30.00      23.40           247.50
            1880            20.00      16.00           242.50
            1881             6.20       4.20            56.60
            1882             3.00       2.40            25.00
Ownership:  1877-1882 CARON LEAD MINING CO.LTD.
            Comment 1882 ABANDONED
Management: Manager 1879-1881 JOHN KITTO & SON
            Chief Agent 1877-1878 JOHN KITTO; 1879-1881 RICH.COUCH; 1882
            JOHN KITTO & SON
Employment:              Underground     Surface        Total
            1877             19             8             27
            1878             22            27             49
            1879             17             8             25
            1880             12            15             27
            1881              8             5             13
            1882              9             4             13


CASTELL                       PONTERWYD                     SN 775813 0065

Production: Lead          Ore(tons) Metal(tons)      Value(£)
            1898            25.00      13.00           200.00
            Zinc          Ore(tons) Metal(tons)      Value(£)
            1857            26.80       0.00            97.30
            1858            54.00       0.00           148.00
            1859             5.30       0.00            15.00
            1860            25.00       0.00            67.50
            1861            15.00       0.00            34.00
            1865            21.00       0.00            63.00
            1894            60.00      23.00           162.00
            1895             5.00       2.00            19.00
            1899           386.00     160.00          2719.00
            1900           399.00     162.00          1919.00
            1901           241.00     100.00           805.00
            1902           295.00     117.00          1283.00
            1903           388.00     145.00          2123.00
            1904           207.00      81.00          1082.00
            1905           258.00     101.00          1740.00
            1906           350.00     137.00          2577.00
            1907           392.00     161.00          2651.00
            1908           121.00      50.00           599.00
            1910            20.00       8.00           120.00
            1911            22.00       9.00           132.00
            1912            70.00      29.00           500.00
            1913           166.00      69.00           953.00
            Comment 1901-1902 NEW CASTELL; 1910 NEW CASTELL; 1911 NEW
            CASTELL VALUE EST.
Ownership:  1892-1893 HY.ENFIELD TAYLOR; 1894-1895 CASTELL MINING
            CO.LTD.; 1896 BAINBRIDGE,BOUNDY & MCILQUHAN; 1897-1909 NEW
            CASTELL MINES LTD.; 1910 JOHN OWEN; 1911 EXECUTORS OF JOHN
            OWEN; 1912-1913 NEW CASTELL BLENDE MINE LTD.
            Comment 1892-1893 OR WEST ESGAIR LLE
Management: Chief Agent 1892-1895 HY.ENFIELD TAYLOR; 1896-1898 JOHN OWEN;
            1899-1908 H.W.FRANCIS; 1909-1910 JOHN OWEN; 1912-1913
            G.L.C.CLAYTON

                                    19

CASTELL                          PONTERWYD                        Continued

Employment:              Underground    Surface      Total
             1892             6            2            8
             1893             3                         3
             1894             6            6           12
             1895             3                         3
             1896             2                         2
             1897             8            2           10
             1898            45           22           77
             1899            42            8           50
             1900            21           15           36
             1901             8            9           17
             1902            16           14           30
             1903            23           16           39
             1904            13            3           16
             1905            24            7           31
             1906            25           17           42
             1907            27           10           37
             1908            20            6           26
             1909                          6            6
             1910–1911        8            4           12
             1912            20           15           35
             1913            26           15           41


CASTELL,DYFFRYRN                 PONTERWYD                                    0066

Production: Zinc            Ore(tons)  Metal(tons)    Value(£)
            1865              95.20        0.00        285.60


CASTLE WARD UNITED                                                           0067

Production: Lead & Silver   Ore(tons)  Lead(tons) Silver(ozs)   Value(£)
            1862              80.00       61.00      290.00        0.00


CEFNGWRION                       TALIESIN                      SN 675932 0068

Production: Lead No detailed return
Ownership:  1864–1865 RICH.JONES & CO.
Management: Chief Agent 1864–1865 RICH.JONES


CEFNGWYN                         TALYBONT                      SN 680870 0069

Production: Lead & Silver   Ore(tons)  Lead(tons) Silver(ozs)   Value(£)
            1875             20.00       15.00      120.00       600.00
            1876              3.00        2.20       16.00         0.00
            1878             21.00       15.70       30.00       220.00
            1879             18.00       13.60       62.00       140.70
            1880             28.00       20.50       36.00       274.10
            1881             29.50       20.50       38.00       269.00
            1882             19.20       14.20        0.00       171.00
            1883             11.20        9.00       45.00        95.00
            1884              1.00        0.80        4.00         7.00
Ownership:  1863–1865 WALKER & CO.; 1877–1881 JOHN B.MANSFIELD; 1882–1886
            CAELAN,CEFNGWYN & KYLAN POTOSI CO.
            Comment 1864–1865 SUSPENDED; 1885 STOPPED APR.1885; 1886
            SUSPENDED
Management: Chief Agent 1863 JOHN HUGHES; 1876–1877 JOHN HUGHES;
            1878–1886 JOHN HUGHES JNR.
            Secretary 1876–1886 JOHN B.MANSFIELD (S)

CEFNGWYN                          TALYBONT                    Continued

Employment:                 Underground    Surface      Total
               1877              10            2           12
               1878              15            7           22
               1879              12            7           19
               1880              13           10           23
               1881              14            8           22
               1882              12            5           17
               1883               9            4           13
               1884               6            2            8
               1885               2                         2
               1886                            1            1


CEFNGYNTLE                                                              0070

Production: Lead            Ore(tons) Metal(tons)    Value(£)
               1851            13.20       10.00         0.00


CEFNMAWR                                                                0071

Production: Lead            Ore(tons) Metal(tons)    Value(£)
               1854            15.80       11.00         0.00


CEREGWYNON                        GOGINAN               SN 684837 0072

Production: Lead            Ore(tons) Metal(tons)    Value(£)
               1852            12.80        9.00         0.00
               1854     No detailed return


CHWAREL LAS                  HALKYN, FLINTSHIRE                        0073

Production: Lead            Ore(tons) Metal(tons)    Value(£)
               1861             6.00        4.00         0.00
               Comment 1861 CHEVARAL LLYS


CLARA                             PONTERWYD             SN 737807 0074

Production: Lead            Ore(tons) Metal(tons)    Value(£)
               1857            12.00        9.00         0.00
               1859-1860 No detailed return
               1861      No detailed return
               1862            38.00       29.00         0.00
               1863            14.00       10.50         0.00
               1867            23.00       17.20         0.00
               1868-1870 No detailed return
               1871            40.00       29.00         0.00
               1872            40.00       28.00         0.00
               1873      No detailed return
               1875            10.00        7.50         0.00
               1876             8.00        6.00         0.00
               1877             5.00        3.20        62.50
               1878             7.00        5.50        70.00
               1881             2.50        1.50        25.00
               Comment 1859-1860 SEE CLARA, FLINTSHIRE; 1861 CLARA
               UNITED:INC.PENPOMPREN; 1862-1863 CLARA UNITED; 1867-1870
               CLARA UNITED; 1871-1873 CLARA CONSOLS; 1875-1878 CLARA
               CONSOLS; 1881 CLARA CONSOLS
               Zinc             Ore(tons) Metal(tons)   Value(£)
               1872            30.00        0.00        90.00

21

Comment 1872 CLARA CONSOLS
Ownership:   1859-1860 LAMERT & CO.; 1861-1865 J.B.BALCOMBE & CO.;
             1870-1872 CLARA CONSOLS CO.; 1873-1882 CLARA CONSOLS CO.LTD.;
             1883 S.STRINGER
             Comment 1861-1865 CLARA UNITED; 1870-1882 CLARA CONSOLS; 1883
             CLARA CONSOLS:SUSPENDED
Management:  Manager 1870-1871 WM.BATTYE; 1872 JAS.PHILLIPS; 1873
             NICH.BRAY; 1874 JAS.PHILLIPS; 1876-1879 WM.BATTYE
             Chief Agent 1859-1860 S.TREVETHAN; 1861-1865 JAS.LESTER;
             1874-1882 NICH.BRAY
             Secretary 1873-1875 WM.BATTYE
Employment:                 Underground    Surface       Total
             1877               9             3            12
             1878               8                           8
             1879-1881          4                           4
             1882               2             3             5


COEDMAWRPOOL                   TREFRIW, CAERNARVON                        0075

Production: Lead          Ore(tons) Metal(tons)   Value(£)
            1852            62.00       49.00        0.00
            1853          No detailed return
            1854             7.00        5.00        0.00


COURT GRANGE                      BOW STREET                  SN 656856 0076

Production: Lead & Silver   Ore(tons) Lead(tons) Silver(ozs)   Value(£)
            1850            181.00     130.00        0.00        0.00
            1851            279.00     216.10        0.00        0.00
            1852            171.00     120.00     3600.00        0.00
            1853             91.10      68.20        0.00        0.00
            1854          No detailed return
            1855             40.10      26.40        0.00        0.00
            1856             22.90      16.00        0.00        0.00
            1857          No detailed return
            1878             36.00      27.00     1620.00      504.00
            1879             36.30      27.00      918.00      580.70
            1880            114.00      84.00     3020.00     1720.00
            1881            137.70     105.40     1910.70     4675.00
            1882             12.00       9.20      240.00      169.00
            1888             12.00       8.00      322.00      152.00
            1890              6.00       4.50      179.00       81.00
            1891              1.00       0.50       25.00        9.00
            Zinc            Ore(tons) Metal(tons)   Value(£)
            1879             15.00       0.00       15.40
            1881             20.00      13.00       29.00
            1882             20.00       8.50       35.00
            1883             10.00       5.50       24.00
            1890             14.00       6.00       67.00
            1891              8.00       2.50       23.00
Ownership:   1863-1865 GEO.PELL & CO.; 1867 JOHN TAYLOR & SONS; 1873-1875
             COURT GRANGE CO.; 1877-1881 COURT GRANGE CO.LTD.; 1882 COURT
             GRANGE UNITED MINES CO.LTD.; 1883-1884 THOS.KEY; 1885
             THOS.KEY & C.O.ROGERS; 1886 C.O.ROGERS; 1887 THOS.KEY;
             1888-1893 COURT GRANGE MINE CO.
             Comment 1864-1865 SUSPENDED; 1882 IN LIQUIDATION; 1884-1886
             SUSPENDED; 1893 ABANDONED IN 1893
Management:  Manager 1867 JAS.GARLAND
             Chief Agent 1863 J.WILLIAMS; 1875 GEO.GREEN; 1877-1881
             JAS.G.GREEN; 1882-1883 S.A.CORBETT; 1888 JOHN OWEN; 1890-1892
             JOHN OWEN; 1893 JAS.LEWIS

COURT GRANGE                    BOW STREET                      Continued

Secretary 1888-1893 GEO.GREEN

| Employment: | Underground | Surface | Total |
|-------------|-------------|---------|-------|
| 1877 | 45 | 20 | 65 |
| 1878 | 50 | 26 | 76 |
| 1879 | 22 | 14 | 36 |
| 1880 | 35 | 21 | 56 |
| 1881 | 34 | 23 | 57 |
| 1882 | 31 | 15 | 46 |
| 1883 |  | 6 | 6 |
| 1887 | 2 |  | 2 |
| 1888 | 2 | 2 | 4 |
| 1889 | 6 |  | 6 |
| 1890-1891 | 2 | 2 | 4 |
| 1892 |  | 2 | 2 |
| 1893 |  | 1 | 1 |


CRAIGNANT BACH                  PONTERWYD                       0077

| Production: Lead & Silver | Ore(tons) | Lead(tons) | Silver(ozs) | Value(£) |
|---------------------------|-----------|------------|-------------|----------|
| 1882 | 10.00 | 8.00 | 0.00 | 95.00 |
| 1883 | 2.80 | 2.20 | 4.00 | 15.00 |

Ownership: 1881-1883 CRAIGNANT BACH LEAD MINING CO.LTD.
Management: Chief Agent 1881-1883 AND.WILLIAMS

| Employment: | Underground | Surface | Total |
|-------------|-------------|---------|-------|
| 1881 | 6 |  | 6 |
| 1882 | 8 | 3 | 11 |
| 1883 | 2 | 2 | 4 |


CRAIGYMWN                   LLANRHAIADR, MONTGOMERY      SJ 077286 0078

| Production: Lead | Ore(tons) | Metal(tons) | Value(£) |
|------------------|-----------|-------------|----------|
| 1851 | 23.00 | 17.00 | 0.00 |

1852-1854 No detailed return
Comment 1851-1854 CRAIGYMWYN


CROWN                           PONTERWYD               SN 762799 0079

Production: Lead No detailed return
           Zinc No detailed return
Ownership: 1873-1874 RICH.HARVEY & CO.; 1875-1878 CROWN MINING CO.;
           1879-1887 CROWN MINING CO.LTD.; 1888-1890 W.J.LAVINGTON;
           1891-1892 CROWN MINING CO.LTD.; 1897-1898 CROWN BLENDE
           SYNDICATE LTD.; 1905-1910 JOHN OWEN
           Comment 1884-1887 SUSPENDED; 1891-1892 SUSPENDED; 1897 CROWN
           BLENDE:RESTARTED JAN.1898; 1898 CROWN BLENDE; 1905-1906 CROWN
           BLENDE; 1907 CROWN BLENDE:IDLE; 1908-1910 CROWN BLENDE
Management: Chief Agent 1875 RICH.HARVEY; 1876-1892 DAVID DANIEL; 1897
           E.H.DAVIES; 1898 JOHN OWEN; 1905-1910 JOHN OWEN
           Secretary 1881-1887 W.J.LAVINGTON (S); 1888-1889 GEO.GREEN;
           1891-1892 W.J.LAVINGTON

| Employment: | Underground | Surface | Total |
|-------------|-------------|---------|-------|
| 1877 | 8 |  | 8 |
| 1878-1880 | 6 |  | 6 |
| 1881-1882 | 7 |  | 7 |
| 1883 | 6 |  | 6 |
| 1884-1885 |  | 1 | 1 |
| 1886 | 3 |  | 3 |
| 1887-1888 | 10 |  | 10 |
| 1889 | 9 |  | 9 |
| 1890 |  | 3 | 3 |

CROWN                          PONTERWYD                        Continued

|        | Underground | Surface | Total |
|--------|-------------|---------|-------|
| 1892   |             | 1       | 1     |
| 1898   | 2           |         | 2     |
| 1905   | 2           | 2       | 4     |
| 1906   | 2           |         | 2     |
| 1908–1909 | 2        |         | 2     |
| 1910   |             | 1       | 1     |

CWMBRANE                                                              0080

Production: Lead      Ore(tons)  Metal(tons)  Value(£)
            1862        44.00      83.00        0.00

CWMBRWYNO                      GOGINAN                    SN 715805 0081

Production: Lead & Silver

| Year | Ore(tons) | Lead(tons) | Silver(ozs) | Value(£) |
|------|-----------|------------|-------------|----------|
| 1845 | 72.00 | 43.00 | 0.00 | 0.00 |
| 1846 | 75.00 | 45.00 | 0.00 | 0.00 |
| 1847 | 36.00 | 24.00 | 0.00 | 0.00 |
| 1848 | 36.00 | 24.00 | 0.00 | 0.00 |
| 1849 | 10.00 | 7.00 | 0.00 | 0.00 |
| 1850 | 13.00 | 0.00 | 0.00 | 0.00 |
| 1851 | 13.90 | 11.50 | 0.00 | 0.00 |
| 1852 | 190.00 | 143.00 | 0.00 | 0.00 |
| 1853 | 314.00 | 236.00 | 450.00 | 0.00 |
| 1854 | 630.00 | 446.00 | 0.00 | 0.00 |
| 1855 | 433.00 | 340.00 | 1000.00 | 0.00 |
| 1856 | 429.50 | 327.00 | 961.00 | 0.00 |
| 1857 | 380.10 | 282.20 | 900.00 | 0.00 |
| 1858 | 362.00 | 288.00 | 919.00 | 0.00 |
| 1859 | 267.00 | 200.00 | 0.00 | 0.00 |
| 1860 | 396.00 | 282.00 | 1415.00 | 0.00 |
| 1861 | 288.00 | 222.00 | 0.00 | 0.00 |
| 1862 | 326.00 | 257.00 | 500.00 | 0.00 |
| 1863 | 236.00 | 192.00 | 384.00 | 0.00 |
| 1864 | 38.20 | 21.60 | 0.00 | 0.00 |
| 1865 | 163.60 | 120.00 | 0.00 | 0.00 |
| 1866 | 140.00 | 104.00 | 0.00 | 0.00 |
| 1867 | 80.00 | 62.50 | 190.00 | 0.00 |
| 1868 | 20.00 | 14.50 | 0.00 | 0.00 |
| 1869 | 89.20 | 66.90 | 0.00 | 0.00 |
| 1870 | 188.00 | 143.00 | 0.00 | 0.00 |
| 1871 | 192.00 | 146.00 | 0.00 | 0.00 |
| 1872 | 195.00 | 146.20 | 0.00 | 0.00 |
| 1873 | 170.10 | 126.50 | 400.00 | 0.00 |
| 1874 | 116.60 | 87.00 | 0.00 | 0.00 |
| 1875 | 5.00 | 3.50 | 0.00 | 0.00 |
| 1876 | 26.00 | 19.50 | 0.00 | 0.00 |
| 1877 | 14.40 | 10.80 | 0.00 | 180.60 |
| 1878 | 13.10 | 7.50 | 0.00 | 123.00 |
| 1880 | 53.20 | 34.30 | 75.00 | 532.00 |
| 1881 | 50.00 | 35.00 | 75.00 | 475.00 |
| 1882 | 15.00 | 12.10 | 0.00 | 120.00 |
| 1888 | 18.00 | 13.00 | 114.00 | 135.00 |

Comment 1845–1873 CEFN CWM BRWYNO; 1874 FOR SILVER SEE CWMYSTWYTH; 1875–1878 CEFN CWM BRWYNO; 1880–1882 CEFN CWM BRWYNO; 1888 CEFN CWM BRWYNO

Zinc         Ore(tons)  Metal(tons)  Value(£)
1854          21.00       0.00        0.00
1855          46.70       0.00        0.00
1856          94.50       0.00        274.10

Zinc              Ore(tons)  Metal(tons)     Value(£)
1857              160.10        0.00          432.20
1858               52.00        0.00          156.00
1859               52.50        0.00          350.00
1860               45.90        0.00          114.50
1861         No detailed return
1862               29.20        0.00           62.00
1864               48.80        0.00          146.40
1865               42.20        0.00           72.70
1866               68.40        0.00          136.70
1869               49.60        0.00          141.30
1870               29.00        0.00          110.20
1871               60.00        0.00          225.00
1872               25.00        0.00           93.80
1873               22.60        0.00           56.60
1876               14.00        0.00           49.00
1882               15.00        7.20           45.00
1888               12.00        4.00           48.00
1892               10.00        3.00           21.00
Comment 1854–1858 CEFN BRWYNO; 1859–1862 CEFN CWM BRWYNO;
1865–1866 CEFN CWM BRYNO
Ownership:   1859–1865 JOHN TAYLOR & SONS; 1867–1875 J.H.MURCHISON & CO.;
1876 GEO.WILLIAMS,E.J.WILLIAMS & JAS.PAULL; 1877
GEO.UNDERWOOD; 1878–1881 HERB.E.UNDERWOOD; 1882–1884
GEO.GREEN; 1886–1889 CARDIGAN UNITED MINES LTD.; 1892–1894
CWM BRWYNO BLENDE & LEAD CO.LTD.; 1905–1913 HY.JENKS
Comment 1859–1865 CEFN BRWYNO; 1867–1875 CEFN BRWYNO; 1884
ABANDONED APR.1884; 1889 SUSPENDED; 1892–1894 SUSPENDED;
1912–1913 IDLE
Management: Manager 1867 JAS.PAULL
Chief Agent 1859 JAS.PAULL; 1860 JOHN PAULL; 1861 JAS.PAULL;
1862–1865 JOHN PAULL; 1868–1881 JAS.PAULL; 1882 ROBT.UREN;
1883–1884 JOHN DAVIS; 1886–1889 A.H.JENKS; 1892–1894
A.H.JENKS; 1905–1910 JOHN MITCHELL
Employment:            Underground    Surface        Total
1877                2           7            9
1880               16          17           33
1881               12           6           18
1882                7           2            9
1883                3                        3
1884                4                        4
1886                8          10           18
1887               12           8           20
1888                6           9           15
1889                            1            1
1892               12           5           17
1905–1911           2                        2


CWMDARREN                    GOGINAN                SN 681834 0082

Production: Lead & Silver    Ore(tons)  Lead(tons)  Silver(ozs)   Value(£)
1851              20.40      14.70        0.00         0.00
1852              10.40       7.30      140.00         0.00
1853              37.70      28.00      440.00         0.00
1854         No detailed return
1855              50.30      33.50        0.00         0.00
1856               2.20       1.40        0.00         0.00
1857         No detailed return
Comment 1853 AGGREGATED
Copper            Ore(tons)  Metal(tons)    Value(£)
1855              41.10        0.00         0.00
1856              23.30        0.00         0.00

| Copper | Ore(tons) | Metal(tons) | Value(£) |
|--------|-----------|-------------|----------|
| 1857 | 29.40 | 0.00 | 0.00 |
| 1858 | 5.00 | 0.00 | 0.00 |

Comment 1855—1857 (P); 1858 (P) FOR CU SEE EAGLE BROOK
Ownership: 1863—1865 W.H.PUNCHARD & CO.; 1866 THOS.SPARGO
Management: Chief Agent 1863—1865 AND.WILLIAMS; 1866 RICH.WILLIAMS

CWMERFIN GOGINAN SN 698829 0084

Production: 

| Lead & Silver | Ore(tons) | Lead(tons) | Silver(ozs) | Value(£) |
|---------------|-----------|------------|-------------|----------|
| 1849 | 116.00 | 78.00 | 0.00 | 0.00 |
| 1850 | 81.00 | 55.50 | 0.00 | 0.00 |
| 1851 | 187.90 | 140.70 | 0.00 | 0.00 |
| 1852 | 259.00 | 180.00 | 1360.00 | 0.00 |
| 1853 | 228.00 | 206.00 | 4274.00 | 0.00 |
| 1854 | 226.00 | 170.00 | 4420.00 | 0.00 |
| 1855 | 247.00 | 190.00 | 3420.00 | 0.00 |
| 1856 | 326.60 | 206.00 | 3330.00 | 0.00 |
| 1857 | 256.00 | 184.00 | 3404.00 | 0.00 |
| 1858 | 448.00 | 344.00 | 7224.00 | 0.00 |
| 1859 | 529.60 | 397.00 | 7682.00 | 0.00 |
| 1860 | 626.00 | 462.50 | 10678.00 | 0.00 |
| 1861 | 692.00 | 498.00 | 12450.00 | 0.00 |
| 1862 | 641.00 | 461.00 | 12910.00 | 0.00 |
| 1863 | 730.00 | 532.00 | 15272.00 | 0.00 |
| 1864 | 750.60 | 530.00 | 6478.00 | 0.00 |
| 1865 | 798.50 | 598.00 | 19136.00 | 0.00 |
| 1866 | 765.00 | 545.00 | 17205.00 | 0.00 |
| 1867 | 747.00 | 535.50 | 16920.00 | 0.00 |
| 1868 | 605.30 | 463.50 | 14353.00 | 0.00 |
| 1869 | 495.10 | 371.00 | 11910.00 | 0.00 |
| 1870 | 421.00 | 315.00 | 9922.00 | 0.00 |
| 1871 | 145.50 | 109.10 | 0.00 | 0.00 |
| 1872 | 8.60 | 6.20 | 180.00 | 0.00 |
| 1873 | 14.60 | 10.90 | 66.00 | 0.00 |
| 1874 | 17.70 | 11.50 | 0.00 | 190.30 |
| 1875 | 27.00 | 20.00 | 0.00 | 0.00 |
| 1876 | 5.00 | 3.70 | 0.00 | 0.00 |
| 1877 | 5.40 | 4.00 | 0.00 | 68.10 |
| 1887 | 13.00 | 9.00 | 0.00 | 127.00 |

Comment 1874 FOR SILVER SEE CWMYSTWYTH

| Zinc | Ore(tons) | Metal(tons) | Value(£) |
|------|-----------|-------------|----------|
| 1863 | 29.00 | 0.00 | 87.50 |
| 1887 | 3.00 | 1.00 | 11.00 |
| 1889 | 3.00 | 1.00 | 14.00 |

| Copper | Ore(tons) | Metal(tons) | Value(£) |
|--------|-----------|-------------|----------|
| 1855 | 7.40 | 0.00 | 0.00 |
| 1871 | 13.20 | 0.80 | 32.00 |

Comment 1855 (P); 1871 (P) COPPER EST.
Ownership: 1859—1867 JOHN TAYLOR & SONS; 1868—1875 CWM ERFIN CO.;
1876—1881 WM.JONES; 1882 W.J.SENNETT; 1883 W.J.SENNETT &
W.SADLER; 1884—1889 W.SADLER; 1890—1896 GEO.BURNELL;
1897—1898 EXECUTORS OF THE LATE GEO.BURNELL; 1899—1904
WM.HUGHES JONES
Comment 1880 NOT WORKED; 1898—1900 SUSPENDED; 1901 NOT WORKED
IN 1901; 1902—1904 NOT WORKED
Management: Manager 1868—1875 JOHN TAYLOR & SONS
Chief Agent 1859—1874 JOHN WILLIAMS; 1875—1878 JOHN PAULL;
1879—1881 WM.JONES; 1882—1884 AND.WILLIAMS; 1885 WM.NORTHEY;
1886—1904 J.H.ROBERTS
Employment:

| | Underground | Surface | Total |
|------|-------------|---------|-------|
| 1877 | | 2 | 2 |

| | Underground | Surface | Total |
|---|---|---|---|
| 1882 | | 5 | 5 |
| 1883 | 2 | 2 | 4 |
| 1884 | 2 | | 2 |
| 1885 | 4 | 2 | 6 |
| 1886 | 8 | 2 | 10 |
| 1887 | 6 | 9 | 15 |
| 1888 | 10 | | 10 |
| 1889 | 9 | | 9 |
| 1890 | 13 | 2 | 15 |
| 1891 | 9 | 1 | 10 |
| 1892 | 8 | 2 | 10 |
| 1893 | 3 | 1 | 4 |
| 1894 | 3 | | 3 |
| 1895 | 1 | 1 | 2 |
| 1896–1897 | 2 | | 2 |

**CWMERFIN,WEST**                  GOGINAN                     SN 675817 0085

Production: Lead             Ore(tons) Metal(tons)    Value(£)
           1868           44.00       33.50        0.00
Ownership: 1862–1867 JOHN TAYLOR & SONS; 1868–1874 WEST CWM ERFIN CO.
Management: Manager 1868–1874 JOHN TAYLOR & SONS
            Chief Agent 1862–1874 JAS.PAULL

**CWMFRON**                      LLANIDLOES, MONTGOMERY       SN 971809 0086

Production: Lead             Ore(tons) Metal(tons)    Value(£)
           1864           5.70        4.50        0.00
            Comment 1864–0550 CWMVRON, MONTGOMERY

**CWMMAWR**                     STRATA FLORIDA                        0087

Production: Lead & Silver    Ore(tons)  Lead(tons) Silver(ozs)    Value(£)
           1913         96.00     75.00     764.00     1289.00
           Zinc          Ore(tons) Metal(tons)    Value(£)
           1913         10.00      4.00       65.00
Ownership: 1911 ST.JAMES' SYNDICATE LTD.; 1912–1913 CAMBRIAN LEAD & ZINC
           MINING CO.LTD.
Management: Chief Agent 1911–1913 THOS.EDWARDS
Employment:             Underground   Surface     Total

| | Underground | Surface | Total |
|---|---|---|---|
| 1911 | 7 | 2 | 9 |
| 1912 | 15 | 20 | 35 |
| 1913 | 25 | 21 | 46 |

**CWMOROG**                     PONTERWYD                        0088

Production: Lead No detailed return
Ownership: 1876 CWMOROG MINING CO.; 1877–1879 CWMOROG MINING CO.LTD.;
           1880–1881 CWMOROG SILVER LEAD MINING CO.LTD.
           Comment 1880 NOT WORKED
Management: Chief Agent 1876–1881 JAS.CORBETT
Employment:             Underground   Surface     Total

| | Underground | Surface | Total |
|---|---|---|---|
| 1877 | 6 | | 6 |

CWMPRYF                              CWM RHEIDOL                                0089

Production: Lead & Silver    Ore(tons)   Lead(tons) Silver(ozs)   Value(£)
            1879               10.00        7.50       0.00        103.00
            1880               30.00       23.20     159.00        360.00
            1881               11.40        7.70      56.00        100.80
Ownership:  1879 CWMPRYF MINING CO.; 1880-1883 CWMPRYF MINING CO.LTD.
            Comment 1880 CWMPRYT; 1881-1883 IN LIQUIDATION
Management: Chief Agent 1879-1881 ABS.FRANCIS; 1882 THOS.& GEO.WILLIAMS;
            1883 JOHN DAVIS
Employment:                  Underground    Surface      Total
            1879                  8            5           13
            1880                 18           18           36
            1881                  4                         4
            1883                  4                         4


CWMSEBON                               GOGINAN                                  0090

Production: Lead & Silver    Ore(tons)   Lead(tons) Silver(ozs)   Value(£)
            1845              197.00      128.00       0.00          0.00
            1846              250.00      168.00       0.00          0.00
            1847              205.00      123.00       0.00          0.00
            1848               31.00       17.00       0.00          0.00
            1849               55.00       33.00       0.00          0.00
            1850               47.00       22.00       0.00          0.00
            1851               17.80        8.70       0.00          0.00
            1852-1854 No detailed return
            1857              146.50      118.00    3894.00          0.00
            1858              203.00      164.00    5084.00          0.00
            1859              140.60      105.00       0.00          0.00
            1860       No detailed return
            1863       No detailed return
            Comment 1859 OR SOUTH DARREN; 1860 SEE SOUTH DARREN; 1863 SEE
            SOUTH DARREN
            Copper           Ore(tons) Metal(tons)    Value(£)
            1845               26.00        0.00       0.00
            1846               35.00        0.00       0.00
            1847               12.00        0.00       0.00
            1858               17.70        0.00       0.00
            1859               14.80        1.30       0.00
            1860               16.80        1.10       0.00
            1864-1865 No detailed return
            Comment 1845-1847 (S); 1858 (S) FOR CU SEE EAGLE BROOK;
            1859-1860 (S) COPPER EST.; 1864-1865 SEE SOUTH DARREN
Ownership:  1859-1877 J.H.MURCHISON & CO.
            Comment 1860-1877 OR SOUTH DARREN
Management: Chief Agent 1859-1869 JOHN BOUNDY; 1870-1871 WM.H.BOUNDY;
            1872-1877 JOHN BOUNDY


CWMSYMLOG                             CWMSYMLOG                                 0091

Production: Lead & Silver    Ore(tons)   Lead(tons) Silver(ozs)   Value(£)
            1863                5.00        4.00     116.00          0.00
            1867                8.00        6.00     213.00          0.00


CWMSYMLOG,NORTH                                                                0092

Production: Lead & Silver    Ore(tons)   Lead(tons) Silver(ozs)   Value(£)
            1868                5.00        4.00     106.00          0.00
            1869-1873 No detailed return

CWMSYMLOG,WEST                    CWMSYMLOG                         SN 690840 0093

Production: Lead No detailed return
Ownership:  1866 SETON & CO.
Management: Chief Agent 1866 AND.WILLIAMS


CWMYSTWYTH                      DEVIL'S BRIDGE                      SN 805747 0094

| Production: Lead & Silver | Ore(tons) | Lead(tons) | Silver(ozs) | Value(£) |
|---|---|---|---|---|
| 1845 | 356.00 | 238.00 | 0.00 | 0.00 |
| 1846 | 588.00 | 382.00 | 0.00 | 0.00 |
| 1847 | 439.00 | 263.00 | 0.00 | 0.00 |
| 1848 | 120.00 | 71.00 | 0.00 | 0.00 |
| 1849 | 583.00 | 333.00 | 0.00 | 0.00 |
| 1850 | 801.00 | 572.00 | 0.00 | 0.00 |
| 1851 | 789.10 | 637.30 | 0.00 | 0.00 |
| 1852 | 1075.00 | 784.00 | 2350.00 | 0.00 |
| 1853 | 1026.00 | 770.00 | 0.00 | 0.00 |
| 1854 | 1120.00 | 840.00 | 0.00 | 0.00 |
| 1855 | 1080.00 | 825.00 | 0.00 | 0.00 |
| 1856 | 1195.00 | 829.00 | 0.00 | 0.00 |
| 1857 | 1281.00 | 953.00 | 0.00 | 0.00 |
| 1858 | 1370.00 | 1069.00 | 0.00 | 0.00 |
| 1859 | 1417.50 | 1052.00 | 0.00 | 0.00 |
| 1860 | 1142.00 | 889.00 | 4400.00 | 0.00 |
| 1861 | 1295.00 | 997.00 | 0.00 | 0.00 |
| 1862 | 1270.00 | 997.00 | 1490.00 | 0.00 |
| 1863 | 1360.00 | 1108.50 | 1652.00 | 0.00 |
| 1864 | 1231.90 | 862.40 | 0.00 | 0.00 |
| 1865 | 1277.90 | 958.00 | 0.00 | 0.00 |
| 1866 | 1070.00 | 824.00 | 0.00 | 0.00 |
| 1867 | 833.00 | 639.00 | 0.00 | 0.00 |
| 1868 | 653.80 | 499.00 | 0.00 | 0.00 |
| 1869 | 580.00 | 449.00 | 0.00 | 0.00 |
| 1870 | 346.10 | 264.50 | 0.00 | 0.00 |
| 1871 | 326.70 | 236.00 | 0.00 | 0.00 |
| 1872 | 263.10 | 197.00 | 0.00 | 0.00 |
| 1873 | 194.00 | 145.50 | 0.00 | 0.00 |
| 1874 | 178.00 | 133.00 | 1950.00 | 2413.00 |
| 1875 | 257.00 | 194.00 | 1372.00 | 3863.80 |
| 1876 | 243.00 | 182.20 | 1275.00 | 3574.80 |
| 1877 | 275.00 | 356.20 | 2492.00 | 3249.00 |
| 1878 | 382.00 | 230.00 | 1150.00 | 3522.90 |
| 1879 | 487.00 | 366.70 | 1833.00 | 4722.50 |
| 1880 | 490.00 | 388.70 | 0.00 | 4488.50 |
| 1881 | 474.00 | 355.00 | 0.00 | 4787.00 |
| 1882 | 360.00 | 280.80 | 0.00 | 3144.00 |
| 1883 | 319.00 | 252.00 | 829.00 | 2366.00 |
| 1884 | 193.00 | 152.50 | 0.00 | 1207.00 |
| 1885 | 158.00 | 118.00 | 0.00 | 1060.00 |
| 1886 | 152.00 | 113.00 | 0.00 | 1210.00 |
| 1887 | 145.00 | 104.00 | 0.00 | 1110.00 |
| 1888 | 143.00 | 106.00 | 0.00 | 1175.00 |
| 1889 | 102.00 | 76.00 | 0.00 | 799.00 |
| 1890 | 91.00 | 67.00 | 0.00 | 694.00 |
| 1891 | 50.00 | 37.00 | 0.00 | 340.00 |
| 1892 | 48.00 | 35.00 | 279.00 | 283.00 |
| 1900 | 90.00 | 68.00 | 478.00 | 900.00 |
| 1901 | 159.00 | 121.00 | 795.00 | 982.00 |
| 1902 | 243.00 | 180.00 | 1215.00 | 1520.00 |
| 1903 | 686.00 | 502.00 | 3430.00 | 4526.00 |
| 1904 | 289.00 | 211.00 | 1445.00 | 1978.00 |
| 1905 | 383.00 | 276.00 | 1340.00 | 2877.00 |
| 1906 | 312.00 | 231.00 | 1170.00 | 3432.00 |

| Lead & Silver | Ore(tons) | Lead(tons) | Silver(ozs) | Value(£) |
|---|---|---|---|---|
| 1907 | 364.00 | 276.00 | 1456.00 | 4754.00 |
| 1908 | 251.00 | 186.00 | 879.00 | 1856.00 |
| 1909 | 74.00 | 53.00 | 222.00 | 527.00 |
| 1911 | 86.00 | 64.00 | 344.00 | 667.00 |
| 1912 | 49.00 | 36.00 | 196.00 | 438.00 |

Comment 1874 SILVER INCLUDES 4 OTHER MINES; 1901-1902 INC
KINGSIDE; 1911 INC KINGSIDE; 1912 SILVER EST.:INC.KINGSIDE

| Zinc | Ore(tons) | Metal(tons) | Value(£) |
|---|---|---|---|
| 1859 | 102.60 | 0.00 | 359.00 |
| 1860 | 77.00 | 0.00 | 175.10 |
| 1861 | No detailed return | | |
| 1863 | 19.40 | 0.00 | 58.50 |
| 1864 | 143.70 | 0.00 | 431.00 |
| 1866 | 47.50 | 0.00 | 94.90 |
| 1870 | 115.80 | 0.00 | 231.60 |
| 1872 | 25.00 | 0.00 | 75.00 |
| 1873 | 60.00 | 0.00 | 180.00 |
| 1874 | 110.00 | 0.00 | 300.00 |
| 1876 | 33.00 | 0.00 | 101.20 |
| 1877 | 50.00 | 0.00 | 187.00 |
| 1878 | 100.00 | 0.00 | 167.50 |
| 1879 | 50.00 | 0.00 | 231.30 |
| 1880 | 263.00 | 0.00 | 749.20 |
| 1881 | 582.00 | 232.80 | 1595.00 |
| 1882 | 396.00 | 194.00 | 1333.00 |
| 1883 | 515.00 | 257.50 | 1818.00 |
| 1884 | 1000.00 | 0.00 | 3888.00 |
| 1885 | 1135.00 | 443.00 | 2959.00 |
| 1886 | 785.00 | 288.00 | 2166.00 |
| 1887 | 690.00 | 253.00 | 1941.00 |
| 1888 | 755.00 | 276.00 | 2606.00 |
| 1889 | 495.00 | 183.00 | 1753.00 |
| 1890 | 306.00 | 112.00 | 1243.00 |
| 1891 | 330.00 | 121.00 | 1353.00 |
| 1892 | 440.00 | 148.00 | 1767.00 |
| 1900 | 229.00 | 91.00 | 973.00 |
| 1901 | 171.00 | 67.00 | 534.00 |
| 1902 | 246.00 | 92.00 | 1016.00 |
| 1903 | 1110.00 | 415.00 | 5272.00 |
| 1904 | 1694.00 | 634.00 | 7992.00 |
| 1905 | 1866.00 | 533.00 | 9487.00 |
| 1906 | 1198.00 | 458.00 | 8386.00 |
| 1907 | 795.00 | 291.00 | 3956.00 |
| 1908 | 1333.00 | 530.00 | 6641.00 |
| 1909 | 669.00 | 277.00 | 3766.00 |
| 1910 | 48.00 | 18.00 | 217.00 |
| 1911 | 235.00 | 86.00 | 1204.00 |
| 1912 | 189.00 | 69.00 | 1042.00 |

Comment 1886-1892 CWMYSTWITH; 1901 INC.KINGSIDE; 1911-1912
INC.KINGSIDE

Ownership:    1859-1867 JOHN TAYLOR & SONS; 1868 CWMYSTWYTH CO.; 1869-1881
CWMYSTWYTH CO.LTD.; 1882-1887 CWMYSTWYTH MINES NEW CO.LTD.;
1888-1893 CWMYSTWYTH CO.LTD.; 1896-1898 BAINBRIDGE,BOUNDY &
MCILQUHAN; 1899-1904 CWMYSTWYTH MINING CO.LTD.; 1905-1908
KINGSIDE ZINC-BLENDE CO.LTD.; 1909-1910 BRUNNER MOND &
CO.LTD.; 1911-1913 KINGSIDE MINES LTD.
Comment 1893 ABANDONED IN 1893; 1896 STARTED JAN.1897; 1913
IDLE

Management: Manager 1862-1865 JAS.ROWE; 1866-1868 THOS.BALL; 1869-1876
JOHN TAYLOR & SONS; 1877-1881 H.H.OAKES
Chief Agent 1859-1861 JAS.ROWE; 1862-1863 J.KENDALL;
1866-1869 SML.KENDALL; 1870-1876 WM.MITCHELL; 1877-1881

JOS.B.ROWSE & ROBT.HANCOCK; 1882-1893 JOS.B.ROWSE; 1896-1901
JOHN OWEN
Secretary 1868 JOHN TAYLOR & SONS; 1877-1889 JOHN TAYLOR &
SONS

| Employment: | Underground | Surface | Total |
|---|---|---|---|
| 1877 | 78 | 54 | 132 |
| 1878 | 68 | 72 | 140 |
| 1879 | 101 | 68 | 169 |
| 1880 | 112 | 61 | 173 |
| 1881 | 78 | 59 | 137 |
| 1882 | 68 | 59 | 127 |
| 1883 | 58 | 52 | 110 |
| 1884 | 45 | 49 | 94 |
| 1885 | 50 | 51 | 101 |
| 1886 | 57 | 46 | 103 |
| 1887 | 66 | 36 | 102 |
| 1888 | 69 | 38 | 107 |
| 1889 | 57 | 26 | 83 |
| 1890 | 46 | 20 | 66 |
| 1891 | 42 | 23 | 65 |
| 1892 | 63 | 20 | 83 |
| 1893 | | 4 | 4 |
| 1896-1897 | 4 | | 4 |
| 1898 | 30 | 50 | 80 |
| 1899 | 30 | 70 | 100 |
| 1900 | 40 | 34 | 74 |
| 1901 | 35 | 25 | 60 |
| 1902 | 72 | 44 | 116 |
| 1903 | 80 | 57 | 137 |
| 1904 | 99 | 39 | 138 |
| 1905 | 127 | 37 | 164 |
| 1906 | 120 | 42 | 162 |
| 1907 | 102 | 31 | 133 |
| 1908 | 92 | 32 | 124 |
| 1909 | 14 | 16 | 30 |
| 1910 | 11 | 11 | 22 |
| 1911 | 43 | 17 | 60 |
| 1912 | 51 | 18 | 69 |

Comment 1911-1912 INC.KINGSIDE

---

CWMYSTWYTH,SOUTH         DEVIL'S BRIDGE         SN 805744 0095

| Production: Lead | Ore(tons) | Metal(tons) | Value(£) |
|---|---|---|---|
| 1878 | 40.00 | 32.70 | 360.00 |

Zinc No detailed return
Ownership: 1876-1878 SOUTH CWMYSTWYTH MINING CO.LTD.; 1900-1904
CWMYSTWYTH MINING CO.LTD.
Comment 1902-1904 NOT WORKED
Management: Chief Agent 1876-1878 JOS.MITCHELL

| Employment: | Underground | Surface | Total |
|---|---|---|---|
| 1877 | 37 | 19 | 56 |
| 1900 | 2 | | 2 |

---

CWMYSTWYTH,WEST         DEVIL'S BRIDGE         SN 795739 0096

| Production: Lead | Ore(tons) | Metal(tons) | Value(£) |
|---|---|---|---|
| 1877 | 10.00 | 8.00 | 125.00 |
| 1878 | 5.00 | 3.70 | 55.00 |
| 1879 | 5.00 | 4.00 | 57.50 |

Ownership: 1880 WEST CWMYSTWYTH MINING CO.; 1881-1884 JOHN FLEMING,
1899-1901 CWMYSTWYTH MINING CO.LTD.

Comment 1884 ABANDONED OCT.1884
Management: Chief Agent 1880 JOS.MITCHELL; 1881-1883 THOS.DAVIDSON; 1884
JOS.B.ROWSE; 1899-1901 JOHN OWEN

Employment:

| | Underground | Surface | Total |
|---|---|---|---|
| 1880 | 16 | 3 | 19 |
| 1881 | 14 | 4 | 18 |
| 1882 | 14 | 3 | 17 |
| 1883 | 13 | 3 | 16 |
| 1884 | 9 | 3 | 12 |
| 1899-1901 | 2 | | 2 |

DALRHIW           RADNOR           0097

Production: Copper

| | Ore(tons) | Metal(tons) | Value(£) |
|---|---|---|---|
| 1858 | No detailed return | | |

Comment 1858 FOR CU SEE EAGLE BROOK

DARREN           GOGINAN           SN 678830 0098

Production: Lead & Silver

| | Ore(tons) | Lead(tons) | Silver(ozs) | Value(£) |
|---|---|---|---|---|
| 1847 | No detailed return | | | |
| 1849 | 29.00 | 20.00 | 0.00 | 0.00 |
| 1850 | 15.00 | 10.00 | 0.00 | 0.00 |
| 1851 | 82.70 | 53.90 | 0.00 | 0.00 |
| 1852 | 15.00 | 11.70 | 275.00 | 0.00 |
| 1853 | 52.90 | 47.00 | 1196.00 | 0.00 |
| 1854 | 37.00 | 28.50 | 800.00 | 0.00 |
| 1855 | 52.00 | 38.00 | 988.00 | 0.00 |
| 1856 | 123.10 | 80.30 | 2130.00 | 0.00 |
| 1857 | 70.30 | 47.50 | 1425.00 | 0.00 |
| 1858 | 51.00 | 37.00 | 1147.00 | 0.00 |
| 1859 | 22.00 | 16.20 | 480.00 | 0.00 |
| 1860 | 22.00 | 14.50 | 0.00 | 0.00 |
| 1861 | No detailed return | | | |
| 1862 | 20.00 | 15.00 | 0.00 | 0.00 |
| 1863 | 12.00 | 9.50 | 237.00 | 0.00 |
| 1864 | 36.00 | 27.00 | 82.00 | 0.00 |
| 1865 | 31.00 | 24.00 | 740.00 | 0.00 |
| 1866 | 24.00 | 18.00 | 684.00 | 0.00 |
| 1870 | 38.00 | 28.50 | 0.00 | 0.00 |
| 1871 | 117.00 | 87.70 | 0.00 | 0.00 |
| 1872 | 75.80 | 56.60 | 0.00 | 0.00 |
| 1873 | 167.00 | 126.00 | 650.00 | 0.00 |
| 1874 | 86.70 | 65.00 | 325.00 | 1651.40 |
| 1875 | 130.60 | 97.70 | 2220.00 | 2449.80 |
| 1876 | 134.00 | 103.50 | 3111.00 | 2595.60 |
| 1877 | 136.00 | 111.00 | 3441.00 | 1836.00 |
| 1878 | 70.00 | 55.50 | 2100.00 | 1050.00 |
| 1879 | 7.50 | 5.20 | 175.00 | 95.20 |

Comment 1847 SEE GOGERDDAN MINES; 1862 GREAT DARREN; 1864
GREAT DARREN; 1870 OLD DARREN; 1871-1879 GREAT DARREN

Copper

| | Ore(tons) | Metal(tons) | Value(£) |
|---|---|---|---|
| 1855 | 11.90 | 0.00 | 0.00 |
| 1856 | 7.30 | 0.00 | 0.00 |
| 1857 | 32.50 | 0.00 | 0.00 |

Comment 1855-1857 (P)

Ownership: 1859-1860 G.FORSTER; 1861-1862 DARREN MINING CO.; 1863-1866
THOS.SPARGO & CO.; 1870-1873 ROBT.GIRDWOOD; 1874
ROBT.GIRDWOOD & GEO.GREEN; 1875-1885 ROBT.GIRDWOOD; 1886-1889
P.BARKER; 1890 THOS.W.WARD
Comment 1861-1866 GREAT DARREN; 1870-1871 OLD DARREN;

DARREN                         GOGINAN                        Continued

1872—1886 GREAT DARREN; 1887—1890 GREAT DARREN:SUSPENDED
Management: Manager 1874—1877 GEO.GREEN
            Chief Agent 1859—1860 JOHN HUMPHREYS; 1861 MAT.FRANCIS;
            1862—1866 RICH.WILLIAMS; 1870—1873 GEO.GREEN; 1874—1889
            WM.JONES; 1890 THOS.W.WARD
Employment:              Underground     Surface        Total
            1877             22            23            45
            1878             12            16            28
            1879—1880         2                           2
            1882              2                           2
            1883—1884         8                           8
            1885              6                           6
            1888                            1             1
            1889                            2             2


DARREN,EAST                    CWMSYMLOG                   SN 700837 0099

Production: Lead & Silver   Ore(tons)   Lead(tons)  Silver(ozs)   Value(£)
            1852             483.00       347.00      6940.00        0.00
            1853             415.00       312.00      7885.00        0.00
            1854             815.00       607.00     15782.00        0.00
            1855             535.00       400.00      7040.00        0.00
            1856            1062.60       780.00     11688.00        0.00
            1857            1050.00       760.00     12540.00        0.00
            1858             870.00       657.00     11166.00        0.00
            1859            1150.80       862.00     13792.00        0.00
            1860             714.00        22.00      8250.00        0.00
            1861            1028.00       781.00     17182.00        0.00
            1862             918.50       706.00     13420.00        0.00
            1863             944.00       745.50     14910.00        0.00
            1864             864.50       639.30     13420.00        0.00
            1865             896.80       672.00     14112.00        0.00
            1866             910.00       692.00     15288.00        0.00
            1867             915.00       695.50     15500.00        0.00
            1868             878.40       658.50     15792.00        0.00
            1869             872.70       675.00     17064.00        0.00
            1870             890.70       667.00     16008.00        0.00
            1871             752.50       560.50     16018.00        0.00
            1872             708.70       481.50     13758.00        0.00
            1873             623.80       468.00     12973.00        0.00
            1874             650.00       490.00     13932.00    11499.10
            1875             630.90       453.40     13988.00    11802.10
            1876             440.00       330.00     10329.00     8114.50
            1877             300.00       225.00      5400.00     4945.50
            1878             450.00       337.50      6750.00     6062.70
            1879             540.00       434.70      9803.00     6899.00
            1880             380.00       320.00      7266.00     5102.20
            1881             168.00       126.00       336.00     1596.00
            1882             215.00       171.60      3440.00     2595.00
            1883             315.00       252.00      5040.00     3296.00
            1884             312.00       249.60      4933.00     3016.00
            1885             229.00       173.00      4269.00     2474.00
            1886             154.00       117.00      3155.00     1898.00
            1887             216.00       164.00      4105.00     2525.00
            1888             175.00       132.00      3180.00     2025.00
            1889              85.00        64.00      1506.00      939.00
            1890             110.00        83.00      1850.00     1302.00
            1891             470.00       352.00      8372.00     4748.00
            1892             260.00       196.00      4632.00     2100.00
            1893             122.00        92.00      2173.00      969.00
            1895             167.00       126.00      3559.00     1273.00
            1896             146.00       111.00      3622.00     1202.00

                                 33

| Lead & Silver | Ore(tons) | Lead(tons) | Silver(ozs) | Value(£) |
|---|---|---|---|---|
| 1897 | 14.00 | 11.00 | 347.00 | 123.00 |
| 1899 | 14.00 | 11.00 | 110.00 | 127.00 |
| 1900 | 18.00 | 13.50 | 141.00 | 165.00 |
| 1901 | 5.00 | 3.00 | 60.00 | 45.00 |

Comment 1886 ORE AND HALVANS; 1887-1889 ORE AND WASTE

| Copper | Ore(tons) | Metal(tons) | Value(£) |
|---|---|---|---|
| 1856 | 27.90 | 0.00 | 41.90 |
| 1857 | 31.20 | 0.00 | 0.00 |
| 1880 | 7.00 | 0.60 | 7.50 |

Comment 1856-1857 (P); 1880 (P)

Ownership: 1859-1867 JOHN TAYLOR & SONS; 1868 EAST DARREN CO.; 1869-1881 EAST DARREN CO.LTD.; 1882-1883 JOHN TAYLOR & SONS; 1884-1885 EAST DARREN MINE CO.LTD.; 1886-1887 JOHN TAYLOR & SONS; 1888 EAST DARREN MINE CO.LTD.; 1889-1893 JAS.THEOBALD; 1894 EAST DARREN MINING CO.; 1895 BOARD & BOUNDY; 1896-1897 EAST DARREN MINING CO.LTD.; 1899-1901 WM.GARLAND
Comment 1884-1885 IN LIQUIDATION; 1888 IN LIQUIDATION; 1897 ABANDONED 1897

Management: Manager 1868-1881 JOHN TAYLOR & SONS
Chief Agent 1859-1876 JAS.GARLAND; 1877-1882 JAS.GARLAND & THOS.GARLAND; 1883-1890 THOS.GARLAND; 1891-1895 H.W.FRANCIS; 1896-1897 JOHN MITCHELL; 1899-1901 WM.GARLAND
Secretary 1877-1881 H.H.OAKES

Employment:

|  | Underground | Surface | Total |
|---|---|---|---|
| 1877 | 64 | 53 | 117 |
| 1878 | 59 | 48 | 107 |
| 1879 | 58 | 62 | 120 |
| 1880 | 59 | 52 | 111 |
| 1881 | 40 | 35 | 75 |
| 1882 | 30 | 33 | 63 |
| 1883 | 28 | 26 | 54 |
| 1884 | 25 | 33 | 58 |
| 1885 | 19 | 38 | 57 |
| 1886 | 24 | 35 | 59 |
| 1887 | 18 | 33 | 51 |
| 1888 | 22 | 29 | 51 |
| 1889 | 55 | 81 | 136 |
| 1890 | 66 | 69 | 135 |
| 1891 | 67 | 50 | 117 |
| 1892 | 67 | 45 | 112 |
| 1893 | 20 | 22 | 42 |
| 1894 | 40 | 21 | 61 |
| 1895 | 37 | 21 | 58 |
| 1896 | 27 | 26 | 53 |
| 1897 | 7 | 8 | 15 |
| 1899 |  | 9 | 9 |
| 1900 |  | 6 | 6 |
| 1901 |  | 5 | 5 |

DARREN, SOUTH                    GOGINAN                    SN 685830 0100

Production:

| Lead & Silver | Ore(tons) | Lead(tons) | Silver(ozs) | Value(£) |
|---|---|---|---|---|
| 1859 | No detailed return |  |  |  |
| 1860 | 98.00 | 68.60 | 0.00 | 0.00 |
| 1861 | 117.00 | 89.00 | 2900.00 | 0.00 |
| 1862 | 84.50 | 65.00 | 1420.00 | 0.00 |
| 1863 | 67.90 | 50.90 | 0.00 | 0.00 |
| 1864 | 228.10 | 167.20 | 0.00 | 0.00 |
| 1865 | 326.90 | 245.00 | 0.00 | 0.00 |
| 1866 | 310.50 | 202.80 | 0.00 | 0.00 |
| 1867 | 276.20 | 207.20 | 0.00 | 0.00 |

| Lead & Silver | Ore(tons) | Lead(tons) | Silver(ozs) | Value(£) |
|---|---|---|---|---|
| 1868 | 354.00 | 265.50 | 10070.00 | 0.00 |
| 1869 | 290.10 | 217.60 | 0.00 | 0.00 |
| 1870 | 250.00 | 187.50 | 0.00 | 0.00 |
| 1871 | 154.00 | 115.50 | 3910.00 | 0.00 |
| 1872 | 108.00 | 81.00 | 0.00 | 0.00 |
| 1873 | 171.30 | 126.00 | 4392.00 | 0.00 |
| 1874 | 152.00 | 118.50 | 4637.00 | 3034.70 |
| 1875 | 133.70 | 102.50 | 3807.00 | 2696.40 |
| 1876 | 113.60 | 85.00 | 3043.00 | 2250.30 |
| 1877 | 180.00 | 145.00 | 4850.00 | 3144.20 |
| 1878 | 475.00 | 356.20 | 13010.00 | 7452.00 |
| 1879 | 485.00 | 390.50 | 13569.00 | 5192.50 |
| 1880 | 570.00 | 420.00 | 14206.00 | 6441.00 |
| 1881 | 450.00 | 336.00 | 10350.00 | 5400.00 |
| 1882 | 540.00 | 415.80 | 15120.00 | 7784.00 |
| 1883 | 505.00 | 393.90 | 15150.00 | 6593.00 |
| 1884 | 355.00 | 277.00 | 10570.00 | 4236.00 |
| 1885 | 300.00 | 222.00 | 8945.00 | 3597.00 |
| 1886 | 200.00 | 152.00 | 5962.00 | 2560.00 |
| 1887 | 120.00 | 91.00 | 3570.00 | 1404.00 |
| 1888 | 85.00 | 65.00 | 2534.00 | 1039.00 |
| 1889 | 135.00 | 103.00 | 4025.00 | 1667.00 |
| 1890 | 140.00 | 106.00 | 4174.00 | 1840.00 |
| 1891 | 105.00 | 80.00 | 3130.00 | 1210.00 |
| 1892 | 185.00 | 142.00 | 5514.00 | 1928.00 |
| 1893 | 11.00 | 8.00 | 328.00 | 113.00 |

Comment 1859 SEE CWMSEBON; 1860 OR CWMSEBON; 1863 OR
CWMSEBON; 1864 AGGREGATED

| Zinc | Ore(tons) | Metal(tons) | Value(£) |
|---|---|---|---|
| 1872 | 175.00 | 0.00 | 433.30 |
| 1878 | 21.10 | 0.00 | 57.20 |

| Copper | Ore(tons) | Metal(tons) | Value(£) |
|---|---|---|---|
| 1860 | 15.00 | 1.00 | 138.50 |
| 1861 | 26.50 | 1.80 | 158.00 |
| 1862 | 26.60 | 1.70 | 140.20 |
| 1863 | 39.70 | 2.20 | 0.00 |
| 1864 | 131.70 | 11.30 | 1143.40 |
| 1865 | 203.40 | 20.20 | 1530.00 |
| 1866 | 171.80 | 14.60 | 0.00 |
| 1867 | 115.30 | 13.70 | 777.60 |
| 1868 | 122.90 | 7.90 | 650.40 |
| 1869 | 132.20 | 6.60 | 989.40 |
| 1870 | 117.00 | 7.00 | 813.70 |
| 1871 | 101.40 | 6.00 | 700.80 |
| 1873 | 71.00 | 4.20 | 254.60 |
| 1874 | 68.10 | 4.10 | 300.00 |
| 1875 | 79.40 | 0.00 | 395.50 |
| 1876 | 42.30 | 0.00 | 0.00 |
| 1877 | 26.70 | 1.60 | 97.30 |
| 1878 | 116.70 | 6.50 | 538.40 |
| 1879 | 156.20 | 8.70 | 624.80 |
| 1880 | 210.00 | 23.50 | 1710.70 |
| 1881 | 192.00 | 21.10 | 1344.00 |
| 1882 | 197.30 | 15.80 | 691.00 |
| 1883 | 151.90 | 12.10 | 404.00 |
| 1884 | 100.00 | 7.00 | 214.00 |
| 1885 | 13.00 | 2.00 | 57.00 |
| 1886 | 10.00 | 1.50 | 50.00 |
| 1887 | 22.00 | 3.00 | 105.00 |
| 1888 | 25.50 | 3.70 | 212.00 |
| 1889 | 15.00 | 2.50 | 77.00 |
| 1890 | 16.00 | 2.50 | 115.00 |

35

Copper          Ore(tons) Metal(tons)     Value(£)
1892              19.00        3.50          90.00
1893               5.25        0.80          34.00
Comment 1860—1863 (P) COPPER EST.; 1864—1865 (P) OR CWMSEBON
COPPER EST.; 1866—1869 (P); 1870—1871 (P) COPPER EST.;
1873—1874 (P) COPPER EST.; 1875—1881 (P)

Ownership:    1878—1881 J.H.MURCHISON & CO.; 1882—1887 SOUTH DARREN MINING
CO.LTD.; 1888—1893 SOUTH DARREN LEAD MINING CO.LTD.
Comment 1860—1877 SEE CWMSEBON; 1892 IN LIQUIDATION; 1893
ABANDONED IN 1893

Management:   Chief Agent 1878—1882 HY.JAMES; 1883—1893 JOHN MITCHELL
Secretary 1882—1886 J.H.MURCHISON (S); 1887—1889 J.H.A.SMITH

Employment:              Underground      Surface       Total
1877              71            37          108
1878              78            53          131
1879              97            56          153
1880              90            59          149
1881              84            56          140
1882              84            58          142
1883              78            43          121
1884              28            24           52
1885              32            27           59
1886              30            31           61
1887              30            26           56
1888              34            22           56
1889              34            23           57
1890              32            18           50
1891              24            15           39
1892              27            11           38
1893                            8            8


DDU                         PONTRHYDFENDIGAID                SN 765697 0101

Production:   Lead            Ore(tons) Metal(tons)     Value(£)
1883—1884 No detailed return
Comment 1883—1884 SEE ESGAIRMWYN
Ownership:    Comment 1883—1889 SEE ESGAIRMWYN
Employment:              Underground      Surface       Total
1883—1885
1887—1889
Comment 1883—1885 SEE ESGAIRMWYN; 1887—1889 SEE ESGAIRMWYN


DE BROKE                      DEVIL'S BRIDGE                       0102

Production:   Lead & Silver   Ore(tons)  Lead(tons) Silver(ozs)   Value(£)
1872             15.00        11.20        0.00         0.00
1873          No detailed return
1874             49.00        38.00        0.00       682.90
1875            109.20        81.50        0.00         0.00
1876            100.00        76.00        0.00      1423.50
1877            221.00       167.00        0.00      2762.50
1878            202.00       162.50        0.00      2038.00
1879             92.00        69.00      207.00       821.30
1880              6.90         5.10       25.00        75.00
1881             33.50        25.00      134.00       335.00
Comment 1874 FOR SILVER SEE CWMYSTWYTH
Ownership:    1872—1881 DE BROKE CO.LTD.
Comment 1877—1881 OR DOLWEN; 1882 SEE MYNACH VALE
Management:   Manager 1872—1874 HY.ENFIELD TAYLOR; 1876—1881 JAS.PHILLIPS
Chief Agent 1872—1874 WM.MITCHELL JNR.; 1875 THOS.HODGE &
SON

36

DE BROKE                        DEVIL'S BRIDGE                    Continued

Employment:                Underground      Surface        Total
             1877               32             14             46
             1878               25             17             42
             1879               16             11             27
             1880                4              1              5
             1881                4              2              6


DEVIL'S BRIDGE                  YSTRAD MEURIG                    SN 718700 0103

Production: Lead No detailed return
Ownership:  Comment 1872-1873 SEE GERTRUDE


DOLCLETTWR                      TALIESIN                         SN 658918 0104

Production: Lead            Ore(tons) Metal(tons)      Value(£)
             1889              3.00        2.00          23.00
             1890              3.00        2.00          18.00
            Zinc            Ore(tons) Metal(tons)      Value(£)
             1888             44.00       15.00         134.00
             1889             63.00       22.00         235.00
             1890             40.00       14.00         173.00
            Comment 1888-1890 INC.LLAINHIR
            Copper          Ore(tons) Metal(tons)      Value(£)
             1872             17.00        0.80           0.00
             1873         No detailed return
             1881         No detailed return
             1888         No detailed return
             1889              5.00        0.50          21.00
             1890              6.00        0.50          26.00
            Comment 1872 (P) COPPER EST.; 1881 SEE LLAINHIR; 1888 SEE
            LLAINHIR; 1889-1890 INC.LLAINHIR
Ownership:  1872-1877 RICH.GIBBS; 1881-1883 JAS.MCILQUHAN &
            JAS.RAWSTHORNE; 1884-1891 DOLCLETTWR & LLAINHIR MINING
            CO.LTD.
            Comment 1881-1883 INC.LLAINHIR; 1884 INC.LLAINHIR:SUSPENDED;
            1885-1886 INC.LLAINHIR; 1887 INC.LLAINHIR:SUSPENDED;
            1888-1889 INC.LLAINHIR; 1890 INC.LLAINHIR:IN LIQUIDATION;
            1891 INC.LLAINHIR:SUSPENDED
Management: Chief Agent 1872-1877 THOS.WILLIAMS; 1881-1883 JAS.MCILQUHAN;
            1884-1891 J.H.CLINT
Employment:                Underground      Surface        Total
             1881                5                             5
             1882-1884                          1              1
             1885               12              8             20
             1886               12              6             18
             1888                8              9             17
             1889               13             10             23
             1890               10              8             18
             1891                               1              1
            Comment 1881-1886 INC.LLAINHIR; 1888-1891 INC.LLAINHIR


DOLFAWR                         ABERYSTWYTH                           0105

Production: Lead No detailed return
Ownership:  1877-1881 C.HERB.STOKES
            Comment 1878 NO RETURN; 1880 NOT WORKED
Management: Manager 1881 JOHN DAVIES
            Chief Agent 1878-1881 C.HERB.STOKES
Employment:                Underground      Surface        Total
             1877                2                             2

DOLGOCH                           GLANDOVEY                        SN 706938 0106

Production: Lead No detailed return
Ownership:  1863-1868 T.JONES & CO.
Management: Chief Agent 1863 S.GOLDSWORTHY; 1864-1868 THOS.GOLDSWORTHY


DOLWEN                          DEVIL'S BRIDGE                     SN 779783 0107

Production: Lead & Silver     Ore(tons)  Lead(tons) Silver(ozs)    Value(£)
            1857                 2.60        1.90      108.00          0.00
Ownership:  1863-1865 J.B.BALCOMBE & CO.; 1869 DOLWEN CO.; 1871 DOLWEN
            CONSOLIDATED CO.; 1872-1873 DOLWEN CO.; 1888-1893 JOHN
            JENKINS & PETER JONES
            Comment 1877-1881 SEE DE BROKE; 1891-1893 SUSPENDED
Management: Manager 1869 J.B.BALCOMBE; 1871-1873 J.B.BALCOMBE
            Chief Agent 1863-1865 JAS.LESTER; 1869 JOHN DAVIS; 1871-1873
            DAVID EVANS
Employment:                Underground    Surface        Total
            1888-1890           2                           2


DOLWEN,EAST                     DEVIL'S BRIDGE                     SN 780784 0108

Production: Lead No detailed return
Ownership:  1870 DOLWEN CO.; 1877-1878 C.HERB.STOKES
            Comment 1878 SUSPENDED
Management: Manager 1870 J.B.BALCOMBE
            Chief Agent 1870 JOHN DAVIS; 1878 C.HERB.STOKES
Employment:                Underground    Surface        Total
            1877                2                           2


DRISGOL                           PONTERWYD                        SN 760883 0109

Production: Manganese          Ore(tons) Metal(tons)     Value(£)
            1874        No detailed return
            Comment 1874 DROSGOL SEE ROYAL MINES
Ownership:  1873-1875 C.HERB.STOKES
            Comment 1874-1875 SEE ALSO ROYAL MINES; 1876-1877 SEE ROYAL
            MINES
Management: Chief Agent 1873-1875 JOHN DAVIES


EAGLE BROOK                       PONTERWYD                        SN 734893 0110

Production: Lead & Silver     Ore(tons)  Lead(tons) Silver(ozs)    Value(£)
            1856              115.00       85.00      687.00          0.00
            1857              152.00      108.00      680.00          0.00
            1858               95.70       73.50      620.00          0.00
            1859               60.00       40.00      368.00          0.00
            1860-1861 No detailed return
            1862               21.00       15.20      100.00          0.00
            1867                5.20        3.50        0.00          0.00
            1868-1869 No detailed return
            1870               25.00       19.00      222.00          0.00
            1871               35.00       26.50      290.00          0.00
            1872               50.00       42.00        0.00          0.00
            1873               40.00       28.00      313.00          0.00
            Copper            Ore(tons) Metal(tons)    Value(£)
            1857               19.00        0.00        0.00
            1858               23.10        5.60        0.00
            1859               20.00        1.80        0.00
            1860                6.00        0.40        0.00
            1867               26.50        2.00        0.00

38

EAGLE BROOK                    PONTERWYD                    Continued

        Comment 1857 (P); 1858 (P)CU INC.DALRHIW,CWMSEBON,CWMDARREN;
        1859-1860 (P); 1867 (P) COPPER EST.
Ownership:  1859 PHILLIPS & CO.; 1860-1867 W.SPOONER & CO.; 1868-1878
        EAGLE BROOK MINING CO.LTD.
Management: Manager 1872-1877 HY.TYACK
        Chief Agent 1859-1867 HY.TYACK; 1868-1871 HY.TYACK &
        WM.BATTYE; 1872-1875 HY.TYACK; 1878 AB.FRANCIS
        Secretary 1873-1877 WM.BATTYE (S)
Employment:             Underground    Surface       Total
        1877               4             1             5
        1878                             8             8


EISTEDDFODD                                                        0111

Production: Lead          Ore(tons) Metal(tons)    Value(£)
        1849              20.70      14.00         0.00
        1850              53.00      35.30         0.00
        1856              14.00      11.00         0.00


ELGAR                         BOW STREET              SN 660862 0112

Production: Lead & Silver  Ore(tons)  Lead(tons) Silver(ozs)  Value(£)
        1889               2.50       2.00        0.00         20.00
        1890               2.00       1.50       27.00         24.00
        Zinc              Ore(tons) Metal(tons)    Value(£)
        1888               1.70       0.70         9.00
        1889               1.50       0.50         6.00
        1890               1.00       0.30         4.00
Ownership:  1863 S.ATWOOD & CO.; 1864-1865 J.ATWOOD & CO.; 1876-1883
        ELGAR MINING CO.LTD.; 1887-1888 JOHN DAVIS & CO.; 1889-1890
        THOS.MOLYNEUX; 1897 PLYNLIMON & HAVAN CO.LTD.
        Comment 1864-1865 SUSPENDED; 1882-1883 SUSPENDED; 1890
        ABANDONED APRIL 1890; 1897 ABANDONED 1897
Management: Chief Agent 1863 JOHN HUGHES; 1876-1883 JAS.G.GREEN;
        1887-1888 JOHN DAVIS; 1889-1890 J.HUGHES OWEN; 1897
        H.W.FRANCIS
Employment:             Underground    Surface       Total
        1877               4                          4
        1878              13                         13
        1879               2             1            3
        1880               2                          2
        1887               4                          4
        1888               2                          2
        1889               4             6           10
        1890               4                          4
        1897               2                          2


ELLA                          YSTRADMEURIG                          0113

Production: Lead No detailed return
Ownership:  1873 ROBT.GIRDWOOD; 1874-1875 ROBT.GIRDWOOD & GEO.GREEN
        Comment 1872 SEE HENDREFELIN; 1875 NOW WEST LISBURNE
Management: Manager 1873-1875 GEO.GREEN
        Chief Agent 1874-1875 G.Y.DUNN & RICH.DUNN


ERGLODD                       TALYBONT                SN 656903 0114

Ownership:  Comment 1882-1883 SEE ERGLODD UNITED


                                39

Production: 
| Lead & Silver | Ore(tons) | Lead(tons) | Silver(ozs) | Value(£) |
|---|---|---|---|---|
| 1882 | 10.00 | 7.50 | 82.00 | 68.00 |
| 1883 | 6.00 | 4.50 | 57.00 | 47.00 |

| Zinc | Ore(tons) | Metal(tons) | Value(£) |
|---|---|---|---|
| 1883 | 12.00 | 5.40 | 43.00 |

Ownership: 1881-1882 WILSON,JOHNSON,DODGE & PHIPPS; 1883-1887 ERGLODD UNITED MINES CO.LTD.
Comment 1882 FORMERLY ERGLODD,PENPOMPREN ....; 1883 FORMERLY ERGLODD,PENPOMPREN .... CEFN ERGLODD & PENNY BANK; 1884 IN LIQUIDATION; 1885-1887 SUSPENDED
Management: Chief Agent 1881 D.C.DAVIES & SON; 1882-1885 EVAN REESE
Employment:
| | Underground | Surface | Total |
|---|---|---|---|
| 1881 | 19 | | 19 |
| 1882 | 12 | 4 | 16 |
| 1883 | 14 | 9 | 23 |

Ownership: Comment 1882-1883 SEE ERGLODD UNITED

Production:
| Zinc | Ore(tons) | Metal(tons) | Value(£) |
|---|---|---|---|
| 1911 | 8.00 | 3.00 | 40.00 |
| 1912 | 26.00 | 10.00 | 130.00 |
| 1913 | 53.00 | 21.00 | 225.00 |

Comment 1911 ERWTOWAN; 1912 ERWTOWAN VALUE EST.; 1913 ERWTOWAN
Ownership: 1911-1913 T.A.FOX
Management: Chief Agent 1911-1913 W.GRAY
Employment:
| | Underground | Surface | Total |
|---|---|---|---|
| 1911 | 4 | 2 | 6 |
| 1912 | 12 | 4 | 16 |
| 1913 | 8 | 4 | 12 |

Production:
| Lead & Silver | Ore(tons) | Lead(tons) | Silver(ozs) | Value(£) |
|---|---|---|---|---|
| 1883 | 6.00 | 4.50 | 54.00 | 47.00 |
| 1886 | No detailed return | | | |
| 1902 | 7.00 | 6.00 | 70.00 | 57.00 |
| 1903 | 9.00 | 7.00 | 102.00 | 73.00 |
| 1904 | 4.00 | 3.00 | 40.00 | 27.00 |

Comment 1886 SEE CAMBRIAN
| Copper | Ore(tons) | Metal(tons) | Value(£) |
|---|---|---|---|
| 1883 | 313.00 | 40.30 | 2000.00 |
| 1885 | 54.00 | 9.00 | 274.00 |
| 1886 | 37.00 | 6.00 | 182.00 |
| 1901 | 46.00 | 9.00 | 669.00 |
| 1902 | 65.00 | 14.00 | 699.00 |
| 1903 | 49.00 | 10.00 | 515.00 |
| 1904 | 21.00 | 5.00 | 167.00 |

Comment 1883 ESGAIR FRAITH; 1885-1886 ESGAIR FRAITH; 1901-1904 ESGAIR FRAITH
Ownership: 1877 CAMBRIAN MINING CO.; 1883 UNITED CAMBRIAN COPPER MINING CO.LTD.; 1885-1888 CAMBRIAN MINING CO.LTD.; 1900-1901 VAV.EARLE; 1902-1908 WELSH COPPER MINING SYNDICATE LTD.
Comment 1883 FORMERLY CAMBRIAN; 1885-1886 OR CAMBRIAN; 1887-1888 OR CAMBRIAN:SUSPENDED; 1889-1893 SEE ESGAIR HIR; 1905-1908 NOT WORKED

Management: Chief Agent 1883 ALB.EDEY; 1885-1886 HY.JAMES; 1900-1902
            WM.NORTHEY
Employment:              Underground    Surface      Total
            1883            40           22          62
            1885            25           12          37
            1886             9            7          16
            1889-1891
            1900            16           21          37
            1901            20           25          45
            1902            38           27          65
            1903            20           16          36
            1904             4            4           8
            Comment 1889-1891 SEE ESGAIR HIR


ESGAIR HIR                        TALYBONT                    SN 735913 0119

Production: Lead & Silver    Ore(tons)  Lead(tons) Silver(ozs)    Value(£)
            1845             41.00       26.00       0.00          0.00
            1846            110.00       71.00       0.00          0.00
            1847             45.00       27.00       0.00          0.00
            1848            116.00       70.00       0.00          0.00
            1849          No detailed return
            1851              5.00        3.50       0.00          0.00
            1862          No detailed return
            1872            133.00      100.00    1155.00          0.00
            1873            290.00      212.00    2453.00          0.00
            1874            164.50      119.50    1562.00       2163.40
            1875             30.30       22.00       0.00          0.00
            1889             20.00       15.00       0.00        173.00
            1891             25.00       19.00     195.00        204.00
            1896             30.00       21.00     445.00        266.00
            1898              6.00        4.25       0.00         42.00
            1899             27.00       19.00       0.00        268.00
            1900              1.00        0.50       0.00         11.00
            1903             12.00        9.00     162.00         93.00
            Copper           Ore(tons) Metal(tons)  Value(£)
            1900             20.00        3.00     250.00
Ownership:  1872-1875 ESGAIR HIR MINING CO.; 1876-1877 GRIF.WILLIAMS &
            SON; 1886 ESGAIR HIR MINING CO.LTD.; 1887 SID.HODGKINSON;
            1888-1890 ESGAIR HIR MINE CO.LTD.; 1891-1893 JOS.FELL;
            1894-1898 WELSH MINING CORPORATION LTD.; 1899 CARDIGAN
            CONSOLIDATED MINE CO.LTD.; 1900-1901 VAV.EARLE; 1902-1908
            WELSH COPPER MINING SYNDICATE LTD.
            Comment 1886-1887 WORK RECOMMENCED MAR.1887; 1889-1891
            INC.ESGAIR FFRAITH; 1892-1893 INC.ESGAIR FFRAITH:SUSPENDED;
            1905-1908 NOT WORKED
Management: Chief Agent 1872-1877 JOHN WILLIAMSON; 1886 HY.JAMES;
            1888-1895 JAS.PHILLIPS; 1896-1902 WM.NORTHEY
            Secretary 1894-1895 C.F.BUTTLE
Employment:              Underground    Surface      Total
            1887            10           11          21
            1888            11            6          17
            1889            11            9          20
            1890            10            7          17
            1891             8            4          12
            1895            27           19          46
            1896            16           24          40
            1897             4                        4
            1898             4           10          14
            1899            12            8          20
            1902             9                        9
            1903            12           10          22

                                  41

Comment 1889-1891 INC.ESGAIR FFRAITH

ESGAIR LLE                          PONTERWYD                          SN 795830 0120

| Production: Lead | Ore(tons) | Metal(tons) | Value(£) |
|---|---|---|---|
| 1850 | 50.00 | 38.00 | 0.00 |
| 1851 | 89.30 | 68.00 | 0.00 |
| 1852 | 65.10 | 48.00 | 0.00 |
| 1853 | 261.40 | 190.00 | 0.00 |
| 1854 | 120.00 | 92.00 | 0.00 |
| 1856 | 42.00 | 28.50 | 0.00 |
| 1857 | 42.00 | 27.70 | 0.00 |
| 1865 | 7.00 | 4.70 | 0.00 |
| 1866 | No detailed return | | |
| 1867 | 10.90 | 8.10 | 0.00 |
| 1869 | 16.00 | 13.00 | 0.00 |
| 1870 | 75.00 | 58.50 | 0.00 |
| 1871 | 159.00 | 118.50 | 0.00 |
| 1872 | 268.00 | 200.00 | 0.00 |
| 1873 | 40.00 | 30.00 | 0.00 |
| Zinc | Ore(tons) | Metal(tons) | Value(£) |
| 1865 | 7.10 | 0.00 | 22.50 |

Comment 1865 ESGAIRLEE

Ownership: 1868-1869 STEP.BARKER; 1870-1871 WEST ESGAIR LLE CO.;
1872-1873 GREAT WEST VAN CO.LTD.; 1874-1876 WEST ESGAIR LLE
MINING CO.LTD.; 1878-1880 STEP.BARKER & ALF.E.WENHAM;
1890-1891 JOHN JAMES & JOHN OWEN; 1892 JOHN OWEN
Comment 1876 IN LIQUIDATION; 1891-1892 SUSPENDED

Management: Manager 1870-1871 JOHN WILLIAMS; 1872-1873 JAS.ROACH; 1874
RICH.HARVEY; 1878-1880 ALF.E.WENHAM
Chief Agent 1868-1871 RICH.HARVEY; 1872-1873 WM.BRANWELL &
RICH.HARVEY; 1875-1876 FRED.WILLIAMS & JAS.WILLIAMS;
1890-1892 JOHN OWEN
Secretary 1874-1876 JOHN LAVINGTON

| Employment: | Underground | Surface | Total |
|---|---|---|---|
| 1890 | 2 | | 2 |

ESGAIR LLE,WEST                     PONTERWYD                          SN 792827 0121

| Production: Lead & Silver | Ore(tons) | Lead(tons) | Silver(ozs) | Value(£) |
|---|---|---|---|---|
| 1874 | 109.00 | 81.70 | 405.00 | 330.10 |
| Zinc | Ore(tons) | Metal(tons) | Value(£) | |
| 1871 | 20.00 | 0.00 | 75.00 | |
| 1872 | 90.00 | 0.00 | 270.00 | |
| 1874 | 53.20 | 0.00 | 154.50 | |
| 1876 | 82.50 | 0.00 | 326.90 | |
| 1877 | 100.00 | 0.00 | 375.00 | |
| 1878 | 170.00 | 0.00 | 635.00 | |
| 1879 | 80.00 | 0.00 | 340.00 | |
| 1880 | 157.00 | 0.00 | 510.50 | |
| 1882 | 390.00 | 187.20 | 1170.00 | |
| 1884 | 80.00 | 0.00 | 235.00 | |
| 1886 | 90.00 | 34.00 | 279.00 | |
| 1887 | 62.00 | 22.00 | 214.00 | |
| 1888 | 114.00 | 40.00 | 462.00 | |
| 1889 | 35.00 | 14.00 | 177.00 | |
| 1890 | 36.00 | 15.00 | 198.00 | |

Comment 1871 WEST ESGAIRLEE

| Copper | Ore(tons) | Metal(tons) | Value(£) |
|---|---|---|---|
| 1874 | 25.00 | 1.70 | 38.20 |

Comment 1874 COPPER EST.

Ownership:  1870–1871 WEST ESGAIR LLE CO.; 1872–1873 GREAT WEST VAN
            CO.LTD.; 1874–1876 WEST ESGAIR LLE MINING CO.LTD.; 1877
            STEP.BARKER & CO.; 1878 STEP.BARKER & ALF.E.WENHAM; 1879–1885
            WEST ESGAIR LLE MINING CO.; 1886–1887 GEO.WILLIAMS; 1888
            GEO.WILLIAMS & CO.; 1889–1891 JOHN PAULL & GEO.WILLIAMS
            Comment 1876 IN LIQUIDATION; 1892–1893 SEE CASTELL
Management: Manager 1870–1871 JOHN WILLIAMS; 1872–1873 JAS.ROACH; 1874
            RICH.HARVEY; 1881 JAS.CORBETT
            Chief Agent 1868–1869 THOS.CORBETT; 1870–1871 RICH.HARVEY;
            1872–1873 WM.BRANWELL & RICH.HARVEY; 1875–1876 FRED.WILLIAMS
            & JAS.WILLIAMS; 1877–1878 JAS.CORBETT; 1879–1888
            ALF.E.WENHAM; 1890–1891 JOHN PAULL
            Secretary 1874–1876 JOHN LAVINGTON (S); 1881 STEP.BARKER;
            1883–1884 ALF.E.WENHAM
Employment:              Underground      Surface        Total
            1877            29              17             46
            1878            25               9             34
            1879            31              12             43
            1880            26              18             44
            1881             4                              4
            1882            26              12             38
            1883            25               4             29
            1884            10               3             13
            1885             2                              2
            1886            15               3             18
            1887–1888        6               4             10
            1889             6               3              9
            1890             4               3              7
            1891             2                              2

ESGAIRMWYN                        YSTRADMEURIG                    SN 755693 0122

| Production: | Lead & Silver | Ore(tons) | Lead(tons) | Silver(ozs) | Value(£) |
|---|---|---|---|---|---|
| | 1852 | 56.00 | 42.50 | 200.00 | 0.00 |
| | 1853 | 40.90 | 31.00 | 99.00 | 0.00 |
| | 1854 | 115.00 | 89.00 | 0.00 | 0.00 |
| | 1855 | 170.00 | 130.00 | 0.00 | 0.00 |
| | 1856 | 154.00 | 109.00 | 120.00 | 0.00 |
| | 1857 | 167.00 | 119.00 | 476.00 | 0.00 |
| | 1859 | 117.10 | 64.00 | 76.00 | 0.00 |
| | 1860 | 137.80 | 74.50 | 0.00 | 0.00 |
| | 1861 | No detailed return | | | |
| | 1870 | 20.00 | 15.50 | 32.00 | 0.00 |
| | 1871 | 62.00 | 46.50 | 0.00 | 0.00 |
| | 1872 | 25.00 | 17.50 | 72.00 | 0.00 |
| | 1873 | 85.00 | 61.00 | 256.00 | 0.00 |
| | 1874 | 24.10 | 18.00 | 72.00 | 259.60 |
| | 1875 | 44.20 | 34.50 | 0.00 | 0.00 |
| | 1876 | 49.10 | 36.80 | 0.00 | 0.00 |
| | 1877 | 72.00 | 51.50 | 156.00 | 900.00 |
| | 1878 | 86.00 | 64.10 | 860.00 | 713.80 |
| | 1879 | 73.00 | 60.70 | 400.00 | 766.50 |
| | 1880 | 37.20 | 26.70 | 157.00 | 420.90 |
| | 1883 | 25.00 | 20.00 | 0.00 | 177.00 |
| | 1884 | 33.00 | 24.70 | 159.00 | 247.00 |
| | 1891 | 20.00 | 14.50 | 56.00 | 136.00 |
| | 1892 | 20.00 | 14.00 | 57.00 | 130.00 |
| | 1893 | 34.00 | 27.00 | 333.00 | 191.00 |
| | 1898 | 102.00 | 77.00 | 542.00 | 823.00 |
| | 1899 | 261.00 | 198.00 | 1386.00 | 2561.00 |
| | 1900 | 196.00 | 149.00 | 821.00 | 2274.00 |
| | 1901 | 223.00 | 169.00 | 1227.00 | 1867.00 |

| Lead & Silver | Ore(tons) | Lead(tons) | Silver(ozs) | Value(£) |
|---|---|---|---|---|
| 1902 | 291.00 | 221.00 | 2619.00 | 2083.00 |
| 1903 | 436.00 | 331.00 | 3924.00 | 3289.00 |
| 1904 | 411.00 | 308.00 | 4665.00 | 3162.00 |
| 1905 | 564.00 | 413.00 | 7896.00 | 5238.00 |
| 1906 | 615.00 | 432.00 | 9102.00 | 7895.00 |
| 1907 | 549.00 | 391.00 | 7807.00 | 7535.00 |
| 1908 | 530.00 | 388.00 | 9010.00 | 4580.00 |
| 1909 | 760.00 | 552.00 | 13098.00 | 6656.00 |
| 1910 | 810.00 | 588.00 | 13310.00 | 7273.00 |
| 1911 | 550.00 | 405.00 | 7700.00 | 5423.00 |
| 1912 | 218.00 | 159.00 | 2470.00 | 2850.00 |
| 1913 | 502.00 | 328.00 | 7379.00 | 6650.00 |

Comment 1883-1884 INC DDU; 1909-1910 INC 2 TONS COPPER

| Zinc | Ore(tons) | Metal(tons) | Value(£) |
|---|---|---|---|
| 1873 | 10.00 | 0.00 | 30.00 |
| 1874 | No detailed return | | |
| 1884 | 16.00 | 0.00 | 30.00 |
| 1898 | 6.00 | 2.00 | 14.00 |
| 1899 | 15.00 | 3.00 | 23.00 |
| 1900 | 15.00 | 4.00 | 29.00 |
| 1902 | 9.00 | 3.00 | 25.00 |
| 1903 | 31.00 | 10.00 | 81.00 |

Ownership:    1859-1865 H.JONES & T.JONES; 1866 H.JONES,T.JONES & CO.;
1870-1882 ROBT.GIRDWOOD; 1883-1885 ROBT.GIRDWOOD & CO.;
1886-1889 P.BARKER & JAS.MCILQUHAN; 1890-1891 CARDIGAN
CONSOLIDATED MINING CO.; 1892-1896 THOS.W.WARD; 1897-1898
CARDIGAN CONSOLIDATED MINING CO.LTD.; 1899-1908 THOS.W.WARD;
1909-1913 ESGAIRMWYN MINING CO.
Comment 1859-1860 ESGERMWYN; 1883-1884 INC.DDU; 1885-1886
INC.DDU:STOPPED MAR.1885; 1887 INC.DDU:SUSPENDED; 1888-1889
INC.DDU:STOPPED MAR.1885; 1889 INC,DDU:STOPPED MAR.1885
Management:   Manager 1870-1877 GEO.GREEN; 1878-1879 WM.A.GREEN; 1880-1882
WM.JONES
Chief Agent 1859-1861 JOHN DAVIES; 1862 THOS.GOLDSWORTHY;
1863-1866 J.GOLDSWORTHY; 1883-1885 WM.JONES; 1890-1895
WM.MITCHELL; 1896-1902 J.H.ROBERTS; 1905-1913 JOHN WILLIAMS

| Employment: | Underground | Surface | Total |
|---|---|---|---|
| 1877 | 15 | 15 | 30 |
| 1878 | 14 | 21 | 35 |
| 1879 | 6 | 11 | 17 |
| 1880 | 6 | 14 | 20 |
| 1881-1882 | 4 | | 4 |
| 1883 | 8 | 6 | 14 |
| 1884 | 6 | 5 | 11 |
| 1885 | 3 | | 3 |
| 1887-1889 | | 1 | 1 |
| 1890 | | 10 | 10 |
| 1891 | 20 | 14 | 34 |
| 1892 | 6 | 8 | 14 |
| 1893 | 4 | 1 | 5 |
| 1894-1895 | | 2 | 2 |
| 1896 | 4 | 5 | 9 |
| 1897 | 7 | 3 | 10 |
| 1898 | 19 | 14 | 33 |
| 1899 | 21 | 15 | 36 |
| 1900 | 22 | 16 | 38 |
| 1901 | 23 | 17 | 40 |
| 1902 | 20 | 17 | 37 |
| 1903 | 22 | 19 | 41 |
| 1904 | 24 | 19 | 43 |
| 1905 | 37 | 24 | 61 |
| 1906 | 38 | 24 | 62 |

|      | Underground | Surface | Total |
|------|-------------|---------|-------|
| 1907 | 37 | 24 | 61 |
| 1908 | 36 | 25 | 61 |
| 1909 | 38 | 29 | 67 |
| 1910 | 40 | 26 | 66 |
| 1911 | 41 | 26 | 67 |
| 1912 | 30 | 22 | 52 |
| 1913 | 37 | 23 | 60 |

Comment 1883–1885 INC.DDU; 1887–1889 INC.DDU

FLORIDA                    PONTRYHDFENDIGAID                    0123

Production: Lead & Silver

|      | Ore(tons) | Lead(tons) | Silver(ozs) | Value(£) |
|------|-----------|------------|-------------|----------|
| 1871 | 55.00  | 42.50  | 0.00   | 0.00   |
| 1872 | 287.00 | 215.20 | 0.00   | 0.00   |
| 1873 | 45.00  | 34.00  | 0.00   | 0.00   |
| 1877 | 10.00  | 7.50   | 0.00   | 125.00 |
| 1878 | 21.80  | 17.00  | 0.00   | 216.90 |
| 1882 | 5.00   | 3.70   | 12.00  | 34.00  |
| 1886 | 20.00  | 15.00  | 57.00  | 157.00 |
| 1887 | 40.00  | 29.00  | 110.00 | 310.00 |
| 1888 | 30.00  | 21.00  | 85.00  | 254.00 |
| 1889 | 30.00  | 21.00  | 0.00   | 256.00 |
| 1890 | 20.00  | 14.00  | 77.00  | 153.00 |
| 1891 | 20.00  | 14.50  | 56.00  | 137.00 |
| 1893 | 10.00  | 7.00   | 0.00   | 59.00  |
| 1894 | 20.00  | 13.25  | 0.00   | 137.00 |
| 1896 | 4.00   | 3.00   | 0.00   | 27.00  |
| 1897 | 12.00  | 7.00   | 94.00  | 77.00  |
| 1898 | 9.00   | 6.50   | 0.00   | 63.00  |
| 1905 | 12.00  | 9.00   | 0.00   | 85.00  |

Zinc

|      | Ore(tons) | Metal(tons) | Value(£) |
|------|-----------|-------------|----------|
| 1871 | 110.00 | 0.00  | 412.50  |
| 1872 | 166.00 | 0.00  | 664.00  |
| 1873 | 76.00  | 0.00  | 304.00  |
| 1875 | 7.00   | 0.00  | 21.00   |
| 1877 | 286.00 | 0.00  | 1072.00 |
| 1878 | 118.90 | 0.00  | 356.80  |
| 1879 | 6.10   | 0.00  | 27.50   |
| 1880 | 27.50  | 0.00  | 72.50   |
| 1886 | 141.00 | 63.00 | 423.00  |
| 1887 | 165.00 | 70.00 | 572.00  |
| 1888 | 100.00 | 45.00 | 372.00  |
| 1889 | 60.00  | 23.00 | 243.00  |
| 1890 | 61.00  | 27.00 | 311.00  |
| 1891 | 61.00  | 27.00 | 310.00  |
| 1892 | 100.00 | 45.00 | 442.00  |
| 1893 | 125.00 | 52.00 | 449.00  |
| 1894 | 44.00  | 18.00 | 110.00  |
| 1896 | 9.00   | 3.00  | 6.00    |
| 1897 | 7.00   | 2.00  | 25.00   |
| 1898 | 41.00  | 16.50 | 185.00  |
| 1905 | 12.00  | 5.00  | 84.00   |

Ownership:  1870–1876 FLORIDA MINING CO.; 1877–1884 RICH.ATTENBOROUGH;
1885 E.MACKAY (TRUSTEE OF BANKRUPTCY COURT); 1886
RICH.ATTENBOROUGH; 1887 RODK.MACKAY (TRUSTEE); 1888–1889
RICH.ATTENBOROUGH; 1890–1894 RICH.ATTENBOROUGH & CO.;
1895–1896 GEO.WESTALL; 1897–1898 GEO.WESTALL & HOR.E.CHURCH

Management: Manager 1870–1876 JOHN WILLIAMS
Chief Agent 1877–1882 ED.HALSE; 1883–1895 RICH.COUCH;
1896–1897 J.JACKSON

FLORIDA                        PONTRYHDFENDIGAID                Continued

Employment:              Underground      Surface        Total
            1877              30             25             55
            1878              15             12             27
            1879               6                             6
            1880               6              2              8
            1881-1882          4              1              5
            1883              4                             4
            1884-1885          4              1              5
            1886               9             10             19
            1887              10             12             22
            1888              14             13             27
            1889              11              8             19
            1890               8              4             12
            1891              10              4             14
            1892              10              5             15
            1893              10             12             22
            1894               6              8             14
            1895                             4              4
            1896                             7              7
            1897              15              8             23
            1898              22              6             28


FOEL FAWR                        MONTGOMERY                    SN 826950 0124

Production: Copper No detailed return
Ownership:  1863-1865 NIGHTENGALE & CO.


FOXPATH                        RHEIDOL VALLEY                  SN 705788 0125

Production: Lead            Ore(tons) Metal(tons)    Value(£)
            1853              60.90        45.60        0.00
            1854              16.00         0.00        0.00
            1855              62.00        40.00        0.00
            1856-1857 No detailed return
            Comment 1856 MINE ABANDONED


FRONFAWNOG                   HOLYWELL, FLINTSHIRE                      0126

Production: Lead & Silver   Ore(tons)   Lead(tons) Silver(ozs)   Value(£)
            1879              50.00        40.00      256.00       525.00


FRONGOCH                      DEVIL'S BRIDGE                  SN 723744 0127

Production: Lead & Silver   Ore(tons)   Lead(tons) Silver(ozs)   Value(£)
            1852              90.00        40.00        0.00        0.00
            1855            1256.00       800.00        0.00        0.00
            1856          No detailed return
            1857            1506.00      1080.00        0.00        0.00
            1858          No detailed return
            1859            1033.00       800.00     5000.00        0.00
            1860            1110.00       953.00     2860.00        0.00
            1861            1422.00      1095.00        0.00        0.00
            1862            1946.00      1517.00     1820.00        0.00
            1863            1498.00      1198.00     1437.00        0.00
            1864            1455.30      1047.50        0.00        0.00
            1865            1540.00      1172.00        0.00        0.00
            1866            1560.00      1186.00        0.00        0.00
            1867            1586.00      1205.50        0.00        0.00
            1868            1170.00       878.00        0.00        0.00

46

| Lead & Silver | Ore(tons) | Lead(tons) | Silver(ozs) | Value(£) |
|---|---|---|---|---|
| 1869 | 1500.00 | 1147.00 | 0.00 | 0.00 |
| 1870 | 1248.00 | 954.00 | 0.00 | 0.00 |
| 1871 | 1314.00 | 1005.00 | 0.00 | 0.00 |
| 1872 | 1145.00 | 870.00 | 0.00 | 0.00 |
| 1873 | 1040.00 | 795.50 | 0.00 | 0.00 |
| 1874 | 850.00 | 646.00 | 0.00 | 0.00 |
| 1875 | 1162.00 | 878.00 | 4265.00 | 0.00 |
| 1876 | No detailed return | | | |
| 1878 | 748.60 | 561.00 | 2529.00 | 7917.00 |
| 1879 | 370.00 | 294.20 | 1176.00 | 3441.00 |
| 1880 | 570.00 | 428.00 | 2140.00 | 5779.20 |
| 1881 | 600.00 | 420.00 | 2250.00 | 5472.50 |
| 1882 | 460.00 | 345.00 | 0.00 | 3943.00 |
| 1883 | 285.00 | 222.30 | 0.00 | 1708.00 |
| 1884 | 260.00 | 202.80 | 0.00 | 1540.00 |
| 1885 | 125.00 | 86.00 | 0.00 | 888.00 |
| 1886 | 104.00 | 68.00 | 0.00 | 850.00 |
| 1887 | 330.00 | 238.00 | 0.00 | 2476.00 |
| 1888 | 310.00 | 218.00 | 0.00 | 2741.00 |
| 1889 | 220.00 | 159.00 | 0.00 | 1793.00 |
| 1890 | 250.00 | 176.00 | 0.00 | 2172.00 |
| 1891 | 390.00 | 274.00 | 0.00 | 2915.00 |
| 1892 | 155.00 | 106.00 | 0.00 | 1008.00 |
| 1893 | 210.00 | 138.00 | 0.00 | 1215.00 |
| 1894 | 205.00 | 136.00 | 0.00 | 1087.00 |
| 1895 | 185.00 | 132.00 | 0.00 | 1078.00 |
| 1896 | 165.00 | 122.00 | 135.00 | 1082.00 |
| 1897 | 147.00 | 108.00 | 0.00 | 1091.00 |
| 1898 | 201.00 | 152.75 | 0.00 | 1558.00 |
| 1899 | 43.00 | 33.00 | 0.00 | 383.00 |
| 1900 | 42.00 | 29.00 | 0.00 | 325.00 |
| 1901 | 333.00 | 237.00 | 499.00 | 1665.00 |
| 1902 | 426.00 | 312.00 | 0.00 | 2500.00 |
| 1903 | 202.00 | 146.00 | 303.00 | 1333.00 |

Comment 1855 FOR SILVER SEE LISBURNE MINES; 1856 SEE LISBURNE
MINES; 1858 SEE EAST LOGYLAS; 1859 AG INC E LOGYLAS &
GLOGFACH; 1874-1875 FOR VALUE SEE LISBURNE MINES; 1876 SEE
LISBURNE MINES

| Zinc | Ore(tons) | Metal(tons) | Value(£) |
|---|---|---|---|
| 1859 | 153.10 | 0.00 | 459.00 |
| 1860 | 52.50 | 0.00 | 125.80 |
| 1861 | 52.00 | 0.00 | 110.00 |
| 1863 | 194.50 | 0.00 | 582.00 |
| 1864 | 107.10 | 0.00 | 321.20 |
| 1871 | 60.00 | 0.00 | 225.00 |
| 1879 | 300.00 | 0.00 | 1300.00 |
| 1880 | 1965.00 | 0.00 | 6760.00 |
| 1881 | 2350.00 | 1057.50 | 6672.50 |
| 1882 | 2350.00 | 1057.50 | 6781.00 |
| 1883 | 2558.00 | 1227.80 | 8569.00 |
| 1884 | 2304.00 | 0.00 | 6179.00 |
| 1885 | 1750.00 | 613.00 | 4797.00 |
| 1886 | 2050.00 | 767.00 | 5442.00 |
| 1887 | 2110.00 | 774.00 | 6660.00 |
| 1888 | 2850.00 | 1066.00 | 10863.00 |
| 1889 | 2260.00 | 827.00 | 9692.00 |
| 1890 | 2550.00 | 1100.00 | 13435.00 |
| 1891 | 2762.00 | 1387.00 | 13985.00 |
| 1892 | 1560.00 | 733.00 | 6360.00 |
| 1893 | 2321.00 | 1054.00 | 7319.00 |
| 1894 | 2645.00 | 1010.00 | 7556.00 |
| 1895 | 2305.00 | 880.00 | 6038.00 |

| Zinc | Ore(tons) | Metal(tons) | Value(£) |
|------|-----------|-------------|----------|
| 1896 | 1769.00   | 661.50      | 5165.00  |
| 1897 | 1509.00   | 564.00      | 5029.00  |
| 1898 | 1649.00   | 610.00      | 6620.00  |
| 1899 | 549.00    | 205.00      | 2196.00  |
| 1900 | 663.00    | 259.00      | 2500.00  |
| 1901 | 1739.00   | 609.00      | 3478.00  |
| 1902 | 2726.00   | 914.00      | 8000.00  |
| 1903 | 1453.00   | 485.00      | 5957.00  |

Comment 1863 FROMGOCH; 1871 FROUGOCH

Ownership: 1860—1867 JOHN TAYLOR & SONS; 1868—1877 LISBURNE MINING
CO.LTD.; 1878—1882 FRONGOCH LEAD MINE CO.LTD.; 1883—1885
FRONGOCH MINING CO.LTD.; 1886—1889 JOHN KITTO & SONS;
1890—1897 JOHN KITTO; 1898 SOCIETE ANONYME MINIERE; 1899—1903
SOCIETE ANONYME DES MINES DE FRONGOCH
Comment 1859 SEE EAST LOGYLAS; 1860—1877 SEE LISBURNE MINES;
1881 SEE ALT GOCH; 1903 ABANDONED AUG.1903

Management: Manager 1862—1863 HY.THOMAS; 1864—1867 THOS.BALL; 1868—1877
JOHN TAYLOR & SONS; 1879—1881 JOHN KITTO & SON
Chief Agent 1860—1861 HY.THOMAS; 1862—1863 THOS.BALL;
1868—1875 THOS.BALL; 1876—1877
D.SIMMONS,R.GLANVILLE,P.GARLAND&H.CLEMES; 1878 JOHN KITTO;
1882—1888 JOHN KITTO & SON; 1889—1894 ABEL PAULL; 1895—1897
JOHN OWEN; 1898 MAX C.STEGEMANN; 1899 B.NOGARE; 1900—1903
G.H.TREFOIS
Secretary 1872—1874 HY.TAYLOR; 1877 H.H.OAKES; 1879—1881
H.R.MOORE (S)

Employment:

| | Underground | Surface | Total |
|------|-------------|---------|-------|
| 1878 | 65  | 23  | 88  |
| 1879 | 106 | 93  | 199 |
| 1880 | 123 | 171 | 294 |
| 1881 | 134 | 176 | 310 |
| 1882 | 127 | 157 | 284 |
| 1883 | 95  | 129 | 224 |
| 1884 | 68  | 120 | 188 |
| 1885 | 49  | 77  | 126 |
| 1886 | 54  | 68  | 122 |
| 1887 | 62  | 80  | 142 |
| 1888 | 69  | 78  | 147 |
| 1889 | 77  | 79  | 156 |
| 1890 | 79  | 81  | 160 |
| 1891 | 98  | 82  | 180 |
| 1892 | 79  | 92  | 171 |
| 1893 | 61  | 72  | 133 |
| 1894 | 60  | 76  | 136 |
| 1895 | 60  | 69  | 129 |
| 1896 | 61  | 66  | 127 |
| 1897 | 70  | 63  | 133 |
| 1898 | 88  | 70  | 158 |
| 1899 | 95  | 133 | 228 |
| 1900 | 145 | 125 | 270 |
| 1901 | 69  | 90  | 159 |
| 1902 | 115 | 120 | 235 |

FRONGOCH,WEST                  DEVIL'S BRIDGE                          0128

Production: Lead

| | Ore(tons) | Metal(tons) | Value(£) |
|------|-----------|-------------|----------|
| 1861 | 34.80 | 24.40 | 0.00 |
| 1863 | 24.00 | 19.00 | 0.00 |
| 1864 | 66.30 | 49.50 | 0.00 |
| 1865 | 22.00 | 16.00 | 0.00 |
| 1866 | No detailed return | | |

| Lead | Ore(tons) | Metal(tons) | Value(£) |
|------|-----------|-------------|----------|
| 1867 | 42.00 | 31.00 | 0.00 |
| 1868 | 30.00 | 21.50 | 0.00 |
| 1869 | 40.00 | 30.00 | 0.00 |
| 1870 | 41.00 | 31.00 | 0.00 |
| 1871 | 36.00 | 28.00 | 0.00 |
| 1872 | 14.00 | 10.50 | 0.00 |
| 1873 | 10.00 | 7.50 | 0.00 |
| 1890 | 54.00 | 38.00 | 432.00 |
| 1891 | 106.00 | 80.00 | 761.00 |
| 1892 | 10.00 | 7.50 | 58.00 |
| 1894 | 5.00 | 3.50 | 20.00 |
| 1898 | 57.00 | 40.50 | 424.00 |
| 1899 | 42.00 | 30.00 | 373.00 |

| Zinc | Ore(tons) | Metal(tons) | Value(£) |
|------|-----------|-------------|----------|
| 1890 | 22.00 | 6.00 | 45.00 |
| 1891 | 154.00 | 45.00 | 453.00 |
| 1892 | 135.00 | 47.00 | 520.00 |
| 1894 | 86.00 | 30.00 | 215.00 |
| 1898 | 902.00 | 344.50 | 4130.00 |
| 1899 | 254.00 | 97.00 | 1674.00 |
| 1900 | 36.00 | 14.00 | 130.00 |

Ownership:   1869–1881 LISBURNE MINING CO.LTD.; 1890–1896 WEST FRONGOCH
MINE CO.LTD.; 1897–1899 W.S.MURRAY; 1900–1903 SOCIETE ANONYME
DES MINES DE FRONGOCH
Comment 1869–1881 SEE LISBURNE MINES; 1903 ABANDONED
AUG.1903
Management: Manager 1869–1881 JOHN TAYLOR & SONS
Chief Agent 1869–1875 THOS.BALL; 1876
D.SIMMONS,R.GLANVILLE,P.GARLAND,& T.BALL; 1877–1881
D.SIMMONS,R.GLANVILLE,P.GARLAND&H.CLEMES; 1890–1891
WM.MITCHELL; 1892–1893 NICH.BRAY; 1894–1896 JOHN MITCHELL;
1897–1898 W.S.MURRAY; 1899 J.C.MURRAY; 1900–1903 G.H.TREFOIS
Secretary 1872–1874 HY.TAYLOR; 1877–1881 H.H.OAKES

Employment:

| | Underground | Surface | Total |
|------|-----------|---------|-------|
| 1877–1889 | | | |
| 1890 | 20 | 8 | 28 |
| 1891 | 24 | 12 | 36 |
| 1892 | 17 | 9 | 26 |
| 1893 | 8 | | 8 |
| 1894 | 8 | 7 | 15 |
| 1895 | 4 | | 4 |
| 1896 | 6 | | 6 |
| 1897 | 33 | 21 | 54 |
| 1898 | 52 | 26 | 78 |
| 1899 | 41 | 20 | 61 |
| 1900 | 28 | | 28 |

Comment 1877–1889 SEE LISBURNE MINES


GELLIRHEIRON                     RHEIDOL VALLEY              SN 703796 0129

Production: Lead & Silver

| | Ore(tons) | Lead(tons) | Silver(ozs) | Value(£) |
|------|-----------|------------|-------------|----------|
| 1856 | 20.00 | 15.00 | 0.00 | 0.00 |
| 1857 | 42.00 | 29.50 | 0.00 | 0.00 |
| 1858 | 42.00 | 31.00 | 0.00 | 0.00 |
| 1859 | 209.00 | 153.00 | 0.00 | 0.00 |
| 1860 | 80.00 | 61.50 | 0.00 | 0.00 |
| 1861 | 90.00 | 69.00 | 552.00 | 0.00 |
| 1862 | 150.00 | 112.50 | 340.00 | 0.00 |
| 1863 | 50.00 | 39.50 | 98.00 | 0.00 |
| 1864 | 23.00 | 17.20 | 47.00 | 0.00 |

1865–1867 No detailed return

GELLIRHEIRON                    RHEIDOL VALLEY              Continued

        Comment 1857 GELLY Y FEIRON; 1858 GELLERHEIRON; 1859-1866
        GELLI'R'EIRON
Ownership:   1859-1865 WM.BATTYE & CO.
        Comment 1863 GELLYIRIERIN; 1886-1889 SEE TY LLWYD
Management: Chief Agent 1859-1865 JOHN RICHARDS
Employment:          Underground     Surface      Total
        1886-1889
        Comment 1886-1889 SEE TY LLWYD


GERTRUDE                        DEVIL'S BRIDGE                        0130

Production: Lead & Silver   Ore(tons)  Lead(tons) Silver(ozs)   Value(£)
        1871            41.00      30.00      0.00          0.00
        1872            48.70      36.50      0.00          0.00
        1873           154.10     115.00      0.00          0.00
        1874            36.20      27.00     84.00        451.90
        1875            10.00       7.50      0.00          0.00
        1876            48.80      36.50      0.00        598.10
        Comment 1874 OR BODCOLL
Ownership:   1871-1872 ROBT.GIRDWOOD; 1873 GERT.R.GIRDWOOD; 1874-1876
        ROBT.GIRDWOOD & GEO.GREEN; 1877-1881 ROBT.GIRDWOOD
        Comment 1872 GERTRUDE BODCOLL OR DEVIL'S BRIDGE; 1873 OR
        DEVIL'S BRIDGE; 1876 OR BODCOLL
Management: Manager 1871-1874 GEO.GREEN
        Chief Agent 1874 RICH.DUNN & S.Y.DUNN; 1875-1876
        RICH.DUNN,S.G.DUNN & S.Y.DUNN; 1877-1881 GEO.GREEN &
        S.Y.DUNN


GLAN CASTELL                    PONTERWYD                            0131

Ownership:   1890-1893 JOHN OWEN
        Comment 1891 SUSPENDED
Management: Chief Agent 1890-1893 JOHN OWEN
Employment:          Underground     Surface      Total
        1890                2                        2
        1892-1893           2                        2


GLANDOVEY                       GLANDOVEY                            0132

Production: Lead No detailed return
Ownership:   1875-1877 TALYBONT CO.
Management: Chief Agent 1875-1877 J.GLANVILLE


GLANRHEIDOL UNITED              RHEIDOL UNITED                       0133

Production: Lead            Ore(tons) Metal(tons)    Value(£)
        1867            72.70      54.50          0.00
        1868      No detailed return
        Comment 1867-1868 GLAN RHEIDOL
        Zinc            Ore(tons) Metal(tons)    Value(£)
        1867            50.70       0.00        120.80
        Comment 1867 GLAN RHEIDOL
Ownership:   Comment 1866-1877 SEE CAEGYNON


GLOG                                                                0134

Production: Lead & Silver   Ore(tons)  Lead(tons) Silver(ozs)   Value(£)
        1865            18.00      13.00     58.00          0.00

50

GLOG                                            Continued

| Lead & Silver | Ore(tons) | Lead(tons) | Silver(ozs) | Value(£) |
|---|---|---|---|---|
| 1866 | 28.00 | 21.00 | 88.00 | 0.00 |
| 1867 | No detailed return | | | |

Comment 1865 CLOG


GLOGFACH              PONTRHYDYGROES              SN 747705 0135

Production: 

| Lead & Silver | Ore(tons) | Lead(tons) | Silver(ozs) | Value(£) |
|---|---|---|---|---|
| 1857 | 2341.50 | 1825.00 | 0.00 | 0.00 |
| 1859–1860 | No detailed return | | | |
| 1861 | 440.00 | 343.00 | 5831.00 | 0.00 |
| 1862 | 775.00 | 612.00 | 9800.00 | 0.00 |
| 1863 | 725.00 | 587.00 | 11740.00 | 0.00 |
| 1864 | 665.60 | 512.40 | 11323.00 | 0.00 |
| 1865 | 646.00 | 494.00 | 10348.00 | 0.00 |
| 1866 | 800.00 | 608.00 | 12800.00 | 0.00 |
| 1867 | 622.00 | 423.00 | 14430.00 | 0.00 |
| 1868 | 473.00 | 357.00 | 9306.00 | 0.00 |
| 1869 | 470.00 | 387.00 | 11410.00 | 0.00 |
| 1870 | 396.00 | 299.00 | 6908.00 | 0.00 |
| 1871 | 500.00 | 382.00 | 10351.00 | 0.00 |
| 1872 | 356.00 | 270.50 | 7668.00 | 0.00 |
| 1873 | 263.00 | 200.00 | 5560.00 | 0.00 |
| 1874 | 200.00 | 152.00 | 4800.00 | 0.00 |
| 1875 | 180.00 | 141.50 | 0.00 | 0.00 |
| 1876 | No detailed return | | | |
| 1880 | 14.00 | 11.00 | 293.00 | 224.00 |

Comment 1859–1860 SEE EAST LOGYLAS; 1874–1875 FOR VALUE SEE
LISBURNE MINES; 1876 SEE LISBURNE MINES
Ownership:   1860–1867 JOHN TAYLOR & SONS; 1868–1871 LISBURNE MINING
CO.LTD.; 1872–1881 LISBURNE MINES CO.LTD.
Comment 1860–1865 SEE LISBURNE MINES; 1868–1881 SEE LISBURNE
MINES
Management: Manager 1862–1863 HY.THOMAS; 1864–1867 THOS.BALL; 1868–1881
JOHN TAYLOR & SONS
Chief Agent 1860–1861 HY.THOMAS; 1862–1863 THOS.BALL;
1868–1875 THOS.BALL; 1876 D.SIMMONS,R.GLANVILLE,P.GARLAND &
T.BALL; 1877–1881 D.SIMMONS,R.GLANVILLE,P.GARLAND&H.CLEMES
Secretary 1872–1874 HY.TAYLOR; 1877–1881 H.H.OAKES
Employment:          Underground     Surface        Total
1877–1881
Comment 1877–1881 SEE LISBURNE MINES


GLOGFAWR              PONTRHYDYGROES              SN 747708 0136

Production: 

| Lead & Silver | Ore(tons) | Lead(tons) | Silver(ozs) | Value(£) |
|---|---|---|---|---|
| 1862 | 23.00 | 16.50 | 117.00 | 0.00 |
| 1864 | 22.30 | 16.60 | 0.00 | 0.00 |
| 1865 | 23.00 | 17.00 | 196.00 | 0.00 |
| 1866 | 38.00 | 29.00 | 255.00 | 0.00 |
| 1867 | 194.00 | 150.00 | 1640.00 | 0.00 |
| 1868 | 246.00 | 188.00 | 2376.00 | 0.00 |
| 1869 | 515.00 | 394.00 | 4761.00 | 0.00 |
| 1870 | 473.00 | 359.50 | 4275.00 | 0.00 |
| 1871 | 331.00 | 250.00 | 3182.00 | 0.00 |
| 1872 | 359.00 | 271.00 | 3400.00 | 0.00 |
| 1873 | 545.00 | 417.00 | 4205.00 | 0.00 |
| 1874 | 671.00 | 513.00 | 5130.00 | 0.00 |
| 1875 | 818.00 | 625.50 | 6119.00 | 0.00 |
| 1876 | No detailed return | | | |
| 1880 | 920.00 | 750.00 | 7646.00 | 11040.00 |

MC-F

```
              Comment 1874-1875 FOR VALUE SEE LISBURNE MINES; 1876 SEE
              LISBURNE MINES
              Copper        Ore(tons) Metal(tons)    Value(£)
              1879            18.00       1.00         37.50
              Comment 1879 (P)
Ownership:    1861-1867 JOHN TAYLOR & SONS; 1868-1871 LISBURNE MINING
              CO.LTD.; 1872-1881 LISBURNE MINES CO.LTD.
              Comment 1861-1881 SEE LISBURNE MINES
Management:   Manager 1862-1863 HY.THOMAS; 1864-1867 THOS.BALL; 1868-1881
              JOHN TAYLOR & SONS
              Chief Agent 1861 HY.THOMAS; 1862-1863 THOS.BALL; 1868-1875
              THOS.BALL; 1876 D.SIMMONS,R.GLANVILLE,P.GARLAND & T.BALL;
              1877-1881 D.SIMMONS,R.GLANVILLE,P.GARLAND&H.CLEMES
              Secretary 1872-1874 HY.TAYLOR; 1877-1881 H.H.OAKES
Employment:              Underground     Surface         Total
              1877-1881
              Comment 1877-1881 SEE LISBURNE MINES
```

GOGERDDAN MINES                    GOGINAN                              0137

```
Production: Lead            Ore(tons) Metal(tons)     Value(£)
            1845             210.00     136.00          0.00
            1846             118.50      77.00          0.00
            1847             194.00     128.00          0.00
            1848             243.00     162.00          0.00
            1849             131.00      87.00          0.00
            1850              35.00      23.00          0.00
            Comment 1847 INC BOG & DAREN
```

GOGINAN                            GOGINAN                    SN 690818 0138

```
Production: Lead & Silver   Ore(tons) Lead(tons) Silver(ozs)   Value(£)
            1845            1768.00    1149 00       0.00        0.00
            1846            1558.00    1013.00       0.00        0.00
            1847            1446.00     951.00       0.00        0.00
            1848            1238.00     816.00       0.00        0.00
            1849            1160.00     766.00       0.00        0.00
            1850            1004.00     717.00       0.00        0.00
            1851             845.40     675.10       0.00        0.00
            1852             556.00     389.00   10892.00        0.00
            1853             375.00     273.00   10025.00        0.00
            1854             276.00     205.00    7176.00        0.00
            1855             187.00     140.00    3400.00        0.00
            1856             339.00     259.00    5180.00        0.00
            1857             344.40     246.00    5656.00        0.00
            1858             272.00     194.00    4510.00        0.00
            1859             304.50     228.00    5700.00        0.00
            1860             333.50     232.00    5769.00        0.00
            1861             365.00     270.00    7020.00        0.00
            1862             257.00     192.70    5010.00        0.00
            1863             194.00     150.00    4530.00        0.00
            1864             154.60     115.50    4570.00        0.00
            1865              99.00      74.00    1558.00        0.00
            1866             259.00     198.00    6224.00        0.00
            1867             372.00     279.00    8055.00        0.00
            1868             350.00     262.00    7860.00        0.00
            1869             402.90     324.00    9251.00        0.00
            1870             338.00     272.00    7112.00        0.00
            1871             292.00     220.50    5716.00        0.00
            1872             256.00     188.00    5049.00        0.00
            1873             150.00     114.00    3240.00        0.00
```

| Lead & Silver | Ore(tons) | Lead(tons) | Silver(ozs) | Value(£) |
|---|---|---|---|---|
| 1874 | 122.00 | 91.50 | 2856.00 | 2138.00 |
| 1875 | 161.60 | 125.50 | 3432.00 | 3078.50 |
| 1876 | 190.00 | 140.00 | 3832.00 | 3430.00 |
| 1877 | 229.00 | 171.70 | 5150.00 | 3655.50 |
| 1878 | 314.00 | 243.00 | 6171.00 | 4043.20 |
| 1879 | 99.00 | 75.20 | 2133.00 | 1164.40 |
| 1880 | 157.00 | 120.00 | 3006.00 | 2140.40 |
| 1881 | 34.00 | 24.50 | 68.00 | 320.00 |
| 1882 | 50.00 | 38.50 | 1155.00 | 646.00 |
| 1883 | 52.00 | 40.50 | 1352.00 | 616.00 |
| 1884 | 117.00 | 89.00 | 2904.00 | 1218.00 |
| 1885 | 106.00 | 79.00 | 1896.00 | 1105.00 |
| 1886 | 63.00 | 43.00 | 1250.00 | 739.00 |

Comment 1875-1886 INC.LEVEL NEWYDD

| Zinc | Ore(tons) | Metal(tons) | Value(£) |
|---|---|---|---|
| 1872 | 26.00 | 0.00 | 78.00 |
| 1880 | 34.00 | 0.00 | 51.00 |

Comment 1880 INC.LEVEL NEWYDD

Ownership: 1859 JOHN TAYLOR & SONS; 1860 T.&H.JONES & CO.; 1861-1867
JOHN TAYLOR & SONS; 1868-1875 GOGINAN CO.; 1876 GOGINAN &
LEVEL NEWYDD MINING CO.; 1877-1881 GOGINAN & LEVEL NEWYDD
MINING CO.LTD.; 1882-1885 GOGINAN SILVER LEAD MINING CO.LTD.;
1886 GOGINAN REALIZATION CO.LTD.
Comment 1876-1881 INC.LEVEL NEWYDD

Management: Manager 1868-1881 JOHN TAYLOR & SONS
Chief Agent 1859-1876 JAS.PAULL; 1877-1882 WM.H.PAULL;
1883-1886 JOHN KITTO & SON

| Employment: | Underground | Surface | Total |
|---|---|---|---|
| 1877 | 63 | 57 | 120 |
| 1878 | 55 | 47 | 102 |
| 1879 | 43 | 32 | 75 |
| 1880 | 23 | 22 | 45 |
| 1881 | 38 | 26 | 64 |
| 1882 | 43 | 25 | 68 |
| 1883 | 19 | 17 | 36 |
| 1884 | 12 | 14 | 26 |
| 1885 | 12 | 12 | 24 |
| 1886 | 8 | 13 | 21 |

Comment 1877-1880 INC.LEVEL NEWYDD

GOGINAN,WEST            GOGINAN             0139

| Production: Lead | Ore(tons) | Metal(tons) | Value(£) |
|---|---|---|---|
| 1857 | 0.80 | 0.60 | 0.00 |
| 1858-1861 No detailed return | | | |
| 1879 | 6.00 | 4.00 | 61.80 |

Ownership: 1874-1878 WEST GOGINAN LEAD MINING CO.LTD.; 1879 WEST GOGINAN
MINING CO.LTD.; 1880 E.W.LAYTON; 1881 NEW WEST GOGINAN MINING
CO.LTD.; 1882-1883 NEW WEST GOGINAN MINING SYNDICATE LTD.
Comment 1859-1860 ABANDONED; 1881-1882 NEW WEST GOGINAN; 1883
NEW WEST GOGINAN; SUSPENDED

Management: Manager 1875-1878 JOHN KITTO
Chief Agent 1874 WM.TREVETHAN; 1875-1876 RICH.COUCH;
1877-1878 WM.TREVETHAN; 1879 JOHN KITTO; 1880 WM.TREVETHAN;
1881 ABS.FRANCIS; 1882-1883 R.DELATORRE
Secretary 1878 E.W.LAYTON

| Employment: | Underground | Surface | Total |
|---|---|---|---|
| 1877 | 14 | 3 | 17 |
| 1878 | 6 | 2 | 8 |
| 1879 | 12 | 2 | 14 |
| 1880 | 4 | | 4 |

|       | Underground | Surface | Total |
|-------|-------------|---------|-------|
| 1881  | 9           |         | 9     |
| 1882  | 6           | 1       | 7     |

GOTHIC                          RHEIDOL VALLEY                SN 697794 0140

Production: Lead

| | Ore(tons) | Metal(tons) | Value(£) |
|------|-----------|-------------|----------|
| 1865 | 6.70 | 4.20 | 0.00 |
| 1866 | No detailed return | | |
| 1867 | 17.00 | 13.00 | 0.00 |
| 1868 | 17.00 | 13.00 | 0.00 |

Ownership: 1890—1893 THOS.WILLIAMS & CO.
Comment 1893 SUSPENDED
Management: Chief Agent 1866—1867 JAS.LESTER; 1890—1893 THOS.WILLIAMS
Employment:

|           | Underground | Surface | Total |
|-----------|-------------|---------|-------|
| 1890—1891 | 4           | 2       | 6     |
| 1892      | 4           |         | 4     |

GRAIGCOCH                       PONTRHYDYGROES               SN 705723 0141

Production: Lead & Silver

| | Ore(tons) | Lead(tons) | Silver(ozs) | Value(£) |
|------|-----------|------------|-------------|----------|
| 1852 | 96.00 | 71.00 | 0.00 | 0.00 |
| 1853 | 80.00 | 56.00 | 0.00 | 0.00 |
| 1854 | 70.00 | 50.00 | 0.00 | 0.00 |
| 1855 | 16.00 | 10.00 | 0.00 | 0.00 |
| 1856 | No detailed return | | | |
| 1869 | 199.00 | 154.00 | 0.00 | 0.00 |
| 1870 | 173.00 | 132.00 | 0.00 | 0.00 |
| 1871 | 212.00 | 160.00 | 0.00 | 0.00 |
| 1872 | 243.00 | 184.50 | 0.00 | 0.00 |
| 1873 | 186.00 | 141.00 | 0.00 | 0.00 |
| 1874 | 141.00 | 104.50 | 0.00 | 0.00 |
| 1875 | 182.00 | 133.00 | 665 00 | 0.00 |
| 1876 | No detailed return | | | |

Comment 1852—1854 GRAIGGOCH; 1855 FOR SILVER SEE LISBURNE
MINES; 1856 SEE LISBURNE MINES; 1869—1870 GRAIGCOCH; 1874—1875
FOR VALUE SEE LISBURNE MINES; 1876 SEE LISBURNE MINES
Ownership: 1861—1867 JOHN TAYLOR & SONS; 1868—1872 LISBURNE MINING
CO.LTD.; 1873—1874 LISBURNE MINES CO.LTD.; 1875 LISBURNE
MINING CO.LTD.; 1876—1881 LISBURNE MINES CO.LTD.
Comment 1861—1865 SEE LISBURNE MINES; 1868—1881 SEE LISBURNE
MINES
Management: Manager 1862—1863 HY.THOMAS; 1864—1867 THOS.BALL; 1868—1881
JOHN TAYLOR & SONS
Chief Agent 1861 HY.THOMAS; 1862—1863 THOS.BALL; 1868—1875
THOS.BALL; 1876 SIMMONS,GLANVILLE,GARLAND,CLEMES&BALL;
1877—1881 D.SIMMONS,R.GLANVILLE,P.GARLAND&H.CLEMES
Secretary 1872—1874 HY.TAYLOR; 1877—1881 H.H.OAKES
Employment:

|           | Underground | Surface | Total |
|-----------|-------------|---------|-------|
| 1877—1881 |             |         |       |

Comment 1877—1881 SEE LISBURNE MINES

GROGWINION                      PONTRHYDYGROES               SN 715721 0142

Production: Lead & Silver

| | Ore(tons) | Lead(tons) | Silver(ozs) | Value(£) |
|------|-----------|------------|-------------|----------|
| 1850 | 20.40 | 15.70 | 0.00 | 0.00 |
| 1851 | 66.50 | 51.50 | 0.00 | 0.00 |
| 1852 | 23.90 | 16.40 | 0.00 | 0.00 |
| 1853 | 32.00 | 24.00 | 0.00 | 0.00 |
| 1854 | No detailed return | | | |

| Lead & Silver | Ore(tons) | Lead(tons) | Silver(ozs) | Value(£) |
|---|---|---|---|---|
| 1855 | 1.90 | 1.20 | 0.00 | 0.00 |
| 1856 | No detailed return | | | |
| 1857 | 7.30 | 5.50 | 0.00 | 0.00 |
| 1858 | 14.00 | 10.00 | 0.00 | 0.00 |
| 1859 | No detailed return | | | |
| 1860 | 166.00 | 0.00 | 0.00 | 0.00 |
| 1861 | No detailed return | | | |
| 1862 | 94.30 | 70.50 | 210.00 | 0.00 |
| 1864 | 44.80 | 33.60 | 198.00 | 0.00 |
| 1865 | 33.20 | 23.00 | 0.00 | 0.00 |
| 1866-1867 | No detailed return | | | |
| 1872 | 39.50 | 29.60 | 0.00 | 0.00 |
| 1873 | 100.00 | 77.00 | 0.00 | 0.00 |
| 1874 | 500.00 | 387.00 | 1548.00 | 6733.00 |
| 1875 | 790.00 | 619.00 | 5372.00 | 11738.20 |
| 1876 | 1078.70 | 840.00 | 7200.00 | 16103.80 |
| 1877 | 1200.00 | 984.00 | 8856.00 | 16200.00 |
| 1878 | 1100.00 | 885.50 | 0.00 | 10133.00 |
| 1879 | 1000.00 | 825.00 | 0.00 | 9867.50 |
| 1880 | 1100.00 | 907.00 | 3628.00 | 11752.50 |
| 1881 | 600.00 | 450.00 | 1950.00 | 5681.70 |
| 1882 | 430.00 | 352.60 | 0.00 | 3963.00 |
| 1883 | 66.80 | 53.50 | 0.00 | 510.00 |
| 1884 | 28.00 | 21.00 | 0.00 | 160.00 |
| 1885 | 61.00 | 44.00 | 0.00 | 378.00 |
| 1886 | 39.00 | 26.00 | 0.00 | 290.00 |
| 1887 | 25.00 | 18.00 | 0.00 | 170.00 |
| 1888 | 5.00 | 3.00 | 0.00 | 36.00 |
| 1889 | 21.00 | 14.00 | 0.00 | 143.00 |

Comment 1851 AGGREGATED; 1872 LATE BRYNYSTWYTH
Ownership: 1859-1862 PARRY,ATWOOD & CO.; 1863-1866 PARRY & ATWOOD;
1872-1875 GROGWINION MINING CO.; 1876-1884 GROGWINION MINING
CO.LTD.; 1885-1886 GROGWINION CONSOLS LEAD MINE CO.LTD.; 1887
JOHN KITTO & SON; 1888-1890 JOHN KITTO
Comment 1881 NORTH GROGWINION
Management: Manager 1872-1878 JOHN KITTO; 1879-1881 JOHN KITTO & SON
Chief Agent 1859-1866 W.TREGONING; 1874-1881 JOHN OWEN;
1882-1887 JOHN KITTO & SON; 1888-1890 JOHN KITTO
Secretary 1872-1881 GEO.BEDFORD (S)

| Employment: | Underground | Surface | Total |
|---|---|---|---|
| 1877 | 117 | 50 | 167 |
| 1878 | 117 | 55 | 172 |
| 1879 | 112 | 56 | 168 |
| 1880 | 122 | 62 | 184 |
| 1881 | 87 | 40 | 127 |
| 1882 | 47 | 29 | 76 |
| 1883 | 25 | 14 | 39 |
| 1884 | 4 | 6 | 10 |
| 1885 | 4 | 1 | 5 |
| 1886 | 2 | 4 | 6 |
| 1887 | 2 | | 2 |
| 1888 | 3 | 1 | 4 |
| 1889 | | 7 | 7 |
| 1890 | 3 | 1 | 4 |

GROGWINION,NORTH               PONTRHYDYGROES               SN 703728 0143

| Production: Lead | Ore(tons) | Metal(tons) | Value(£) |
|---|---|---|---|
| 1882 | 60.30 | 48.30 | 526.00 |
| 1883 | 1.90 | 1.50 | 15.00 |

Ownership: 1881-1883 NORTH GROGWINION MINING CO.LTD.; 1884-1886

GROGWINION CONSOLS LEAD MINING CO.; 1887 JOHN KITTO & SON;
1888-1889 JOHN KITTO
Comment 1881 SEE GROGWINION; 1884-1889 SUSPENDED
Management: Chief Agent 1881-1887 JOHN KITTO & SON; 1888-1889 JOHN KITTO
Employment:

| | Underground | Surface | Total |
|---|---|---|---|
| 1881 | 11 | 18 | 29 |
| 1882 | 28 | 14 | 42 |
| 1883 | | 5 | 5 |

GWAITHCOCH    LLANAFAN    SN 705842 0144

Production: Lead

| | Ore(tons) | Metal(tons) | Value(£) |
|---|---|---|---|
| 1860 | 35.00 | 25.70 | 0.00 |
| 1861 | 29.30 | 20.50 | 0.00 |
| 1862 | 20.00 | 14.70 | 0.00 |
| 1863 | 20.00 | 15.50 | 0.00 |

Comment 1860-1862 GWAITHGOCH
Ownership: 1861-1865 JOHN TAYLOR & SONS
Comment 1861-1865 SEE LISBURNE MINES
Management: Manager 1862-1863 HY.THOMAS; 1864-1865 THOS.BALL
Chief Agent 1861 HY.THOMAS; 1862-1863 THOS.BALL

GWARCWMBACH    TALYBONT    SN 676918 0145

Production: Lead No detailed return
Ownership: 1913 F.E.BOYCOTT
Employment:

| | Underground | Surface | Total |
|---|---|---|---|
| 1913 | 6 | | 6 |

HAFOD    PONTRHYDYGROES    SN 762727 0146

Production: Lead No detailed return
Ownership: 1861-1865 HAFOD MINING CO.
Comment 1864-1865 SUSPENDED
Management: Chief Agent 1861-1865 CHAS.ROWE

HAFOD,EAST    PONTRHYDYGROES    SN 765726 0147

Production: Lead    Ore(tons) Metal(tons)  Value(£)
1868-1873 No detailed return
Ownership: 1860 HAND & CO.; 1861-1871 W.SPOONER & CO.
Management: Chief Agent 1860 SAMP.MITCHELL; 1861-1871 R.RIDGE
Secretary 1868-1871 WM.BATTYE

HAFOD,NORTH    PONTRYHYDGROES    SN 755737 0148

Production: Lead No detailed return
Ownership: 1861-1865 THOS.SPARGO
Comment 1864-1865 SUSPENDED
Management: Chief Agent 1861 AB.FRANCIS; 1862-1863 RICH.WILLIAMS

HAVAN    TALYBONT    SN 730880 0149

Production: Lead & Silver

| | Ore(tons) | Lead(tons) | Silver(ozs) | Value(£) |
|---|---|---|---|---|
| 1864 | 261.50 | 195.50 | 977.00 | 0.00 |
| 1865 | 210.00 | 164.00 | 0.00 | 0.00 |
| 1866 | 93.00 | 73.00 | 0.00 | 0.00 |

| Lead & Silver | Ore(tons) | Lead(tons) | Silver(ozs) | Value(£) |
|---|---|---|---|---|
| 1867 | 42.00 | 31.50 | 0.00 | 0.00 |
| 1889 | 7.00 | 5.00 | 0.00 | 55.00 |
| 1890 | 10.00 | 7.50 | 58.00 | 92.00 |

Comment 1864–1866 HAFAN INC.HENFWLCH; 1867 HAFAN; 1889–1890 HAFAN INC.HENFWLCH

| Zinc | Ore(tons) | Metal(tons) | Value(£) |
|---|---|---|---|
| 1890 | 4.00 | 0.70 | 9.00 |

Comment 1890 HAFAN INC.HENFWLCH

| Copper | Ore(tons) | Metal(tons) | Value(£) |
|---|---|---|---|
| 1867 | 13.80 | 0.90 | 0.00 |
| 1890 | 11.00 | 1.00 | 0.00 |

Comment 1867 (P) HAFAN; 1890 HAFAN–INC.HENFWLCH

Ownership: 1862–1865 W.H.PUNCHARD; 1866 SETON & CO.; 1868–1869 J.P.THOMAS; 1870–1874 STRAUSBERG & CO.; 1875–1877 COLONEL STRAUSBERG; 1882–1883 SIR PRYCE P.PRYSE; 1889–1895 THOS.MOLYNEUX; 1896–1901 PLYNLIMON & HAVAN CO.LTD.
Comment 1862–1866 INC.HENFWLCH; 1868–1877 INC.HENFWLCH; 1882 INC.HENFWLCH; 1883 INC.HENFWLCH:SUSPENDED; 1889–1892 INC.HENFWLCH; 1893 INC.HENFWLCH:SUSPENDED; 1894 INC.HENFWLCH; 1895–1900 INC.HENFWLCH:SUSPENDED; 1901 INC.HENFWLCH:NOT WORKED IN 1901

Management: Chief Agent 1862 MAT.FRANCIS; 1863–1866 GEO.JONES; 1868–1869 JAS.LESTER; 1870–1874 W.PROSSER; 1875–1877 EVAN RICHARDS; 1882 JOHN EVANS; 1889 J.HUGHES OWEN; 1890–1895 JOHN DAVIS; 1896 FRED.WILLIAMS; 1897–1898 H.W.FRANCIS

| Employment: | Underground | Surface | Total |
|---|---|---|---|
| 1882 | 4 | 1 | 5 |
| 1889 | 10 | 2 | 12 |
| 1890 | 8 | 8 | 16 |
| 1891 | 8 | | 8 |
| 1892 | 4 | 4 | 8 |
| 1894 | 8 | 4 | 12 |

Comment 1882 INC.HENFWLCH; 1889–1892 INC.HENFWLCH; 1894 INC.HENFWLCH


HENDREFELIN            DEVIL'S BRIDGE                0150

| Production: Lead | Ore(tons) | Metal(tons) | Value(£) |
|---|---|---|---|
| 1870 | 20.00 | 15.00 | 0.00 |

Ownership: 1870–1872 ROBT.GIRDWOOD
Comment 1872 OR ELLA
Management: Manager 1870–1872 GEO.GREEN


HENFWLCH              TALYBONT            SN 737884 0151

Production: Lead & Silver    Ore(tons)   Lead(tons) Silver(ozs)    Value(£)
1864–1866 No detailed return
1889–1890 No detailed return
Comment 1864–1866 SEE HAVAN; 1889–1890 SEE HAVAN
Zinc            Ore(tons) Metal(tons)     Value(£)
1890       No detailed return
Comment 1890 SEE HAVAN
Copper          Ore(tons) Metal(tons)     Value(£)
1890       No detailed return
Comment 1890 SEE HAVAN

Ownership: Comment 1862–1866 SEE HAVAN; 1868–1877 SEE HAVAN; 1882–1883 SEE HAVAN; 1889–1901 SEE HAVAN

| Employment: | Underground | Surface | Total |
|---|---|---|---|
| 1882 | | | |
| 1889–1892 | | | |

|  | Underground | Surface | Total |
|--|-------------|---------|-------|
| 1894 |  |  |  |

Comment 1882 SEE HAVAN; 1889-1892 SEE HAVAN; 1894 SEE HAVAN


HENFWLCH,EAST             LLANBADARNFAWR            0152

Ownership: 1882 S.STRINGER
Management: Chief Agent 1882 AND.WILLIAMS
Employment:

|  | Underground | Surface | Total |
|--|-------------|---------|-------|
| 1882 | 2 |  | 2 |


KINGSIDE               CWMYSTWYTH            0153

Production: Lead & Silver

|  | Ore(tons) | Lead(tons) | Silver(ozs) | Value(£) |
|--|-----------|------------|-------------|----------|
| 1888 | 97.00 | 72.00 | 0.00 | 828.00 |
| 1889 | 108.00 | 80.00 | 0.00 | 919.00 |
| 1890 | 82.00 | 61.00 | 0.00 | 692.00 |
| 1891 | 96.00 | 71.00 | 0.00 | 721.00 |
| 1892 | 27.00 | 20.00 | 155.00 | 179.00 |
| 1901-1902 No detailed return |  |  |  |  |
| 1911-1912 No detailed return |  |  |  |  |
| 1913 | 1.00 | 1.00 | 4.00 | 12.00 |

Comment 1901-1902 SEE CWMYSTWYTH; 1911-1912 SEE CWMYSTWYTH

Zinc

|  | Ore(tons) | Metal(tons) | Value(£) |
|--|-----------|-------------|----------|
| 1892 | 10.00 | 3.00 | 17.00 |
| 1901 | No detailed return |  |  |
| 1911-1912 No detailed return |  |  |  |
| 1913 | 61.00 | 25.00 | 360.00 |

Comment 1901 SEE CWMYSTWYTH; 1911-1912 SEE CWMYSTWYTH
Ownership: 1886-1893 KINGSIDE MINING CO.LTD.; 1911-1913 KINGSIDE MINES
LTD.
Comment 1886 STARTED JAN.1887; 1893 ABANDONED IN 1893
Management: Manager 1886-1887 JOHN TAYLOR & SONS
Chief Agent 1886-1893 JOS.B.ROWSE
Employment:

|  | Underground | Surface | Total |
|--|-------------|---------|-------|
| 1887 | 27 | 32 | 59 |
| 1888 | 47 | 24 | 71 |
| 1889 | 40 | 20 | 60 |
| 1890 | 28 | 10 | 38 |
| 1891 | 25 | 13 | 38 |
| 1892 | 15 | 11 | 26 |
| 1893 |  | 1 | 1 |
| 1911-1912 |  |  |  |
| 1913 | 24 | 19 | 43 |

Comment 1911-1912 SEE CWMYSTWYTH


KYLAN POTOSI                                 0154

Production: Lead No detailed return
Ownership: 1863-1865 WALKER & CO.
Comment 1864-1865 SUSPENDED
Management: Chief Agent 1863 JOHN HUGHES


LERI VALLEY               TALYBONT            SN 675883 0155

Production: Lead

|  | Ore(tons) | Metal(tons) | Value(£) |
|--|-----------|-------------|----------|
| 1901 | 15.00 | 11.00 | 100.00 |
| 1910 | 24.00 | 18.00 | 176.00 |

LERI VALLEY                          TALYBONT                      Continued

        Zinc            Ore(tons) Metal(tons)    Value(£)
        1910              73.00      26.00        330.00
        Comment 1910 LERY VALLEY
Ownership:  1904-1908 ED.EVANS; 1909 LONG MINING CO.LTD.; 1910-1912 LERI
        MINING CO.LTD.; 1913 LERY MINING CO.LTD.
        Comment 1902-1903 SEE PENDINAS; 1912-1913 IDLE
Management: Chief Agent 1904-1908 ED.EVANS
Employment:          Underground    Surface          Total
        1904-1906         2                           2
        1907             6                           6
        1908             2                           2
        1909            16            5              21
        1910            16           19              35
        1913                          1               1


LERRY                                TALYBONT                         0156

Production: Lead           Ore(tons) Metal(tons)    Value(£)
        1856             23.90      15.90          0.00
        1857             60.10      45.00          0.00
        1858             79.70      58.50          0.00
        1859          No detailed return
        1860             10.00       6.50          0.00
        1861          No detailed return
        Zinc           Ore(tons) Metal(tons)    Value(£)
        1865             25.00       0.00         75.00
        Copper         Ore(tons) Metal(tons)    Value(£)
        1857              5.20       0.00          0.00
        Comment 1857 (P)
Ownership:  1859-1860 ATKINS,REVIS & CO.
Management: Chief Agent 1859-1860 CHAS.WILLIAMS


LEVEL NEWYDD                         GOGINAN                  SN 707818 0157

Production: Lead & Silver  Ore(tons) Lead(tons) Silver(ozs)    Value(£)
        1849          No detailed return
        1852             75.00      57.00         0.00          0.00
        1853             25.00      18.00         0.00          0.00
        1875-1886 No detailed return
        Comment 1849 SEE LEVEL NEWYDD, FLINTSHIRE; 1875-1886 SEE
        GOGINAN
        Zinc           Ore(tons) Metal(tons)    Value(£)
        1880          No detailed return
        Comment 1880 SEE GOGINAN
Ownership:  Comment 1876-1881 SEE GOGINAN
Employment:          Underground    Surface          Total
        1877-1880
        Comment 1877-1880 SEE GOGINAN


LISBURNE MINES                     PONTRHYDYGROES                       0158

Production: Lead & Silver  Ore(tons) Lead(tons) Silver(ozs)    Value(£)
        1845           2492.00    1623.00         0.00          0.00
        1846           2650.00    1722.00         0.00          0.00
        1847           2028.00    1338.00         0.00          0.00
        1848           2454.00    1624.00         0.00          0.00
        1849           2733.00    1804.00         0.00          0.00
        1850           3345.00    2389.00         0.00          0.00
        1851           3406.10    2753.10         0.00          0.00
        1852           3186.00    2293.00      8972.00          0.00

                                     59

| Lead & Silver | Ore(tons) | Lead(tons) | Silver(ozs) | Value(£) |
|---|---|---|---|---|
| 1853 | 2752.00 | 2066.00 | 4000.00 | 0.00 |
| 1854 | 2595.00 | 1653.00 | 0.00 | 0.00 |
| 1855 | 0.00 | 0.00 | 2150.00 | 0.00 |
| 1856 | 2821.40 | 2023.00 | 3458.00 | 0.00 |
| 1874 | 0.00 | 0.00 | 0.00 | 28665.40 |
| 1875 | 0.00 | 0.00 | 0.00 | 35613.10 |
| 1876 | 2342.00 | 1756.00 | 10536.00 | 35244.00 |
| 1877 | 2101.00 | 1575.00 | 9450.00 | 27784.60 |
| 1878 | 1861.70 | 1396.00 | 8376.00 | 19963.80 |
| 1879 | 948.00 | 740.00 | 8523.00 | 10299.80 |
| 1880 | 976.00 | 733.50 | 3566.00 | 11432.00 |
| 1881 | 1005.00 | 750.00 | 3550.00 | 10150.50 |
| 1882 | 855.00 | 633.40 | 5037.00 | 8994.00 |
| 1883 | 745.00 | 600.50 | 5140.00 | 6713.00 |
| 1884 | 601.00 | 480.80 | 3300.00 | 4619.00 |
| 1885 | 660.00 | 502.00 | 3835.00 | 5593.00 |
| 1886 | 448.00 | 340.00 | 2155.00 | 4305.00 |
| 1887 | 572.00 | 443.00 | 2560.00 | 5136.00 |
| 1888 | 558.00 | 428.00 | 2776.00 | 5205.00 |
| 1889 | 570.00 | 412.00 | 3125.00 | 5193.00 |
| 1890 | 395.00 | 283.00 | 1905.00 | 3244.00 |
| 1891 | 428.00 | 319.00 | 1729.00 | 3249.00 |
| 1892 | 331.00 | 251.50 | 1261.00 | 2198.00 |
| 1893 | 312.00 | 237.00 | 1189.00 | 1975.00 |
| 1909 | 82.50 | 65.00 | 412.00 | 702.00 |
| 1910 | 522.00 | 382.00 | 2871.00 | 4471.00 |
| 1911 | 519.00 | 404.00 | 2595.00 | 4882.00 |
| 1912 | 637.00 | 508.00 | 3185.00 | 7277.00 |
| 1913 | 667.00 | 532.00 | 3003.00 | 8010.00 |

Comment 1855 E LOGYLAS FRONGOCH & GRAIGCOCH; 1874-1875 SEE
SEPARATE MINES

| Zinc | Ore(tons) | Metal(tons) | Value(£) |
|---|---|---|---|
| 1854 | 200.00 | 0.00 | 0.00 |
| 1855 | 315.00 | 0.00 | 0.00 |
| 1856 | 264.10 | 0.00 | 797.30 |
| 1857 | 284.60 | 0.00 | 923.20 |
| 1858 | 105.00 | 0.00 | 288.50 |
| 1859 | 168.00 | 0.00 | 458.00 |
| 1860 | 57.30 | 0.00 | 110.30 |
| 1861 | 50.00 | 0.00 | 120.50 |
| 1871 | 61.60 | 0.00 | 124.70 |

Ownership: 1877-1888 JOHN TAYLOR & SONS; 1889-1892 LISBURNE MINES
CO.LTD.; 1893-1898 PETER & THOS.GARLAND & WM.MITCHELL;
1899-1903 J.A.&THOS.GARLAND & JAS.MCILQUHAN; 1907-1913
LISBURNE DEVELOPMENT SYNDICATE LTD.
Comment 1877 THE LISBURNE MINES INCLUDE:; 1878 EAST LOGYLAS,
LOGYLAS, FRONGOCH,; 1879 GLOGFACH, GLOGFAWR, GRAIGCOCH,; 1880
GWAITHCOCH, WEST FRONGOCH.; 1902-1903 NOT WORKED
Management: Chief Agent 1877-1898 PETER GARLAND; 1909-1913 R.R.NANCARROW
Secretary 1893-1898 JAS.MCILQUHAN

| Employment: | Underground | Surface | Total |
|---|---|---|---|
| 1877 | 211 | 208 | 419 |
| 1878 | 125 | 99 | 224 |
| 1879 | 129 | 104 | 233 |
| 1880 | 113 | 67 | 180 |
| 1881 | 132 | 59 | 191 |
| 1882 | 87 | 57 | 144 |
| 1883 | 53 | 43 | 96 |
| 1884 | 50 | 48 | 98 |
| 1885 | 53 | 53 | 106 |
| 1886 | 54 | 59 | 113 |
| 1887 | 64 | 64 | 128 |

LISBURNE MINES                    PONTRHYDYGROES                   Continued

|           | Underground | Surface | Total |
|-----------|-------------|---------|-------|
| 1888      | 66          | 60      | 126   |
| 1889      | 53          | 56      | 109   |
| 1890      | 50          | 44      | 94    |
| 1891      | 35          | 39      | 74    |
| 1892      | 29          | 27      | 56    |
| 1893      | 30          | 29      | 59    |
| 1894-1901 | 2           |         | 2     |
| 1907      | 55          | 4       | 59    |
| 1908      | 31          | 8       | 39    |
| 1909      | 26          | 14      | 40    |
| 1910      | 47          | 20      | 67    |
| 1911      | 50          | 25      | 75    |
| 1912      | 67          | 19      | 86    |
| 1913      | 55          | 29      | 84    |

Comment 1877 AGGREGATE: INCLUDING; 1878 EAST LOGYLAS,
LOGYLAS, FRONGOCH,; 1879 GLOGFACH, GLOGFAWR, GRAIGCOCH,; 1880
GWAITHCOCH, WEST FRONGOCH.


LISBURNE,NEW                     PONTRHYDYGROES                  SN 748686 0159

Production: Lead & Silver    Ore(tons)  Lead(tons) Silver(ozs)   Value(£)
            1857              6.20       4.60       30.00         0.00
            1858-1861 No detailed return
            1864              7.00       5.50        0.00         0.00
            Comment 1864 FOR SILVER SEE SILVER MOUNTAIN
Ownership:  1875 GEO.PELL
            Comment 1859-1860 ABANDONED; 1875 NEW LISBURN
Management: Chief Agent 1875 JOS.BALL


LISBURNE,SOUTH                    YSTRADMEURIG                          0160

Production: Lead & Silver    Ore(tons)  Lead(tons) Silver(ozs)   Value(£)
            1860             64.50      48.00      468.00         0.00
            1864              6.20       4.80       34.00         0.00
            1865             45.00      34.00        0.00         0.00
            1866-1868 No detailed return
            Zinc              Ore(tons) Metal(tons)  Value(£)
            1862             25.00       0.00         67.50
            1864            198.90       0.00        597.00
            1865             99.50       0.00        298.50
            1872            154.00       0.00        577.00
            1873             72.00       0.00        216.00
            1874             No detailed return
            1877             30.00       0.00        112.50
            1878             20.00       0.00         70.00
            Comment 1862 SOUTH LISBURN; 1864 SOUTH LISBURN
Ownership:  1859-1860 J.HANMER & CO.; 1861-1866 A.P.DAVIES; 1876
            RICH.ATTENBOROUGH & ? VICKERS; 1877-1883 RICH.ATTENBOROUGH
            Comment 1880 NOT WORKED; 1882 SUSPENDED
Management: Manager 1880-1881 AND.HALSE
            Chief Agent 1859-1860 JAS.KEMP; 1861-1865 J.KNEEBONE; 1866
            J.SOCHIN; 1877-1882 ED.HALSE; 1883 RICH.COUCH
Employment:                  Underground  Surface     Total
            1877                 4                        4
            1878-1879            2                        2
            1880-1881                        1            1
            1883                 1                        1

Production: Lead No detailed return
Ownership: 1880–1884 WEST LISBURNE MINING CO.LTD.
           Comment 1875 SEE ELLA; 1884 STOPPED MAR.1884
Management: Chief Agent 1880–1881 NICH.BRAY; 1882–1884 WM.NORTHEY
           Secretary 1880–1881 RICH.ATTENBOROUGH; 1883–1884 WM.BATTYE
           (S)

| Employment: | Underground | Surface | Total |
|---|---|---|---|
| 1880 | | 6 | 6 |
| 1881 | 2 | 12 | 14 |
| 1882 | 4 | 8 | 12 |
| 1883 | 2 | | 2 |
| 1884 | 2 | 1 | 3 |

LLAINHIR          TALIESIN          0162

| Production: Lead & Silver | Ore(tons) | Lead(tons) | Silver(ozs) | Value(£) |
|---|---|---|---|---|
| 1885 | 5.00 | 4.00 | 15.00 | 30.00 |
| 1886 | 5.00 | 3.50 | 8.00 | 33.00 |

| Zinc | Ore(tons) | Metal(tons) | Value(£) |
|---|---|---|---|
| 1888–1890 No detailed return | | | |

Comment 1888–1890 SEE DOLCLETTWR

| Copper | Ore(tons) | Metal(tons) | Value(£) |
|---|---|---|---|
| 1881 | 20.00 | 2.20 | 121.50 |
| 1885 | 14.00 | 2.00 | 52.00 |
| 1886 | 15.00 | 1.00 | 40.00 |
| 1888 | 3.50 | 0.20 | 14.00 |
| 1889–1890 No detailed return | | | |

Comment 1881 LATE DOLCLETTWR; 1888 & DOLCLETTWR; 1889–1890
SEE DOLCLETTWR
Ownership: 1880 LLAINHIR MINE CO.; 1881 JAS.MCILQUHAN & JAS.RAWSTHORNE
           Comment 1881 SEE ALSO DOLCLETTWR; 1882–1891 SEE DOLCLETTWR
Management: Manager 1881 EVAN DANIEL
           Chief Agent 1880 JAS.W.HENHAM

| Employment: | Underground | Surface | Total |
|---|---|---|---|
| 1880 | 10 | 5 | 15 |
| 1881–1886 | | | |
| 1888–1891 | | | |

Comment 1881–1886 SEE DOLCLETTWR; 1888–1891 SEE DOLCLETTWR

LLANBADARN                  0164

| Production: Lead | Ore(tons) | Metal(tons) | Value(£) |
|---|---|---|---|
| 1848 | 33.00 | 18.00 | 0.00 |
| 1849 | No detailed return | | |

LLANCYNFELYN          TALIESIN          SN 650920 0165

| Production: Lead | Ore(tons) | Metal(tons) | Value(£) |
|---|---|---|---|
| 1846 | 4.00 | 2.75 | 0.00 |

LLANERCH          TALYBONT          SN 694859 0166

| Production: Lead | Ore(tons) | Metal(tons) | Value(£) |
|---|---|---|---|
| 1856 | 4.40 | 2.90 | 0.00 |
| 1857 | No detailed return | | |

Comment 1856 LLANARCH; 1857 LLANARSH
Ownership: 1898 JOS.EVANS; 1899–1903 MRS.EVANS
           Comment 1899–1900 SUSPENDED; 1901 NOT WORKED IN 1901,
1902–1903 NOT WORKED

LLANERCH                    TALYBONT                    Continued

Employment:                 Underground    Surface      Total
            1898                2                          2


LLANFAIR                    LAMPETER                    SN 627513 0167

Production: Lead & Silver    Ore(tons)   Lead(tons)  Silver(ozs)    Value(£)
            1845              158.00       103.00        0.00          0.00
            1846              242.00       157.00        0.00          0.00
            1847              291.00       189.00        0.00          0.00
            1848               80.00        53.00        0.00          0.00
            1849              206.00       134.00        0.00          0.00
            1850               88.00        67.50        0.00          0.00
            1851—1854 No detailed return
            Comment 1849—1850 LLANFAIR CLYDOGAN; 1853 LLANFAIR CLYDOGAN
Ownership:  1859—1865 JOHN TAYLOR & SONS
            Comment 1862—1865 SUSPENDED
Management: Chief Agent 1859—1861 THOS.BALL


LLANFYRNACH                 LLANFYRNACH, PEMBROKESHIRE                0168

Production: Lead & Silver    Ore(tons)   Lead(tons)  Silver(ozs)    Value(£)
            1858               42.00        30.70       184.00         0.00
            1859               96.00        65.00       390.00         0.00
            1860              186.00       158.00      1108.00         0.00
            1861               43.00        29.00       263.00         0.00
            Comment 1859—1860 LLANFYRNECH
Ownership:  1859—1860 WM.BATTYE
            Comment 1859 LLANFYNECH; 1860 WINDING UP
Management: Chief Agent 1859—1860 ? PASCOE


LLANGANFELIN                TALIESIN                                 0169

Production: Lead            Ore(tons) Metal(tons)     Value(£)
            1855              21.00       14.00          0.00
            1856—1857 No detailed return


LLANYMARON                                                          0170

Production: Lead            Ore(tons) Metal(tons)     Value(£)
            1848              11.00        5.00          0.00
            1849     No detailed return


LLANYMAWN                                                           0171

Production: Lead            Ore(tons) Metal(tons)     Value(£)
            1850     No detailed return


LLAWRCWMBACH                TALYBONT                    SN 708854 0172

Production: Lead & Silver    Ore(tons)   Lead(tons)  Silver(ozs)    Value(£)
            1851               1.70         1.20         0.00          0.00
            1852               4.00         2.80         0.00          0.00
            1853     No detailed return
            1854              12.00         9.20        37.00          0.00
            1859     No detailed return
            1860              66.20        45.50       210.00          0.00
            1861     No detailed return

| Lead & Silver | Ore(tons) | Lead(tons) | Silver(ozs) | Value(£) |
|---|---|---|---|---|
| 1864 | 21.60 | 15.70 | 85.00 | 0.00 |
| 1865 | 31.00 | 21.00 | 48.00 | 0.00 |
| 1866 | No detailed return | | | |
| 1867 | 16.10 | 12.00 | 0.00 | 0.00 |
| 1870 | 11.00 | 8.50 | 27.00 | 0.00 |
| 1871 | 18.00 | 14.00 | 56.00 | 0.00 |
| 1872 | 8.00 | 6.00 | 23.00 | 0.00 |
| 1873 | 20.00 | 15.00 | 85.00 | 0.00 |
| 1874 | 22.90 | 17.50 | 105.00 | 330.90 |
| 1875 | 15.50 | 4.00 | 0.00 | 0.00 |
| 1876 | 32.50 | 24.40 | 240.00 | 0.00 |
| 1877 | 16.60 | 13.00 | 130.00 | 224.10 |
| 1878 | 7.50 | 5.50 | 0.00 | 73.20 |
| 1879 | 16.50 | 12.20 | 0.00 | 154.00 |

Comment 1859 SEE LLAWRCWMBACH, MONTGOMERY; 1860 SEE ALSO
LLAWRCWMBACH, MONTGOMERY

Ownership: 1859-1875 C.E.HAYWARD & CO.; 1876-1883 C.E.HAYWARD
Comment 1883 SUSPENDED

Management: Manager 1872-1882 JOH.PHILLIPS
Chief Agent 1859-1860 PETER GARLAND; 1861-1867 S.TREGONING;
1868 W.H.TREGONING; 1869-1871 JAS.LESTER; 1883 JOH.PHILLIPS

Employment:

| | Underground | Surface | Total |
|---|---|---|---|
| 1877-1878 | 6 | 2 | 8 |
| 1879 | 6 | 1 | 7 |
| 1880 | 6 | | 6 |
| 1881 | 1 | | 1 |
| 1882 | | 1 | 1 |

LLECHWEDHELIG                     TALYBONT                 SN 683848 0173

Production: Lead

| | Ore(tons) | Metal(tons) | Value(£) |
|---|---|---|---|
| 1853 | 3.40 | 2.50 | 0.00 |

LLECHWYDDEN                       PENRHYNCOCH                        0174

Production: Lead & Silver

| | Ore(tons) | Lead(tons) | Silver(ozs) | Value(£) |
|---|---|---|---|---|
| 1853 | 161.30 | 118.00 | 590.00 | 0.00 |
| 1854 | 23.00 | 17.20 | 0.00 | 0.00 |

LLERY TEIFY                                                           0175

Production: Zinc

| | Ore(tons) | Metal(tons) | Value(£) |
|---|---|---|---|
| 1872 | 11.00 | 0.00 | 33.00 |

LLETTYHEN                         PENRHYNCOCH              SN 694849 0176

Production: Lead & Silver

| | Ore(tons) | Lead(tons) | Silver(ozs) | Value(£) |
|---|---|---|---|---|
| 1851 | 22.90 | 17.20 | 0.00 | 0.00 |
| 1852 | 27.00 | 19.00 | 0.00 | 0.00 |
| 1853 | 75.00 | 56.20 | 0.00 | 0.00 |
| 1854 | No detailed return | | | |
| 1855 | 2.70 | 1.80 | 0.00 | 0.00 |
| 1856 | 10.30 | 7.00 | 112.00 | 0.00 |
| 1857 | 2.10 | 1.50 | 24.00 | 0.00 |

LLWYNMALEES                    YSTRADMEURIG                    SN 689678 0178

| Production: Lead & Silver | Ore(tons) | Lead(tons) | Silver(ozs) | Value(£) |
|---|---|---|---|---|
| 1845 | 60.00 | 39.00 | 0.00 | 0.00 |
| 1847 | 49.00 | 32.00 | 0.00 | 0.00 |
| 1848 | 51.00 | 33.00 | 0.00 | 0.00 |
| 1849 | 32.00 | 21.00 | 0.00 | 0.00 |
| 1850 | 100.00 | 67.50 | 0.00 | 0.00 |
| 1851 | 59.60 | 45.00 | 0.00 | 0.00 |
| 1855 | 71.00 | 50.00 | 620.00 | 0.00 |
| 1856 | 101.40 | 82.50 | 987.00 | 0.00 |
| 1857 | 100.80 | 67.00 | 741.00 | 0.00 |
| 1858 | 15.00 | 10.50 | 147.00 | 0.00 |
| 1859-1861 No detailed return | | | | |
| 1862 | 40.00 | 30.00 | 530.00 | 0.00 |
| 1863 | 40.00 | 30.50 | 488.00 | 0.00 |
| 1864 | 26.50 | 20.00 | 301.00 | 0.00 |
| 1865-1866 No detailed return | | | | |
| 1867 | 40.60 | 30.40 | 0.00 | 0.00 |

Comment 1845 LLWYNMALYS; 1847-1850 LLWYNMALYS; 1851 LLRYN
MALERS

| Zinc | Ore(tons) | Metal(tons) | Value(£) |
|---|---|---|---|
| 1864 | 20.50 | 0.00 | 60.00 |

Ownership:    1859-1865 BEAVAN & CO.; 1866-1867 WM.WILLIAMS & CO.;
              1868-1871 LLWYNMALEES MINING CO.LTD.
Management:   Chief Agent 1859-1871 NICH.BRAY
              Secretary 1868-1871 WM.BATTYE


LLWYNTEIFY                     PONTERWYD                      SN 748794 0179

Ownership:    Comment 1886-1889 SEE BWLCHGWYN
Employment:                Underground    Surface      Total
              1886-1888
              Comment 1886-1888 SEE BWLCHGWYN


LLYWERNOG                      PONTERWYD                      SN 733810 0180

| Production: Lead & Silver | Ore(tons) | Lead(tons) | Silver(ozs) | Value(£) |
|---|---|---|---|---|
| 1845 | 48.00 | 30.00 | 0.00 | 0.00 |
| 1865 | 30.30 | 22.50 | 0.00 | 0.00 |
| 1866 | 78.20 | 58.50 | 0.00 | 0.00 |
| 1867 | No detailed return | | | |
| 1870 | 20.00 | 15.00 | 120.00 | 0.00 |
| 1871 | 80.00 | 60.00 | 0.00 | 0.00 |
| 1872 | 60.00 | 31.00 | 0.00 | 0.00 |
| 1873 | No detailed return | | | |

Comment 1865 OLLEWERNAY; 1866-1867 LLEWERNOG

| Zinc | Ore(tons) | Metal(tons) | Value(£) |
|---|---|---|---|
| 1865 | 14.50 | 0.00 | 73.60 |

Comment 1865 LLEWERNAY
Ownership:    1860 JONES,HUGHES & CO.; 1861-1871 J.B.BALCOMBE & CO.;
              1872-1873 LLYWERNOG CO.LTD.; 1874-1875 J.B.BALCOMBE & CO.
              Comment 1860-1869 LLYWERNOG UNITED
Management:   Manager 1872-1875 JOHN EVANS
              Chief Agent 1860 JOHN HUGHES; 1861-1865 JAS.LESTER; 1866-1869
              JOHN DAVIES; 1870-1871 JOHN DAVIS; 1872-1873 JOHN DAVIES
              Secretary 1872-1873 J.B.BALCOMBE


LODGE PARK                     GLANDOVEY                      SN 665926 0181

Ownership.    1895-1897 SIR PRYCE P.PRYSE
              Comment 1896-1897 SUSPENDED

LODGE PARK                    GLANDOVEY                        Continued

Management: Chief Agent 1896-1897 SIR PRYCE P.PRYSE
Employment:                 Underground    Surface        Total
            1895                 2                           2


LOGYLAS                       PONTRHYDYGROES                   SN 739722 0182

Production: Lead No detailed return
Ownership:  1861-1867 JOHN TAYLOR & SONS
            Comment 1861-1867 SEE LISBURNE MINES
Management: Manager 1862-1863 HY.THOMAS; 1864-1867 THOS.BALL
            Chief Agent 1861 HY.THOMAS; 1862-1863 THOS.BALL


LOGYLAS,EAST                  PONTRHYDYGROES                   SN 739722 0183

Production: Lead & Silver     Ore(tons)    Lead(tons)  Silver(ozs)    Value(£)
            1855               1146.00      730.00        0.00          0.00
            1856         No detailed return
            1857                902.00      647.00     2588.00          0.00
            1858               2294.00     1789.00     8945.00          0.00
            1859               1267.00      950.00        0.00          0.00
            1860               1218.00     1001.00     6006.00          0.00
            1861                907.00      698.00        0.00          0.00
            1862                775.00      597.00     2390.00          0.00
            1863                562.00      449.50     1798.00          0.00
            1864                737.50      550.00     2608.00          0.00
            1865                788.00      592.00     2521.00          0.00
            1866                771.00      598.00     3145.00          0.00
            1867                785.00      589.00        0.00          0.00
            1868                615.00      453.00     2247.00          0.00
            1869                505.00      367.00     1930.00          0.00
            1870                370.00      276.00      870.00          0.00
            1871                214.00      158.50      457.00          0.00
            1872                129.00       95.00      300.00          0.00
            1873                148.00      107.00      635.00          0.00
            1874                 97.00       72.00      450.00          0.00
            1875                 18.00       13.50      126.00          0.00
            1876         No detailed return
            1879                 44.00       33.00      135.00        462.00
            1880                 12.00        9.00       56.00        135.60
            Comment 1855 FOR SILVER SEE LISBURNE; 1856 SEE LISBURNE; 1858
            INC FRONGOCH; 1859 INC GLOGFACH -AG SEE FRONGOCH; 1860 INC
            GLOGFACH; 1874-1875 FOR VALUE SEE LISBURNE; 1876 SEE
            LISBURNE
Ownership:  1859-1860 JOHN TAYLOR & SONS; 1868-1881 LISBURNES MINING
            CO.LTD.
            Comment 1859 INC.FRONGOCH; 1860 SEE LISBURNE MINES; 1868-1881
            SEE LISBURNE MINES
Management: Manager 1868-1881 JOHN TAYLOR & SONS
            Chief Agent 1859 JOHN EDDY; 1860 HY.THOMAS; 1868-1875
            THOS.BALL; 1876-1881 SIMMONS,GLANVILLE,GARLAND,CLEMES&BALL
            Secretary 1872-1874 HY.TAYLOR; 1877-1881 H.H.OAKES
Employment:                 Underground    Surface        Total
            1877-1881
            Comment 1877-1881 SEE LISBURNE MINES


LOVEDEN NO.1                  GLANDOVEY                        SN 657904 0999

Production: Lead & Silver     Ore(tons)    Lead(tons)  Silver(ozs)    Value(£)
            1854                 60.00       46.00      788.00          0.00
            1855                 40.00       30.00      582.00          0.00

                                   66

LOVEDEN NO.1                        GLANDOVEY                      Continued

Lead & Silver       Ore(tons)  Lead(tons) Silver(ozs)    Value(£)
1856-1857 No detailed return
1859                4.30       3.20        0.00           0.00
1860-1862 No detailed return
Comment 1855-1857 LOVEDEN UNITED; 1859-1862 LOVEDEN UNITED


LOVEDEN NO.2                        TALYBONT                    SN 668941 0184

Production: Lead & Silver     Ore(tons)   Lead(tons) Silver(ozs)    Value(£)
            1901              80.00       61.00       240.00         560.00
            1902              101.00      80.00       0.00           661.00
            1903              244.00      185.00      0.00           1614.00
            1904              87.00       68.00       0.00           679.00
            1905              7.00        5.00        0.00           60.00
            1908              51.00       41.00       0.00           357.00
            1909              155.00      122.00      535.00         1370.00
            1910              102.00      78.00       0.00           841.00
            1911              66.00       50.00       0.00           512.00
            Zinc              Ore(tons)   Metal(tons)     Value(£)
            1903              5.00        1.00            8.00
Ownership:  1899 JOHN JENKINS; 1900-1902 LOVEDEN MINE LTD.; 1903-1907
            LOVEDEN MINING CO.(1903) LTD.; 1908-1910 SCOTTISH CARDIGAN
            LEAD MINES LTD.; 1911-1912 CARDIGAN MINING CO.LTD.
            Comment 1899-1901 FORMERLY PENRHYN GERWEN; 1906 NOT WORKED;
            1907 IDLE; 1912 ABANDONED
Management: Chief Agent 1899 JOHN JENKINS; 1900-1902 T.C.COTHERILL;
            1903-1907 HAR.TWITE; 1908 THOS.E.HARDY; 1909-1911 K.FERGUSON;
            1912 J.MCKENDRICK
Employment:                 Underground     Surface        Total
            1899            6                              6
            1900            7               3              10
            1901            17              6              23
            1902            12              10             22
            1903            33              14             47
            1904            32              12             44
            1905            34              12             46
            1906-1907                       1              1
            1908            30              10             40
            1909            15              14             29
            1910            25              17             42
            1911            42              23             65


MAY                                 CWMYSTWYTH                           0185

Production: Lead No detailed return
Ownership:  1911-1913 MAY MINING CO.LTD.
            Comment 1911-1912 OPENING; 1913 CLOSED MAY 1913
Management: Chief Agent 1911-1912 R.ART.THOMAS; 1913 R.THOMAS
Employment:                 Underground     Surface        Total
            1912            14              2              16
            1913            11              3              14


MELINDWR                            GOGINAN                              0186

Production: Lead & Silver     Ore(tons)   Lead(tons) Silver(ozs)    Value(£)
            1874              25.00       19.00       0.00           351.90
            1875              100.00      75.00       275.00         1041.90
            1876              34.90       26.00       90.00          473.50
            1877              16.00       12.00       60.00          206.00
            1878              10.70       7.00        28.00          101.80

                                      67
MC-G

```
          Comment 1874-1875 MELINDWR VALLEY
Ownership:  1873 MELINDWR MINING CO.; 1874-1875 MELINDWR VALLEY LEAD
          MINING CO.; 1876-1880 MELINDWR LEAD MINING CO.LTD.
          Comment 1873 MELINDDWR; 1874 MELINDUR VALLEY; 1875 MELINDWR
          VALLEY
Management: Manager 1873-1878 JOHN KITTO; 1879-1880 JOHN KITTO & SON
          Chief Agent 1874-1880 WM.TREVETHAN
          Secretary 1873-1878 E.C.RAVENSCROFT (S); 1879-1880 H.R.MOORE
          (S)
```

| Employment: | Underground | Surface | Total |
|---|---|---|---|
| 1877 | 4 | 3 | 7 |
| 1878 | 10 | 6 | 16 |
| 1879 | 6 |  | 6 |


MELINLLYNPAIR　　　　　　　　MERIONETH　　　　　　　　0187

| Production: | Lead & Silver | Ore(tons) | Lead(tons) | Silver(ozs) | Value(£) |
|---|---|---|---|---|---|
|  | 1852 | 20.00 | 15.00 | 120.00 | 0.00 |
|  | 1853 | 45.00 | 35.00 | 260.00 | 0.00 |
|  | 1854 | No detailed return |  |  |  |


MOEL GLOMEN　　　　　　　　TALYBONT　　　　　　　SN 697874 0188

| Production: | Lead | Ore(tons) | Metal(tons) | Value(£) |
|---|---|---|---|---|
|  | 1865 | 0.80 | 0.50 | 0.00 |
|  | 1866-1867 | No detailed return |  |  |


MONYDD GORDDU　　　　　　　　BOW STREET　　　　　　SN 667862 0189

| Production: | Lead & Silver | Ore(tons) | Lead(tons) | Silver(ozs) | Value(£) |
|---|---|---|---|---|---|
|  | 1874 | 25.00 | 18.00 | 0.00 | 0.00 |
|  | 1875 | 5.00 | 4.00 | 0.00 | 0.00 |
|  | 1876 | 90.60 | 68.00 | 0.00 | 1282.60 |
|  | 1877 | 71.10 | 49.50 | 999.00 | 960.30 |
|  | 1878 | 70.00 | 52.50 | 1540.00 | 753.00 |
|  | 1879 | 180.00 | 135.00 | 978.00 | 1890.00 |
|  | 1880 | 240.00 | 193.00 | 875.00 | 2712.00 |
|  | 1881 | 165.00 | 113.00 | 3135.00 | 2005.40 |
|  | 1882 | 8.00 | 76.40 | 1376.00 | 1098.00 |
|  | 1883 | 37.80 | 30.40 | 682.00 | 376.00 |
|  | 1884 | 9.00 | 0.00 | 140.00 | 83.00 |

Comment 1882-1884 MYNYDD GORDDU

| Zinc | Ore(tons) | Metal(tons) | Value(£) |
|---|---|---|---|
| 1875 | 2.00 | 0.00 | 10.00 |
| 1876 | 19.90 | 0.00 | 100.00 |
| 1877 | 20.00 | 0.00 | 76.00 |
| 1878 | 20.00 | 0.00 | 50.00 |
| 1879 | 20.00 | 0.00 | 85.00 |
| 1880 | 40.00 | 0.00 | 120.00 |
| 1881 | 52.20 | 27.00 | 133.50 |
| 1883 | 8.60 | 3.60 | 10.00 |

```
          Comment 1875 MONYD GORDU; 1880-1881 MONYD GORDDU; 1883 MYNYDD
          GORDDU
Ownership:  1876-1884 MONYDD GORDDU CO.LTD.; 1885 GREEN,WHITE & CO.
          Comment 1882 MYNYDD GORDDU; 1883 IN LIQUIDATION; 1884-1885
          SUSPENDED
Management: Manager 1881 JNO.PELL
          Chief Agent 1875-1876 RICH.ROWSE; 1877-1880 JAS.GREEN;
          1881-1885 THOS.KEMP
```

MONYDD GORDDU               BOW STREET             Continued

| Employment: | Underground | Surface | Total |
|---|---|---|---|
| 1877 | 32 | 10 | 42 |
| 1878 | 22 | 24 | 46 |
| 1879 | 32 | 11 | 43 |
| 1880 | 40 | 18 | 58 |
| 1881 | 40 | 14 | 54 |
| 1882 | 40 | 15 | 55 |
| 1883 | 6 | 4 | 10 |


MOUNTAIN LAKE            TALYBONT            SN 712910 0190

Production: Lead No detailed return
Ownership: 1862 JOHN JONES,ATWOOD & CO.; 1863-1865 THOMSON & CO.
Management: Chief Agent 1863-1865 W.TREGONING


MYNACH VALE              DEVIL'S BRIDGE           0191

| Production: Lead & Silver | Ore(tons) | Lead(tons) | Silver(ozs) | Value(£) |
|---|---|---|---|---|
| 1882 | 96.50 | 4.90 | 0.00 | 53.00 |
| 1883 | 25.30 | 19.20 | 0.00 | 184.00 |
| 1884 | 31.00 | 23.25 | 0.00 | 193.00 |
| 1885 | 20.00 | 14.00 | 0.00 | 140.00 |
| 1886 | 19.00 | 14.00 | 0.00 | 151.00 |
| 1887 | 2.50 | 1.75 | 7.00 | 18.00 |

Ownership: 1882-1890 MYNACH VALE MINING CO.LTD.
        Comment 1882 FORMERLY DE BROKE; 1889 SUSPENDED: RESTARTED
        MAR.1890; 1890 STOPPED JULY 1890
Management: Chief Agent 1882-1890 JAS.PHILLIPS

| Employment: | Underground | Surface | Total |
|---|---|---|---|
| 1882 | 12 | 3 | 15 |
| 1883 | 11 | 2 | 13 |
| 1884 | 4 | 3 | 7 |
| 1885 | 6 | | 6 |
| 1886 | 4 | 1 | 5 |
| 1887 | 3 | | 3 |
| 1888 | | 1 | 1 |
| 1890 | 1 | 1 | 2 |


NANT                                            0192

| Production: Lead & Silver | Ore(tons) | Lead(tons) | Silver(ozs) | Value(£) |
|---|---|---|---|---|
| 1879 | 10.00 | 7.00 | 40.00 | 105.00 |


NANT SYDDION            PONTERWYD            SN 774790 0193

Production: Lead No detailed return
            Zinc No detailed return
Ownership: 1898-1910 JOHN OWEN; 1911-1913 W.A.GREEN & F.E.BOYCOTT
        Comment 1898 SUSPENDED; 1901 NOT WORKED IN 1901; 1902-1904
        NOT WORKED; 1908-1913 IDLE
Management: Chief Agent 1898-1910 JOHN OWEN

| Employment: | Underground | Surface | Total |
|---|---|---|---|
| 1899-1900 | 2 | | 2 |
| 1905 | 4 | | 4 |
| 1906-1907 | 2 | | 2 |
| 1910 | | 1 | 1 |

NANTCARIDYN                                                                    0194

Production: Lead No detailed return
Ownership:  1868 ROBT.NORTHEY
Management: Chief Agent 1868 ROBT.NORTHEY


NANTCLYN                              BOW STREET                               0195

Production: Lead No detailed return
Ownership:  1876—1877 C.HERB.STOKES; 1879 C.HERB.STOKES
            Comment 1879 NANTLLYN
Management: Manager 1876—1877 JAS.JAMES
            Chief Agent 1879 C.HERB.STOKES
Employment:                 Underground     Surface       Total
            1879                2                           2


NANTEOS                               PONTERWYD                                0196

Production: Lead & Silver     Ore(tons)   Lead(tons) Silver(ozs)    Value(£)
            1848               50.00        30.00       0.00         0.00
            1849              177.00       106.00       0.00         0.00
            1850              308.00       206.50       0.00         0.00
            1851              459.00       338.10       0.00         0.00
            1852              452.00       334.50       0.00         0.00
            1853              125.00        89.00       0.00         0.00
            1854              112.00        84.50       0.00         0.00
            1855              126.00        95.00       0.00         0.00
            1856              224.60       170.00       0.00         0.00
            1857              303.60       232.50       0.00         0.00
            1858              211.40       161.70       0.00         0.00
            1859              203.70       151.00       0.00         0.00
            1860              306.60       198.50     702.00         0.00
            1861              152.00       111.00     444.00         0.00
            1862               62.80        47.80     191.00         0.00
            1870               50.00        37.50       0.00         0.00
            1871—1872 No detailed return
            Comment 1855—1859 INC.PENRHIW; 1861—1862 INC PENRHIW
Ownership:  1859—1865 J.H.MURCHISON & CO.
            Comment 1859—1863 INC.PENRHIW; 1864—1865
            INC.PENRHIW:SUSPENDED
Management: Chief Agent 1859—1863 HY.BOUNDY


NANTEOS CONSOLS                       PONTERWYD                                0197

Production: Zinc              Ore(tons) Metal(tons)    Value(£)
            1870               28.00       0.00         84.00


NANTY                                 MONTGOMERY                    SN 852823 0198

Production: Lead & Silver     Ore(tons)   Lead(tons) Silver(ozs)    Value(£)
            1855               84.00        64.00     176.00         0.00
            1856               56.30        42.80     112.00         0.00
            1857—1860 No detailed return
            1861              240.10       180.00       0.00         0.00
Ownership:  1860—1861 JOHN TAYLOR & SONS
Management: Chief Agent 1860—1861 JOHN WILLIAMS

| Production: | Lead & Silver | Ore(tons) | Lead(tons) | Silver(ozs) | Value(£) |
|---|---|---|---|---|---|
| | 1845 | 120.00 | 72.00 | 0.00 | 0.00 |
| | 1846 | 57.25 | 33.00 | 0.00 | 0.00 |
| | 1847 | 79.00 | 48.00 | 0.00 | 0.00 |
| | 1848 | 17.00 | 10.00 | 0.00 | 0.00 |
| | 1849—1854 No detailed return | | | | |
| | 1855 | 30.00 | 24.00 | 0.00 | 0.00 |
| | 1856 | 115.00 | 80.00 | 0.00 | 0.00 |
| | 1857 | 76.20 | 48.00 | 0.00 | 0.00 |
| | 1858 | 38.00 | 24.00 | 0.00 | 0.00 |
| | 1859 | 42.00 | 35.00 | 0.00 | 0.00 |
| | 1860 | 36.00 | 27.00 | 0.00 | 0.00 |
| | 1863 | 21.90 | 16.40 | 0.00 | 0.00 |
| | 1864 | 11.70 | 8.70 | 0.00 | 0.00 |
| | 1865—1867 No detailed return | | | | |
| | 1881 | 19.50 | 14.50 | 0.00 | 192.50 |
| | 1882 | 124.00 | 101.70 | 0.00 | 992.00 |
| | 1883 | 89.20 | 70.40 | 0.00 | 730.00 |
| | 1884 | 1.00 | 0.00 | 0.00 | 6.00 |
| | 1885 | 6.00 | 4.00 | 31.00 | 42.00 |
| | 1886 | 1.00 | 0.75 | 5.00 | 5.00 |
| | 1888 | 2.75 | 2.00 | 14.00 | 25.00 |
| | 1889 | 4.00 | 3.00 | 20.00 | 31.00 |
| | 1890 | 2.00 | 1.50 | 10.00 | 17.00 |
| | 1893 | 6.00 | 4.00 | 29.00 | 37.00 |
| | 1895 | 6.00 | 4.00 | 29.00 | 37.00 |

Comment 1860 NANTYCREIA; 1863—1867 NANTYCRIA; 1881 NANTYCREIA

| Zinc | Ore(tons) | Metal(tons) | Value(£) |
|---|---|---|---|
| 1854 | 43.50 | 0.00 | 0.00 |
| 1855 | 128.00 | 0.00 | 0.00 |
| 1856 | 684.40 | 0.00 | 2738.00 |
| 1857 | 728.30 | 0.00 | 2446.50 |
| 1858 | 756.00 | 0.00 | 2592.40 |
| 1859 | 854.20 | 0.00 | 2565.10 |
| 1860 | 779.00 | 0.00 | 2284.50 |
| 1861 | 750.00 | 0.00 | 1850.00 |
| 1862 | 169.00 | 0.00 | 418.80 |
| 1863 | 514.50 | 0.00 | 1523.00 |
| 1864 | 275.50 | 0.00 | 891.40 |
| 1865 | 200.00 | 0.00 | 775.00 |
| 1880 | 30.00 | 0.00 | 68.80 |
| 1881 | 170.00 | 68.00 | 467.50 |
| 1882 | 136.00 | 65.30 | 476.00 |
| 1883 | 80.40 | 44.20 | 354.00 |
| 1884 | 47.00 | 0.00 | 161.00 |
| 1885 | 36.00 | 14.00 | 63.00 |
| 1887 | 11.00 | 4.00 | 64.00 |
| 1888 | 71.00 | 29.00 | 335.00 |
| 1889 | 49.00 | 20.00 | 240.00 |
| 1890 | 32.00 | 13.00 | 193.00 |
| 1891 | 55.00 | 22.50 | 366.00 |
| 1892 | 44.00 | 18.00 | 209.00 |
| 1893 | 93.00 | 38.00 | 422.00 |
| 1894 | 59.00 | 24.00 | 236.00 |
| 1895 | 20.00 | 8.00 | 81.00 |

Comment 1855 NANTYCRIA; 1857 NANTYCRIA; 1858 NANTYCRIAU;
1860—1865 NANTYCRIA; 1881—1885 NANTYCRIA; 1887—1895
NANTYCRIA

Ownership: 1859—1865 T.& H.JONES & CO.; 1881 NANTYCREIAU MINING CO.;
1882 T.S.G.KIRKPATRICK; 1883—1884 GEO.GREEN; 1885 NANTYCREIAU
MINING CO., 1886 GEO.GREEN & T.S.G.KIRKPATRICK; 1887—1898
NANTYCREIAU MINING CO.; 1899 WM.A.GREEN; 1900—1902 JOHN OWEN;

```
              1903 WM.A.GREEN & JOHN OWEN; 1904-1909 JOHN OWEN; 1910-1913
              WM.A.GREEN
              Comment 1882-1895 NANTYCRIA; 1896-1900 NANTYCRIA : SUSPENDED;
              1901-1902 NANTYCRIA; 1903-1904 NANTYCRIA : NOT WORKED;
              1905-1911 NANTYCRIA; 1912-1913 NANTYCRIA : IDLE
Management:   Chief Agent 1859-1861 JOS.DAVIES; 1862 THOS.GOLDSWORTHY;
              1863-1865 J.GOLDSWORTHY; 1881-1883 ROBT.UREN; 1886-1889
              RICH.JONES; 1890-1895 EVAN JONES; 1900 JOHN OWEN; 1902-1909
              JOHN OWEN
              Secretary 1887-1894 GEO.GREEN (S)
```

| Employment: | Underground | Surface | Total |
|---|---|---|---|
| 1881 | 10 | 7 | 17 |
| 1882 | 20 | 8 | 28 |
| 1883 | 8 | 3 | 11 |
| 1884 | 8 | 2 | 10 |
| 1885 | 6 | 2 | 8 |
| 1886 | 4 |  | 4 |
| 1887 | 4 | 2 | 6 |
| 1888 | 8 | 3 | 11 |
| 1889 | 8 | 2 | 10 |
| 1890-1891 | 2 | 5 | 7 |
| 1892 | 4 | 8 | 12 |
| 1893 | 2 | 9 | 11 |
| 1894 | 4 | 8 | 12 |
| 1895 | 6 | 4 | 10 |
| 1901-1902 | 2 |  | 2 |
| 1905 | 4 |  | 4 |
| 1906-1909 | 2 |  | 2 |

NANTYEAR                                                                        0200

| Production: Copper | Ore(tons) | Metal(tons) | Value(£) |
|---|---|---|---|
| 1857 | 12.80 | 0.00 | 0.00 |
| Comment 1857 (P) | | | |

NANTYGLO                                                                        0201

| Production: Zinc | Ore(tons) | Metal(tons) | Value(£) |
|---|---|---|---|
| 1873 | 80.00 | 0.00 | 240.00 |
| 1874 | No detailed return | | |

PANTANHIRION                        LLANFANAN                                   0202

```
Production:   Lead No detailed return
Ownership:    1880 CROSSWOOD MINING LANDS CO.LTD.
Management:   Chief Agent 1880-1881 JOHN KITTO
```

| Employment: | Underground | Surface | Total |
|---|---|---|---|
| 1880 | 9 | | 9 |

PANTMAWR                            CWM RHEIDOL                        SN 704786 0203

| Production: Lead & Silver | Ore(tons) | Lead(tons) | Silver(ozs) | Value(£) |
|---|---|---|---|---|
| 1845 | No detailed return | | | |
| 1856 | 22.00 | 16.70 | 97.00 | 0.00 |
| 1857 | 21.00 | 15.70 | 0.00 | 0.00 |
| 1858-1862 | No detailed return | | | |
| 1866 | 30.00 | 23.00 | 0.00 | 0.00 |
| 1867 | No detailed return | | | |

```
              Comment 1845 SEE PANTMAWR MONTGOMERY; 1858-1860 PANTYMAWR;
```

PANTMAWR                          CWM RHEIDOL                        Continued

          1861 NOW KNOWN AS SILVER BANK; 1862 RHEIDOL VALLEY; 1866-1867
          PANTSHAWR
Ownership:  1859 MAT.FRANCIS & CO.
          Comment 1859 PANTYMAWR
Management: Chief Agent 1859 JOHN JONES


PANTYGO,WEST                    HALKYN, FLINTSHIRE                      0204

Production: Lead              Ore(tons) Metal(tons)     Value(£)
          1872                  10.00      7.50         0.00
          1873              No detailed return


PENCLAYEN                       RHEIDOL VALLEY                         0205

Production: Lead              Ore(tons) Metal(tons)     Value(£)
          1853                 147.80    110.80         0.00


PENCRAIGDDU                       GOGINAN                             0206

Production: Lead              Ore(tons) Metal(tons)     Value(£)
          1856                   9.20      6.10         0.00
          1857              No detailed return
          Comment 1857 PANCRAIG DDU
Ownership:  1863-1871 C.E.HAYWARD & CO.; 1875 C.E.HAYWARD
          Comment 1875 PENCRAYDDU; 1876-1884 SEE CAENANT; 1885-1890 SEE
          BWLCH UNITED
Management: Chief Agent 1863-1867 S.TREGONING; 1868 W.H.TREGONING;
          1869-1871 JAS.LESTER; 1875 JAS.PHILLIPS
Employment:                 Underground     Surface       Total
          1878-1883
          1885
          1887
          Comment 1878-1883 SEE CAENANT; 1885 SEE BWLCH UNITED; 1887
          SEE BWLCH UNITED


PENDINAS                          TALYBONT                            0207

Production: Lead No detailed return
Ownership:  1892-1893 ED.EVANS; 1896-1903 ED.EVANS
          Comment 1893 ABANDONED IN 1893; 1902-1903 OR LERI VALLEY
Management: Chief Agent 1892-1893 ED.EVANS; 1896-1903 ED.EVANS
Employment:                 Underground     Surface       Total
          1892-1893            2                            2
          1896-1903            2                            2


PENDMAS                           TALYBONT                            0208

Production: Lead No detailed return
Management: Chief Agent 1867-1868 J.EVANS


PENFORRDDGOCH                     GLANDOVEY                           0209

Production: Lead No detailed return
Ownership:  1866-1868 ART.DEAN & CO.
Management: Chief Agent 1866-1868 RICH.JONES


                                    73

Production: Lead & Silver    Ore(tons)  Lead(tons) Silver(ozs)    Value(£)
            1845              24.00      15.00      0.00           0.00
            1857               3.10       2.20      0.00           0.00
            1864              64.20      48.10      0.00           0.00
            1865              86.10      64.50      0.00           0.00
            1866              22.00      16.50      0.00           0.00
            1867         No detailed return
            Comment 1845 PENY BANC; 1857 PENY BANC; 1864 PENY BANC,AG SEE
            SILVER MOUNTAIN; 1865-1867 PENY BANC
Ownership:  1863-1867 D.HOBSON & CO.
            Comment 1882-1883 SEE ERGLODD UNITED
Management: Chief Agent 1863-1865 S.GLEDHILL; 1866-1867 J.GLEDHILL


PENPOMPREN                    TALYBONT                       SN 657908 0211

Production: Lead & Silver    Ore(tons)  Lead(tons) Silver(ozs)    Value(£)
            1855              12.20       8.00      0.00           0.00
            1856-1861 No detailed return
            1862             100.00      77.00      1000.00        0.00
            1866              90.00      68.00      1286.00        0.00
            1867              22.00      17.00       260.00        0.00
            1868-1872 No detailed return
            1890              18.00      13.00      0.00           145.00
            Comment 1861 NOW PART OF CLARA UNITED MINES
            Zinc             Ore(tons) Metal(tons)    Value(£)
            1867              43.30       0.00        105.40
            1890              33.00      10.00        140.00
Ownership:  1861-1865 PENPOMPREN CO.LTD.; 1866-1867 D.HOBSON & CO.;
            1889-1891 PENPOMPREN MINE SYNDICATE; 1897-1898 FRED.WILLIAMS
            & OTHERS; 1899-1904 R.D.JENKINS
            Comment 1859-1860 ABANDONED; 1882-1883 SEE ERGLODD UNITED;
            1891 SUSPENDED; 1900 SUSPENDED; 1901 NOT WORKED IN 1901;
            1902-1904 NOT WORKED
Management: Manager 1889-1891 W.STAINTON
            Chief Agent 1861 CHAS.WILLIAMS; 1862 JOHN HUMPHREYS;
            1863-1867 J.GLEDHILL; 1889-1891 W.STAINTON; 1897-1904
            FRED.WILLIAMS
Employment:                 Underground    Surface        Total
            1889               12              4           16
            1890               16             12           28
            1898                7                           7
            1899                2                           2


PENRHIW                       PONTERWYD                      SN 737787 0212

Production: Lead & Silver    Ore(tons)  Lead(tons) Silver(ozs)    Value(£)
            1845              46.00      27.00      0.00           0.00
            1850              20.00      14.80      0.00           0.00
            1851               3.00      20.20      0.00           0.00
            1855-1859 No detailed return
            1861-1862 No detailed return
            1888              10.00       7.00       47.00         80.00
            1889              20.00      15.00       97.00        164.00
            1890              31.00      22.00      150.00        252.00
            1891              32.00      23.00      153.00        256.00
            1892              55.00      39.00      265.00        368.00
            1893              41.00      29.00      198.00        284.00
            1894              13.00       9.25       63.00         90.00
            1895              31.00      22.00      149.00        186.00
            1910              31.00      23.00      0.00           233.00
            1911              30.00      23.00      0.00           235.00

| Lead & Silver | Ore(tons) | Lead(tons) | Silver(ozs) | Value(£) |
|---|---|---|---|---|
| 1912 | 40.00 | 30.00 | 160.00 | 350.00 |

Comment 1850–1851 PENRHEW; 1855–1859 SEE NANTEOS; 1861–1862
SEE NANTEOS; 1888–1894 INC.YSTUMTUEN; 1895 INC YSTUMTUEN

| Zinc | Ore(tons) | Metal(tons) | Value(£) |
|---|---|---|---|
| 1888 | 73.00 | 30.00 | 288.00 |
| 1889 | 164.00 | 67.00 | 754.00 |
| 1890 | 69.00 | 28.00 | 277.00 |
| 1891 | 67.00 | 27.00 | 318.00 |
| 1892 | 65.00 | 26.00 | 258.00 |
| 1893 | 50.00 | 20.00 | 170.00 |
| 1894 | 62.00 | 25.00 | 196.00 |
| 1896 | 31.00 | 4.00 | 31.00 |
| 1910 | 100.00 | 34.00 | 350.00 |
| 1911 | 60.00 | 21.00 | 242.00 |
| 1912 | 10.00 | 3.00 | 30.00 |

Comment 1888–1894 INC.YSTUMTUEN; 1896 INC.YSTUMTUEN &
TYNYFRON
Ownership: 1886–1889 PENRHIW & YSTUMTUEN MINES CO.; 1890–1899
PENRHIW,YSTUMTUEN & TYNYFRON MINES CO.; 1908 BOOTH,BROOKS &
RICHARDS; 1909–1912 ABERYSTWYTH SILVER LEAD MINES LTD.; 1913
RICH.RICHARDS
Comment 1859–1865 SEE NANTEOS; 1869 SEE BWLCHGWYN; 1886–1888
INC.YSTUMTUEN; 1889–1895 INC.YSTUMTUEN & TYNYFRON; 1896–1899
INC.YSTUMTUEN & TYNYFRON : SUSPENDED
Management: Chief Agent 1886 GEO.GREEN; 1887–1895 EVAN JONES; 1908–1911
R.RICHARDS; 1912 F.C.MOORWOOD
Secretary 1887–1894 GEO.GREEN (S)

| Employment: | Underground | Surface | Total |
|---|---|---|---|
| 1886 | 4 | | 4 |
| 1887 | 7 | 3 | 10 |
| 1888 | 19 | 12 | 31 |
| 1889 | 17 | 8 | 25 |
| 1890 | 7 | 6 | 13 |
| 1891 | 9 | 7 | 16 |
| 1892 | 9 | 5 | 14 |
| 1893 | 9 | 8 | 17 |
| 1894 | 8 | 7 | 15 |
| 1895 | | 5 | 5 |
| 1908 | 4 | 8 | 12 |
| 1909 | 8 | 13 | 21 |
| 1910 | 12 | 14 | 26 |
| 1911 | 12 | 6 | 18 |
| 1912 | 8 | 2 | 10 |
| 1913 | 9 | 2 | 11 |

Comment 1886–1888 INC.YSTUMTUEN; 1889–1895 INC.YSTUMTUEN &
TYNYFRON


PENRHYN GERWEN     GLANDOVEY     0213

Production: Lead No detailed return
Ownership: 1881–1883 C.HERB.STOKES; 1898 JOHN JENKINS
Comment 1883 SUSPENDED; 1899–1901 SEE LOVEDEN
Management: Chief Agent 1881–1883 C.HERB.STOKES

| Employment: | Underground | Surface | Total |
|---|---|---|---|
| 1881 | 6 | | 6 |
| 1882 | 4 | | 4 |

PENRHYNGWM                    CAERNARVONSHIRE                        0214

Production: Lead No detailed return
Ownership:  1880—1881 PENRHYN MINING CO.
Management: Chief Agent 1880—1881 NICH.BRAY


PENRHYNWDDU                     FLINTSHIRE                           0215

Production: Lead & Silver    Ore(tons)   Lead(tons) Silver(ozs)    Value(£)
            1854               23.00        16.20      97.00          0.00
            1855               20.00        14.00      70.00          0.00
            1856—1857 No detailed return
            Comment 1854 PENRHYN; 1856—1857 PENRHYNWDDU


PENSARN                         TALIESIN                   SN 668912 0216

Production: Lead           Ore(tons) Metal(tons)    Value(£)
            1871           No detailed return
            1874           No detailed return
            Comment 1871 LENSARN — SEE BRYNARIAN; 1874 SEE BRYNARIAN
            Zinc           Ore(tons) Metal(tons)    Value(£)
            1872           No detailed return
            1874—1875 No detailed return
            Comment 1872 SEE BRYNARIAN; 1874—1875 SEE BRYNARIAN
Ownership:  Comment 1872—1877 SEE BRYNARIAN


PENYBONTPREN                    TALIESIN                             0217

Production: Lead           Ore(tons) Metal(tons)    Value(£)
            1847             42.00      23.50          0.00
            1848             38.00      22.00          0.00
            1849             12.00       7.00          0.00
            Comment 1847 AGGREGATED


PENYCEFN                        TALYBONT                   SN 656856 0218

Production: Lead & Silver    Ore(tons)   Lead(tons) Silver(ozs)    Value(£)
            1845               36.00        23.00       0.00          0.00
            1846               46.00        29.00       0.00          0.00
            1852               64.00        48.00       0.00          0.00
            1853           No detailed return
            1854               90.00        63.00    1470.00          0.00
            1856               24.00        18.80     637.00          0.00
            1857           No detailed return
            1869               18.00        11.00     418.00          0.00
            1870—1873 No detailed return
            Zinc           Ore(tons) Metal(tons)    Value(£)
            1870           No detailed return
            Comment 1870 SEE PENYCEFN, MONTGOMERY


PLYNLIMON                       PONTERWYD                  SN 795855 0219

Production: Lead & Silver    Ore(tons)   Lead(tons) Silver(ozs)    Value(£)
            1866               60.00        46.00       0.00          0.00
            1867              245.00       190.50       0.00          0.00
            1868              347.10       260.00       0.00          0.00
            1869              350.00       266.00       0.00          0.00
            1870              148.10       111.00       0.00          0.00
            1871              277.00       307.70       0.00          0.00
            1872              355.80       236.50       0.00          0.00

                                 76

PLYNLIMON                     PONTERWYD                    Continued

| Lead & Silver | Ore(tons) | Lead(tons) | Silver(ozs) | Value(£) |
|---|---|---|---|---|
| 1873 | 169.80 | 129.00 | 0.00 | 0.00 |
| 1874 | 403.90 | 303.00 | 0.00 | 5462.70 |
| 1875 | 322.00 | 240.50 | 1200.00 | 4648.90 |
| 1876 | 142.00 | 108.00 | 535.00 | 2042.70 |
| 1877 | 160.00 | 129.50 | 647.00 | 2129.00 |
| 1878 | 85.00 | 68.50 | 0.00 | 869.70 |
| 1887 | 40.00 | 29.00 | 0.00 | 405.00 |
| 1888 | 52.00 | 34.00 | 173.00 | 468.00 |
| 1889 | 48.00 | 34.00 | 0.00 | 392.00 |
| 1890 | 30.00 | 20.00 | 0.00 | 253.00 |
| 1891 | 25.00 | 19.00 | 0.00 | 180.00 |
| 1895 | 10.00 | 8.00 | 0.00 | 65.00 |

Comment 1872-1877 PLYNLIMMON
Ownership:   1864-1866 GEO.WILLIAMS; 1867-1868 ROYAL PLYNLIMON MINING CO.;
             1869-1873 PLYNLIMON MINING CO.; 1874-1880 PLYNLIMON MINING
             CO.LTD.; 1882 PLYNLIMON MINING CO.LTD.; 1883-1892 WM.THOMAS;
             1893-1897 ELIZ.THOMAS
             Comment 1864-1866 PLINLIMON; 1874-1880 PLYNLIMMON; 1882
             PLYNLIMMON : SUSPENDED; 1883-1887 PLYNLIMMON; 1892-1893
             SUSPENDED; 1897 ABANDONED 1897
Management:  Manager 1867-1871 JOHN PAULL; 1872-1880 JOHN GARLAND
             Chief Agent 1864-1865 RICH.WILLIAMS; 1866 JOHN PAULL; 1882
             J.H.MURCHISON; 1883-1884 WM.BRANWELL; 1886-1888 WM.THOMAS;
             1889-1892 JOHN OWEN
             Secretary 1871-1880 J.H.MURCHISON (S)

| Employment: | Underground | Surface | Total |
|---|---|---|---|
| 1877 | 45 | 21 | 66 |
| 1878 | 31 | 27 | 58 |
| 1883 | | 14 | 14 |
| 1884 | 7 | | 7 |
| 1885 | | 1 | 1 |
| 1886 | | 4 | 4 |
| 1887 | 10 | 20 | 30 |
| 1888 | 4 | 14 | 18 |
| 1889 | 2 | 16 | 18 |
| 1890 | 10 | 2 | 12 |
| 1891 | 9 | 5 | 14 |
| 1892 | | 2 | 2 |
| 1894 | | 2 | 2 |
| 1895 | 3 | 2 | 5 |
| 1896 | | 2 | 2 |


PLYNLIMON,SOUTH               PONTERWYD              SN 794841 0220

Production: Lead No detailed return

| Zinc | Ore(tons) | Metal(tons) | Value(£) |
|---|---|---|---|
| 1878 | 20.00 | 0.00 | 65.50 |

             Comment 1878 SOUTH PLYNLIMMON
Ownership:   Comment 1874-1875 SOUTH PLYNLIMMON
Management:  Manager 1871 SML.RICHARDS
             Chief Agent 1872-1874 JOHN WALTERS; 1875 WM.ROWLANDS


PONTERWYD                     PONTERWYD                         0221

Production: Lead          Ore(tons) Metal(tons)    Value(£)

| | Ore(tons) | Metal(tons) | Value(£) |
|---|---|---|---|
| 1857 | 2.80 | 2.10 | 0.00 |
| 1872 | 244.00 | 183.00 | 0.00 |

             1858-1861 No detailed return
Ownership:   1859-1860 JONES,HUGHES & CO.; 1861-1865 J.B.BALCOMBE & CO.,
             1868-1869 ? LAMERT; 1870-1871 LLYWERNOG CO.LTD.

Management:   Manager 1870–1871 J.B.BALCOMBE
             Chief Agent 1859–1860 JOHN HUGHES; 1861–1865 JAS.LESTER;
             1868–1869 JAS.LESTER; 1870–1871 JOHN DAVIS

POWELL             PONTERWYD           SN 728809 0222

Production: Lead & Silver

| | Ore(tons) | Lead(tons) | Silver(ozs) | Value(£) |
|---|---|---|---|---|
| 1864 | 20.00 | 15.00 | 0.00 | 0.00 |
| 1865 | 20.00 | 13.00 | 0.00 | 0.00 |
| 1866 | 40.00 | 29.00 | 0.00 | 0.00 |
| 1867 | 170.00 | 127.50 | 0.00 | 0.00 |
| 1868 | 360.00 | 269.00 | 0.00 | 0.00 |
| 1869 | 326.00 | 240.00 | 1200.00 | 0.00 |
| 1870 | 235.00 | 177.50 | 0.00 | 0.00 |
| 1871 | 350.00 | 269.00 | 0.00 | 0.00 |
| 1872 | 90.00 | 68.00 | 0.00 | 0.00 |
| 1873 | 20.00 | 15.00 | 0.00 | 0.00 |
| 1874 | 174.20 | 130.60 | 0.00 | 2370.30 |
| 1875 | 134.50 | 100.50 | 450.00 | 0.00 |
| 1876 | 220.00 | 167.00 | 751.00 | 3043.00 |
| 1877 | 270.00 | 202.00 | 1010.00 | 3375.00 |
| 1878 | 122.10 | 90.00 | 0.00 | 1247.50 |
| 1880 | 20.50 | 18.00 | 0.00 | 197.80 |
| 1881 | 75.00 | 55.50 | 0.00 | 682.00 |
| 1882 | 110.00 | 85.80 | 0.00 | 976.00 |
| 1883 | 112.00 | 86.20 | 0.00 | 780.00 |
| 1884 | 89.00 | 67.60 | 0.00 | 578.00 |
| 1885 | 86.00 | 64.00 | 328.00 | 645.00 |
| 1886 | 66.00 | 47.00 | 249.00 | 501.00 |
| 1887 | 55.00 | 41.20 | 152.00 | 457.00 |
| 1888 | 63.00 | 47.00 | 177.00 | 545.00 |
| 1889 | 61.00 | 46.00 | 0.00 | 527.00 |
| 1890 | 51.00 | 39.00 | 0.00 | 428.00 |

Comment 1864 FOR SILVER SEE SILVER MOUNTAIN; 1865–1867 POWEL
UNITED; 1868–1872 POWELL UNITED; 1873–1878 POWELL
CONSOLIDATED; 1882 POWELL CONSOLIDATED

Zinc

| | Ore(tons) | Metal(tons) | Value(£) |
|---|---|---|---|
| 1868 | 30.00 | 0.00 | 60.00 |
| 1869 | 20.00 | 0.00 | 35.00 |
| 1870 | 15.00 | 0.00 | 30.00 |
| 1873 | 30.00 | 0.00 | 90.00 |
| 1875 | 30.00 | 0.00 | 90.00 |
| 1876 | 30.00 | 0.00 | 120.00 |
| 1877 | 40.00 | 0.00 | 150.00 |
| 1878 | 35.00 | 0.00 | 105.00 |
| 1881 | 22.00 | 8.50 | 60.50 |
| 1882 | 35.00 | 19.20 | 119.00 |
| 1883 | 45.00 | 22.50 | 167.00 |
| 1884 | 30.00 | 0.00 | 87.00 |
| 1885 | 15.00 | 6.00 | 45.00 |
| 1886 | 25.00 | 9.00 | 63.00 |
| 1887 | 44.00 | 16.00 | 167.00 |
| 1888 | 45.00 | 16.00 | 175.00 |
| 1889 | 34.00 | 13.00 | 160.00 |
| 1890 | 33.00 | 14.00 | 173.00 |

Comment 1868–1870 POWELL UNITED; 1873 POWELL UNITED;
1875–1876 POWELL CONSOLIDATED; 1877 POWELL CONSOLS; 1878
POWELL UNITED

Ownership:   1863–1867 WM.ROWLANDS & CO.; 1868–1871 POWELL UNITED MINES
          CO.LTD.; 1872–1878 POWELL CONSOLIDATED MINES CO.LTD.;
          1881–1884 POWELL CONSOLIDATED MINES CO.LTD.; 1885–1892 POWELL
          MINES CO.

Comment 1863-1867 POWEL UNITED; 1868-1871 POWELL UNITED;
1872-1878 POWELL CONSOLIDATED; 1881-1884 POWELL CONSOLIDATED
Management: Manager 1873-1878 NICH.BRAY
Chief Agent 1863-1866 S.TREVETHAN; 1867 NICH.BRAY; 1868-1871
JOHN TREVETHAN; 1872 NICH.BRAY; 1881-1892 NICH.BRAY
Secretary 1873-1878 G.H.MOSS (S)

| Employment: | Underground | Surface | Total |
|---|---|---|---|
| 1877 | 36 | 29 | 65 |
| 1878 | 12 | 8 | 20 |
| 1879 | 1 |  | 1 |
| 1880 | 13 | 8 | 21 |
| 1881 | 14 | 11 | 25 |
| 1882 | 20 | 12 | 32 |
| 1883 | 6 | 5 | 11 |
| 1884 | 8 | 5 | 13 |
| 1885 | 10 | 7 | 17 |
| 1886 | 8 | 5 | 13 |
| 1887 | 10 | 6 | 16 |
| 1888 | 8 | 8 | 16 |
| 1889 | 13 | 7 | 20 |
| 1890 | 10 | 7 | 17 |
| 1891 | 2 |  | 2 |
| 1892 |  | 1 | 1 |

PWLL CARREG                                                      0223

| Production: Lead | Ore(tons) | Metal(tons) | Value(£) |
|---|---|---|---|
| 1853 | 4.40 | 3.30 | 0.00 |

PWLL ROMAN                    TALIESIN              SN 657915 0224

| Production: Lead | Ore(tons) | Metal(tons) | Value(£) |
|---|---|---|---|
| 1856 | 1.70 | 1.10 | 0.00 |
| 1857 | No detailed return | | |
| Zinc No detailed return | | | |
| Copper | Ore(tons) | Metal(tons) | Value(£) |
| 1856 | 0.50 | 0.00 | 0.00 |

Comment 1856 (P) PWIL ROMAN
Ownership: 1860-1865 GLEDHILL & CO.; 1868-1871 CHAS.WILLIAMS & CO.
Comment 1864-1865 SUSPENDED
Management: Chief Agent 1860 CHAS.WILLIAMS; 1861-1862 T.WHITEHEAD; 1863
CHAS.WILLIAMS; 1868-1871 CHAS.WILLIAMS

PWLLYRHENAID                  GOGINAN                SN 706823 0225

| Production: Lead | Ore(tons) | Metal(tons) | Value(£) |
|---|---|---|---|
| 1855 | 166.60 | 116.10 | 0.00 |
| 1856-1857 No detailed return | | | |

RED ROCK                    PONTRHYDYGROES                      0226

| Production: Lead & Silver | Ore(tons) | Lead(tons) | Silver(ozs) | Value(£) |
|---|---|---|---|---|
| 1877 | 40.00 | 30.00 | 150.00 | 500.00 |
| 1878 | 200.00 | 157.00 | 0.00 | 1853.00 |
| 1879 | 160.00 | 129.50 | 0.00 | 1345.00 |
| 1880 | 160.00 | 128.00 | 0.00 | 1544.00 |
| 1881 | 140.00 | 98.00 | 0.00 | 1278.10 |
| 1882 | 74.80 | 57.60 | 0.00 | 674.00 |
| 1886 | 59.00 | 38.00 | 0.00 | 368.00 |

| Lead & Silver | Ore(tons) | Lead(tons) | Silver(ozs) | Value(£) |
|---|---|---|---|---|
| 1887 | 59.00 | 42.00 | 0.00 | 320.00 |
| 1888 | 40.00 | 25.00 | 0.00 | 278.00 |
| 1889 | 12.00 | 8.00 | 0.00 | 75.00 |

Comment 1888 VALUE INC RHEIDOL UNITED

| Zinc | Ore(tons) | Metal(tons) | Value(£) |
|---|---|---|---|
| 1888 | 14.00 | 4.00 | 18.00 |
| 1889 | 11.00 | 3.00 | 30.00 |

Ownership: 1876-1885 RED ROCK LEAD MINES CO.LTD.; 1886-1887 JOHN KITTO & SON; 1888 JOHN KITTO; 1889 JOHN KITTO & SON; 1890-1892 JOHN KITTO
Comment 1883-1885 SUSPENDED; 1890-1892 SUSPENDED
Management: Chief Agent 1876-1877 JOHN KITTO; 1878 JOHN KITTO & JOHN OWEN; 1879-1882 JOHN KITTO & SON & FRANK KITTO; 1883-1887 JOHN KITTO & SON; 1888-1892 JOHN KITTO

Employment:
| | Underground | Surface | Total |
|---|---|---|---|
| 1877 | 42 | 13 | 55 |
| 1878 | 38 | 19 | 57 |
| 1879 | 41 | 15 | 56 |
| 1880 | 32 | 15 | 47 |
| 1881 | 27 | 17 | 44 |
| 1882 | 14 | 9 | 23 |
| 1886 | 1 | 10 | 11 |
| 1887 | 3 | 5 | 8 |
| 1888 | | 6 | 6 |
| 1889 | | 2 | 2 |

RHEIDOL                        RHEIDOL UNITED                      0227

Production:
| Lead & Silver | Ore(tons) | Lead(tons) | Silver(ozs) | Value(£) |
|---|---|---|---|---|
| 1865 | 10.00 | 6.00 | 0.00 | 0.00 |
| 1866 | 11.00 | 8.00 | 0.00 | 0.00 |
| 1867 | 60.00 | 37.00 | 155.00 | 0.00 |
| 1868 | 20.00 | 15.50 | 0.00 | 0.00 |

Barytes No detailed return

| Zinc | Ore(tons) | Metal(tons) | Value(£) |
|---|---|---|---|
| 1862 | 112.50 | 0.00 | 275.60 |
| 1865 | 211.00 | 0.00 | 633.00 |
| 1867 | 128.70 | 0.00 | 257.40 |
| 1876 | 47.00 | 0.00 | 141.00 |

Ownership: 1872 CHAS.ELEY; 1873-1877 RHEIDOL MINING CO.; 1878 RHEIDOL MINING CO.LTD.
Comment 1878 IN LIQUIDATION
Management: Chief Agent 1872-1878 JOHN RIDGE
Secretary 1874-1877 CHAS.ELEY (S)

Employment:
| | Underground | Surface | Total |
|---|---|---|---|
| 1877 | 6 | 9 | 15 |

RHEIDOL UNITED                    CWM RHEIDOL                      0228

Production:
| Lead & Silver | Ore(tons) | Lead(tons) | Silver(ozs) | Value(£) |
|---|---|---|---|---|
| 1855 | 45.00 | 33.00 | 0.00 | 0.00 |
| 1856 | 145.10 | 107.50 | 0.00 | 0.00 |
| 1857 | 42.00 | 28.50 | 0.00 | 0.00 |
| 1858 | 39.00 | 23.50 | 0.00 | 0.00 |
| 1859 | 18.20 | 11.50 | 0.00 | 0.00 |
| 1860 | 41.80 | 25.20 | 0.00 | 0.00 |
| 1861 | 41.00 | 28.00 | 84.00 | 0.00 |
| 1869-1873 No detailed return | | | | |
| 1876 | 5.00 | 3.70 | 0.00 | 0.00 |
| 1877 | 11.00 | 8.00 | 48.00 | 148.50 |

| Lead & Silver | Ore(tons) | Lead(tons) | Silver(ozs) | Value(£) |
|---|---|---|---|---|
| 1882 | 4.20 | 2.40 | 0.00 | 29.00 |
| 1883 | 9.20 | 5.50 | 0.00 | 63.00 |
| 1884 | 7.00 | 4.80 | 0.00 | 42.00 |
| 1885 | 26.00 | 17.00 | 100.00 | 161.00 |
| 1886 | 25.00 | 16.00 | 94.00 | 180.00 |
| 1887 | 17.00 | 11.00 | 0.00 | 125.00 |
| 1888 | 5.00 | 3.00 | 19.00 | 0.00 |
| 1889 | 2.00 | 1.50 | 0.00 | 16.00 |

Comment 1888 FOR VALUE SEE RED ROCK

| Zinc | Ore(tons) | Metal(tons) | Value(£) |
|---|---|---|---|
| 1855 | 66.30 | 0.00 | 0.00 |
| 1856 | 53.60 | 0.00 | 133.80 |
| 1857 | 157.50 | 0.00 | 510.30 |
| 1858 | 634.50 | 0.00 | 1386.30 |
| 1859 | 1254.00 | 0.00 | 4389.00 |
| 1860 | 1193.90 | 0.00 | 3775.20 |
| 1861 | 940.50 | 0.00 | 2300.00 |
| 1882 | 49.60 | 21.50 | 117.00 |
| 1883 | 106.40 | 40.40 | 241.00 |
| 1884 | 11.00 | 0.00 | 25.00 |
| 1885 | 50.00 | 15.00 | 78.00 |
| 1886 | 15.00 | 5.00 | 24.00 |
| 1887 | 25.00 | 7.00 | 75.00 |
| 1888 | 10.00 | 3.00 | 55.00 |
| 1889 | 41.00 | 12.00 | 86.00 |
| 1890 | 28.00 | 9.00 | 137.00 |

Comment 1888 VALUE INC.WEMYS

Ownership:    1859 PHILLIPS & CO.; 1860 W.SPOONER; 1861–1881 W.SPOONER &
              CO.; 1882–1883 HY.WORSALDINE; 1884–1890 VERE POWYS; 1891
              DAVID LLOYD & MRS.C.JONES
Management:   Chief Agent 1859 JOHN RIDGE; 1860–1881 R.RIDGE; 1882–1884
              ROBT.PEARCE; 1885–1888 D.LAMBERT; 1890–1891 D.LAMBERT

| Employment: | Underground | Surface | Total |
|---|---|---|---|
| 1882 | 14 | 15 | 29 |
| 1883 | 14 | 18 | 32 |
| 1884 | 8 | 10 | 18 |
| 1885 | 11 | 9 | 20 |
| 1886 | 10 | 10 | 20 |
| 1887 | 12 | 9 | 21 |
| 1888 | 6 | 5 | 11 |
| 1889–1890 | 6 | 3 | 9 |
| 1891 | | 1 | 1 |

RHEIDOL,NORTH                    RHEIDOL VALLEY                         0229

| Production: Zinc | Ore(tons) | Metal(tons) | Value(£) |
|---|---|---|---|
| 1877 | 20.00 | 0.00 | 75.00 |

RHEIDOL,VALE OF                  RHEIDOL VALLEY                         0230

Production: Lead No detailed return
Management: Chief Agent 1868–1874 JOHN PAULL

RHYSCOG                          LLANDDEWI BREFI              SN 680540 0231

Production: Lead No detailed return
            Copper No detailed return
Ownership.  1861–1875 A.MARSDON & CO.
Management: Chief Agent 1861–1875 A.MARSDON

ROYAL MINES                          PONTERWYD                                0232

Production: Manganese        Ore(tons)  Metal(tons)      Value(£)
            1874               40.00       0.00           160.00
            Comment 1874 CAMDDWR MAWR & DRISGOL
Ownership:  1874-1879 C.HERB.STOKES
            Comment 1874-1877 DRISGOL & CAMDDWR MAWR; 1878-1879 NO
            RETURN
Management: Chief Agent 1874-1877 ABEL PAULL; 1878-1879 C.HERB.STOKES
Employment:               Underground     Surface          Total
            1879               2                              2


SEVERN                          LLANIDLOES, MONTGOMERY          SN 860878 0233

Production: Lead             Ore(tons)  Metal(tons)      Value(£)
            1857               5.00        3.70           0.00
            Copper           Ore(tons)  Metal(tons)      Value(£)
            1857              17.10        0.00           0.00
            Comment 1857 (P)


SILVER BANK                     RHEIDOL VALLEY                              0234

Production: Lead & Silver    Ore(tons)  Lead(tons)  Silver(ozs)    Value(£)
            1861             No detailed return
            Comment 1861 SEE PANTMAWR


SILVER BANK,WEST                RHEIDOL VALLEY                              0235

Production: Lead No detailed return
Ownership:  1861-1865 WEST SILVER BANK MINING CO.
            Comment 1864-1865 SUSPENDED
Management: Chief Agent 1861-1863 RICH.WILLIAMS


SILVER BROOK                    GOGINAN                                     0236

Ownership:  1886-1887 SILVER BROOK MINING CO.LTD.
            Comment 1886 FORMERLY SILVER STREAM; 1887 FORMERLY SILVER
            STREAM : SUSPENDED
Management: Chief Agent 1886-1887 WM.JONES
            Secretary 1886-1887 F.E.BRIGGS (S)


SILVER MOUNTAIN                 TALIESIN                                    0237

Production: Lead & Silver    Ore(tons)  Lead(tons)  Silver(ozs)    Value(£)
            1863              10.00       8.00        0.00          0.00
            1864             120.50      93.50      960.00          0.00
            1865              13.10       9.00        0.00          0.00
            1866-1867 No detailed return
            Comment 1863 SILVER MOUNTAINS; 1864 AG:INC.4 OTHER MINES


SILVER STREAM                   GOGINAN                                     0238

Production: Lead & Silver    Ore(tons)  Lead(tons)  Silver(ozs)    Value(£)
            1883              9.00        7.20       144.00         85.00
Ownership:  1881-1885 SILVER STREAM MINING CO.LTD.; 1899 JOHN OWEN;
            1900-1910 SILVER STREAM MINING CO.; 1911-1913 W.B.BEBB
            Comment 1886-1887 SEE SILVER BROOK; 1899 STARTED IN 1900;
            1909-1913 IDLE
Management: Chief Agent 1881-1885 WM.JONES; 1899-1910 JOHN OWEN

                                   82

SILVER STREAM                    GOGINAN                    Continued

Employment:              Underground    Surface      Total
            1881             13                        13
            1882-1883         6           6            12
            1884-1885         2                         2
            1900             2                         2
            1901             3           5             8
            1902             3           2             5
            1903             6           6            12
            1904             4           2             6
            1905                         2             2
            1906-1909         2                         2
            1910                         1             1


SNOW BROOK              LLANIDLEOS, MONTGOMERY          SN 827874 0239

Production: Lead & Silver    Ore(tons)  Lead(tons)  Silver(ozs)   Value(£)
            1859              32.50      25.00       300.00        0.00
            1860              24.00      18.50       173.00        0.00
            1861       No detailed return


STRATA FLORIDA              PONTRHYDFENDIGAID                     0240

Ownership:  1904 JOS.PHILLIPS & CO.
Management: Chief Agent 1904 THOS.EDWARDS
Employment:              Underground    Surface      Total
            1904              3           6            9


SWYDDFFYNON                 SWYDDFFYNON                          0241

Production: Lead            Ore(tons) Metal(tons)    Value(£)
            1864             4.00      3.00          0.00
            Comment 1864 FOR SILVER SEE SILVER MOUNTAIN


TALIESIN                    TALIESIN                             0242

Production: Lead & Silver    Ore(tons)  Lead(tons)  Silver(ozs)   Value(£)
            1854              82.00      62.20       682.00        0.00
            1855             142.00     106.00      1587.00        0.00
            1856               7.50       5.00        50.00        0.00
            1857       No detailed return
            1867              14.00      10.50        80.00        0.00
            1868-1872 No detailed return
Ownership:  1863-1867 BURKE & CO.
Management: Chief Agent 1863 GEO.GREEN; 1866-1867 J.GLEDHILL


TALYBONT                    TALYBONT                             0243

Production: Lead & Silver    Ore(tons)  Lead(tons)  Silver(ozs)   Value(£)
            1845              25.00      16.00         0.00         0.00
            1875              10.40       8.00         0.00         0.00
            1876              25.40      18.90         0.00       373.40
            1877              20.00      15.20        98.00       270.00
            1878               5.00       3.70        20.00        50.00
            1879              20.00      15.00        75.00       190.00
            1880              20.00      15.00       100.00       225.00
            1886              50.00      38.00       366.00       437.00
            1887             126.00      97.00         0.00      1134.00
            1888              45.00      34.00       486.00       473.00

                                 83

| Lead & Silver | Ore(tons) | Lead(tons) | Silver(ozs) | Value(£) |
|---|---|---|---|---|
| 1889 | 21.00 | 16.00 | 269.00 | 210.00 |
| 1890 | 23.00 | 18.00 | 203.00 | 216.00 |
| Copper | Ore(tons) | Metal(tons) | Value(£) | |
| 1857 | 2.70 | 0.00 | 0.00 | |

Comment 1857 (P) TALLYBONT

Ownership: 1876–1879 TALYBONT SILVER LEAD MINING CO.; 1880–1881 TALYBONT
SILVER LEAD MINING CO.LTD.; 1886–1890 TALYBONT SILVER LEAD
MINING CO.; 1895 THOS.MOLYNEUX & JOHN DAVIS; 1896–1898
PLYNLIMON & HAVAN CO.LTD.
Comment 1881 SEE ALLTYCRIB; 1886–1890 FORMERLY ALLTYCRIB &
NORTH CARDIGAN; 1897–1898 OR ALLTYCRIB : SUSPENDED

Management: Chief Agent 1876–1881 THOS.GLANVILLE; 1886–1889 A.H.JENKS;
1895 JOHN DAVIS; 1896 FRED.WILLIAMS; 1897–1898 H.W.FRANCIS

| Employment: | Underground | Surface | Total |
|---|---|---|---|
| 1877 | 17 | 3 | 20 |
| 1878 | 14 | 1 | 15 |
| 1879 | 14 | 4 | 18 |
| 1880 | 16 | | 16 |
| 1886 | 30 | 13 | 43 |
| 1887 | 16 | 8 | 24 |
| 1888 | 8 | 6 | 14 |
| 1889 | 10 | 4 | 14 |
| 1890 | 4 | | 4 |
| 1895 | | 4 | 4 |
| 1896 | 4 | | 4 |
| 1897 | 2 | | 2 |


TANYBWLCH                         PWELLHELI, CAERNARVON                        0244

| Production: Zinc | Ore(tons) | Metal(tons) | Value(£) |
|---|---|---|---|
| 1880 | 40.00 | 0.00 | 140.00 |


TANYRALLT                         TALYBONT                                     0245

| Production: Lead & Silver | Ore(tons) | Lead(tons) | Silver(ozs) | Value(£) |
|---|---|---|---|---|
| 1869 | 56.00 | 37.00 | 156.00 | 0.00 |
| 1870 | 87.00 | 64.00 | 167.00 | 0.00 |
| 1871 | 32.00 | 23.50 | 0.00 | 0.00 |
| 1872–1873 No detailed return | | | | |
| 1874 | 10.20 | 7.60 | 120.00 | 165.00 |
| 1875 | 46.00 | 35.00 | 175.00 | 0.00 |
| 1876 | 95.00 | 71.20 | 451.00 | 870.00 |
| 1877 | 35.00 | 27.00 | 275.00 | 472.50 |
| 1878 | 22.00 | 16.50 | 198.00 | 181.40 |
| 1879 | 30.00 | 22.00 | 121.00 | 309.00 |
| 1880 | 40.00 | 31.50 | 301.00 | 480.00 |
| 1881 | 110.00 | 75.00 | 550.00 | 1076.60 |
| 1882 | 95.30 | 73.40 | 734.00 | 858.00 |
| 1883 | 36.10 | 28.50 | 288.00 | 267.00 |
| 1884 | 30.00 | 23.70 | 235.00 | 198.00 |
| 1885 | 21.00 | 15.00 | 160.00 | 144.00 |
| 1886 | 4.00 | 3.00 | 35.00 | 33.00 |

Ownership: 1873–1881 TANYRALLT MINING CO.; 1882–1885 CHAS.WILLIAMS &
CO.; 1886–1887 HY.MALLERY; 1888–1891 JOHN JENKINS
Comment 1869–1871 SEE TANYRALLT, CAERNARVON; 1873–1877
TANYRALT : FORMERLY WEST ALLTYCRIB

Management: Manager 1874–1879 C.HERB.STOKES
Chief Agent 1873 C.HERB.STOKES & JAS.LEEDHAM; 1874–1876 JOHN
DAVIES; 1877 JOHN SPRAGUE, 1878 JOHN DAVIES, 1879–1881 JOHN
DAVIES & CHAS.WILLIAMS; 1882–1885 CHAS.WILLIAMS; 1886–1887

TANYRALLT                TALYBONT          Continued

Employment:

| | JOHN DAVIES; 1890–1891 JOHN JENKINS | | |
|---|---|---|---|
| | Underground | Surface | Total |
| 1877 | 12 | 10 | 22 |
| 1878 | 10 | 6 | 16 |
| 1879 | 8 | 8 | 16 |
| 1880 | 9 | 4 | 13 |
| 1881 | 14 | 3 | 17 |
| 1882 | 12 | 3 | 15 |
| 1883 | 8 | 3 | 11 |
| 1884 | 2 | 6 | 8 |
| 1885 | 6 | | 6 |
| 1886 | 7 | | 7 |
| 1887 | 4 | | 4 |
| 1888–1890 | 2 | | 2 |
| 1891 | | 2 | 2 |


TEMPLE                PONTERWYD          SN 749792 0246

Production:

| Lead | Ore(tons) | Metal(tons) | Value(£) |
|---|---|---|---|
| 1887 | 3.25 | 2.50 | 20.00 |
| Zinc | Ore(tons) | Metal(tons) | Value(£) |
| 1881 | 20.00 | 8.00 | 50.00 |

Comment 1881 TEMPLE LEAD

Ownership: 1876–1877 TEMPLE LEAD MINING CO.; 1878–1883 TEMPLE LEAD
MINING CO.LTD.; 1886–1889 CARDIGAN UNITED MINES LTD.; 1908
BOOTH,BROOKS & RICHARDS; 1909–1912 ABERYSTWYTH SILVER LEAD
MINES LTD.; 1913 RICH.RICHARDS
Comment 1883 SUSPENDED; 1889 SUSPENDED; 1911–1913 IDLE

Management: Chief Agent 1876–1877 CHAS.THOMAS; 1878–1881 JOHN H.CROUCHER;
1882 JOHN DAVIES; 1886–1889 A.H.JENKS; 1908–1911 R.RICHARDS;
1912 F.C.MOORWOOD

Employment:

| | Underground | Surface | Total |
|---|---|---|---|
| 1877 | | 4 | 4 |
| 1878 | 24 | 18 | 42 |
| 1879 | 33 | 12 | 45 |
| 1880 | 20 | 14 | 34 |
| 1881 | 12 | 4 | 16 |
| 1882 | 4 | | 4 |
| 1886 | 16 | 1 | 17 |
| 1887 | 12 | 5 | 17 |
| 1888 | 11 | 2 | 13 |
| 1889 | | 1 | 1 |
| 1908 | 4 | 2 | 6 |
| 1909 | 4 | | 4 |
| 1910 | 2 | | 2 |
| 1913 | 1 | | 1 |


THOMAS UNITED             GOGINAN             0247

Production:

| Lead & Silver | Ore(tons) | Lead(tons) | Silver(ozs) | Value(£) |
|---|---|---|---|---|
| 1855 | 42.00 | 32.00 | 1088.00 | 0.00 |
| 1856 | 32.50 | 24.00 | 296.00 | 0.00 |
| 1857 | No detailed return | | | |
| Copper | Ore(tons) | Metal(tons) | Value(£) | |
| 1855 | 12.60 | 0.00 | 0.00 | |
| 1856 | 6.10 | 0.00 | 0.00 | |

Comment 1855–1856 (P)

85

TRERDDOLE                 TRER DDOLE                SN 662924 0248

Production: Copper        Ore(tons) Metal(tons)    Value(£)
           1856           1.90       0.00        0.00
           Comment 1856 (P)

TY LLWYD                RHEIDOL VALLEY            SN 695798 0249

| Production: Lead & Silver | Ore(tons) | Lead(tons) | Silver(ozs) | Value(£) |
|---|---|---|---|---|
| 1855 | 21.80 | 14.60 | 0.00 | 0.00 |
| 1856 | 45.00 | 34.20 | 151.00 | 0.00 |
| 1857 | 3.70 | 2.80 | 0.00 | 0.00 |
| 1860 | 10.50 | 7.00 | 0.00 | 0.00 |
| 1861 | No detailed return | | | |
| 1865 | 2.10 | 1.70 | 0.00 | 0.00 |
| 1866 | No detailed return | | | |
| 1875 | 40.00 | 32.50 | 201.00 | 0.00 |
| 1876 | 3.20 | 2.20 | 10.00 | 43.10 |
| 1877 | 14.00 | 10.50 | 50.00 | 175.00 |
| 1878 | 7.20 | 5.40 | 25.00 | 76.00 |

           Comment 1877-1878 NEW TYLLWYD
Ownership: 1863-1865 ATWOOD & CO.; 1873-1876 TY LLWYD SILVER LEAD MINING
           CO.; 1877-1878 TY LLWYD SILVER LEAD MINING CO.LTD.; 1886-1889
           CARDIGAN UNITED MINES LTD.; 1890 W.STAINTON
           Comment 1864-1865 SUSPENDED; 1873-1875 TYLLWYD; 1876-1878 NEW
           TYLLWYD; 1886-1888 INC.GELLIRHEIRON; 1889 INC.GELLIRHEIRON :
           SUSPENDED
Management: Chief Agent 1863 W.TREGONING; 1873-1876 JOHN PAULL; 1877 EVAN
           RICHARDS; 1878 WALT.EDDY; 1886-1889 A.H.JENKS; 1890
           W.STAINTON
           Secretary 1877 JOHN B.BALL (S)

| Employment: | Underground | Surface | Total |
|---|---|---|---|
| 1877 | 4 | | 4 |
| 1878 | 10 | 4 | 14 |
| 1886 | 10 | | 10 |
| 1887 | 6 | | 6 |
| 1888-1889 | | 1 | 1 |
| 1890 | | 3 | 3 |

           Comment 1886-1889 INC.GELLIRHEIRON

TY NANT                TALYBONT             SN 696890 0250

Production: Lead No detailed return
Ownership: 1863-1865 EVAN JONES
           Comment 1864-1865 SUSPENDED
Management: Chief Agent 1863 EVAN JONES

TYGWYN               DEVIL'S BRIDGE           SN 776777 0251

Production: Lead No detailed return
Ownership: 1869-1871 TYGWYN CO.LTD.
Management: Manager 1869-1871 JOHN TAYLOR & SONS
           Chief Agent 1869-1871 WM.MITCHELL JNR.

TYNYFRON             CWM RHEIDOL            SN 723786 0252

Production: Lead        Ore(tons) Metal(tons)    Value(£)
           1901     No detailed return
           Comment 1901 SEE YSTUMTUEN
           Zinc        Ore(tons) Metal(tons)    Value(£)
           1879         17.00      0.00       52.80

CWM RHEIDOL Continued

| Zinc | Ore(tons) | Metal(tons) | Value(£) |
|------|-----------|-------------|----------|
| 1880 | 20.00 | 0.00 | 65.00 |
| 1881 | 8.20 | 2.50 | 14.50 |
| 1896 | No detailed return | | |
| 1901 | No detailed return | | |

Comment 1896 SEE PENRHIW; 1901 SEE YSTUMTUEN

Ownership: 1868–1875 ROBT.NORTHEY; 1876–1878 NICH.BRAY & JAS.PHILLIPS; 1879–1881 TYNFRON LEAD MINING CO.; 1882–1887 NICH.BRAY & JAS.PHILLIPS; 1900–1908 RHEIDOL MINING CO.LTD.
Comment 1868 TANYFRON; 1878 TYNFRON; 1883–1887 SUSPENDED; 1889–1899 SEE PENRHIW

Management: Chief Agent 1868–1875 ROBT.NORTHEY; 1877 JOHN H.CROUCHER; 1878 JAS.PHILLIPS; 1879 J.P.THOMAS; 1880–1881 EVAN JONES; 1882–1887 JAS.PHILLIPS; 1900–1902 F.DE BAL; 1903–1908 HY.NOTTINGHAM

Employment:
| | Underground | Surface | Total |
|------|-------------|---------|-------|
| 1877–1878 | 2 | | 2 |
| 1879 | 5 | | 5 |
| 1880 | 2 | 2 | 4 |
| 1881–1882 | 2 | | 2 |
| 1889–1895 | | | |
| 1900 | 8 | | 8 |
| 1903 | 71 | 32 | 103 |
| 1904 | 78 | 36 | 114 |
| 1905 | 70 | 36 | 106 |
| 1906 | 10 | 3 | 13 |
| 1907 | 72 | 37 | 109 |
| 1908 | 32 | 31 | 63 |

Comment 1889–1895 SEE PENRHIW; 1903–1904 INC.YSTUMTUEN; 1907–1908 INC.YSTUMTUEN


TALYBONT SN 645895 0253

Ownership: 1911–1913 TALYBONT LEAD MINES LTD.
Comment 1913 IDLE

Employment:
| | Underground | Surface | Total |
|------|-------------|---------|-------|
| 1911 | 2 | | 2 |
| 1912 | 4 | | 4 |


PONTERWYD 0254

Production:
| Lead & Silver | Ore(tons) | Lead(tons) | Silver(ozs) | Value(£) |
|---------------|-----------|------------|-------------|----------|
| 1873–1874 | No detailed return | | | |
| 1875 | 93.00 | 69.00 | 300.00 | 0.00 |
| 1876 | 40.00 | 30.00 | 130.00 | 0.00 |
| 1877 | 35.00 | 26.20 | 105.00 | 437.20 |
| 1880 | 23.00 | 18.00 | 0.00 | 222.00 |
| 1881 | 77.50 | 58.10 | 0.00 | 664.00 |
| 1882 | 26.00 | 19.50 | 0.00 | 208.00 |
| 1884 | 14.00 | 10.50 | 0.00 | 78.00 |
| 1890 | 32.00 | 24.00 | 218.00 | 280.00 |
| 1891 | 36.00 | 27.00 | 138.00 | 293.00 |
| 1892 | 32.00 | 24.00 | 106.00 | 220.00 |

Comment 1873–1874 SEE GREAT WEST VAN, MONTGOMERY; 1875 SEE ALSO GREAT WEST VAN, MONTGOMERY; 1877 SEE ALSO GREAT WEST VAN, MONTGOMERY; 1884 LEAD EST

Ownership: 1872–1876 MAT.GREEN; 1877–1883 GREAT WEST VAN CO.LTD.; 1884–1887 WEST ESGAIR LLE MINING CO.; 1890 GREAT WEST VAN MINING CO.; 1891–1892 MENDIPS CO.LTD.
Comment 1887 SUSPENDED, 1892 IN LIQUIDATION

Management: Manager 1872–1874 JAS.ROACH; 1881 JAS.CORBETT

Chief Agent 1872-1874 W.BRANWELL; 1875-1876 W.BRANWELL &
THOS.HODGE; 1877-1879 W.BRANWELL; 1880 ALF.E.WENHAM;
1882-1887 ALF.E.WENHAM; 1890-1892 RICH.CLARIDGE
Secretary 1883-1887 ALF.E.WENHAM (S); 1890 J.D.A.NORRIS

| Employment: | Underground | Surface | Total |
|---|---|---|---|
| 1877 | 14 | 5 | 19 |
| 1880 | 24 | 15 | 39 |
| 1881 | 24 | 9 | 33 |
| 1882-1883 | 6 | 1 | 7 |
| 1884 | | 1 | 1 |
| 1890 | 25 | 12 | 37 |
| 1891 | 22 | 14 | 36 |
| 1892 | 22 | 10 | 32 |

VAUGHAN                           GOGINAN                       SN 694848 0255

Production:

| Lead & Silver | Ore(tons) | Lead(tons) | Silver(ozs) | Value(£) |
|---|---|---|---|---|
| 1877 | 20.00 | 15.50 | 333.00 | 287.50 |
| 1878 | 177.00 | 133.70 | 2601.00 | 2063.40 |
| 1879 | 100.00 | 72.50 | 1404.00 | 1058.50 |
| 1880 | 78.00 | 52.00 | 1055.00 | 621.70 |
| 1881 | 20.00 | 15.00 | 270.00 | 182.00 |
| 1909 | 20.00 | 14.00 | 300.00 | 168.00 |
| 1910 | 3.00 | 2.00 | 45.00 | 24.00 |

| Zinc | Ore(tons) | Metal(tons) | Value(£) |
|---|---|---|---|
| 1879 | 26.00 | 0.00 | 84.50 |
| 1880 | 38.00 | 0.00 | 72.50 |
| 1881 | 18.00 | 6.50 | 22.50 |
| 1909 | 182.00 | 55.00 | 728.00 |
| 1910 | 18.00 | 7.00 | 126.00 |

Comment 1879 VAUGHANS
Ownership:    1869-1881 VAUGHAN MINING CO.LTD.; 1882-1883 JOHN TAYLOR &
SONS; 1884-1887 VAUGHAN MINES CO.LTD.; 1907-1911 ST.JAMES'
SYNDICATE LTD.; 1912-1913 CAMBRIAN LEAD & ZINC MINING
CO.LTD.
Comment 1884-1887 SUSPENDED
Management:   Manager 1869-1881 JOHN TAYLOR & SONS
Chief Agent 1869-1876 JAS.GARLAND; 1877 JAS.GARLAND &
WM.GARLAND; 1878 WM.GARLAND; 1882-1887 THOS.GARLAND;
1907-1913 THOS.EDWARDS
Secretary 1877 H.H.OAKES; 1878-1881 JAS.GARLAND

| Employment: | Underground | Surface | Total |
|---|---|---|---|
| 1877 | 18 | 21 | 39 |
| 1878 | 29 | 27 | 56 |
| 1879 | 14 | 11 | 25 |
| 1880 | 16 | 13 | 29 |
| 1881 | 4 | 7 | 11 |
| 1882-1883 | 4 | | 4 |
| 1908 | 17 | 14 | 31 |
| 1909 | 28 | 16 | 44 |
| 1910 | 15 | 5 | 20 |
| 1911 | 6 | 1 | 7 |
| 1912-1913 | 1 | | 1 |

WELSH BROKEN HILL                                              0256

Ownership:    1891-1893 WELSH BROKEN HILL CO.; 1894 C.HERB.STOKES
Comment 1892-1894 SUSPENDED
Management:   Chief Agent 1891-1894 C.HERB.STOKES

| Employment: | Underground | Surface | Total |
|---|---|---|---|
| 1891 | 2 | | 2 |

WELSH POTOSI                    TALYBONT                    SN 735913 0257

Production: Lead & Silver    Ore(tons)   Lead(tons)  Silver(ozs)   Value(£)
            1854               200.00       155.00      1286.00       0.00
            1855               470.00       362.00      2896.00       0.00
            1856               516.00       387.50      3101.00       0.00
            1857               167.20       126.00       752.00       0.00
            1858     No detailed return
            1865-1866 No detailed return
            Comment 1858 SEE CARDIGAN CONSOLS; 1865-1866 SEE BLAENCAELAN
Ownership:  Comment 1863-1866 SEE BLAENCAELAN; 1868 SEE BLAENCAELAN


WEMYS                         DEVIL'S BRIDGE               SN 717742 0258

Production: Lead & Silver    Ore(tons)   Lead(tons)  Silver(ozs)   Value(£)
            1882               110.00        71.50        0.00       906.00
            1883               150.00       112.50        0.00      1090.00
            1884                80.00        60.00      306.00       486.00
            1885                86.00        61.00      242.00       578.00
            1886                98.00        70.00      277.00       775.00
            1887                47.00        33.50      177.00       329.00
            1888                36.00        26.00      137.00       265.00
            1889                31.00        22.00        0.00       215.00
            Comment 1882-1889 WEMYSS
            Zinc             Ore(tons)   Metal(tons)    Value(£)
            1882                45.00        19.80       99.00
            1883               125.00        50.00      311.00
            1884                45.00         0.00       92.00
            1885                72.00        21.00      116.00
            1886                30.00         8.00       29.00
            1887                26.00         8.00       39.00
            1888                17.00         5.00        0.00
            1889                26.00         7.00       45.00
            Comment 1882-1887 WEMYSS; 1888 FOR VALUE SEE RHEIDOL UNITED;
            1889 WEMYSS
Ownership:  1880-1881 WEMYS MINING CO.LTD.; 1882 WEMYS MINES LTD.;
            1883-1887 WEMYSS MINES LTD.; 1888 D.D.WEMYSS; 1889
            W.H.WEMYSS
            Comment 1883-1889 WEMYSS
Management: Chief Agent 1880-1881 RICH.GLANVILLE; 1882-1887 WM.MITCHELL;
            1888-1889 JAS.MITCHELL
            Secretary 1881 DAVID HUGHES
Employment:                 Underground     Surface        Total
            1880                25            26             51
            1881                20            18             38
            1882                24            17             41
            1883                22            14             36
            1884                 6             5             11
            1885                 6             6             12
            1886                 6             7             13
            1887                 4             6             10
            1888                 5             5             10
            1889                 4             6             10


WILLOW BANK                     TALYBONT                            0259

Production: Lead No detailed return
Ownership:  1860-1865 J.H.MURCHISON & CO.
            Comment 1863-1865 SUSPENDED
Management: Chief Agent 1860-1862 T.BOUNDY

YNYS                          TALIESIN                          0260

Production: Lead            Ore(tons) Metal(tons)    Value(£)
            1876              5.00       3.70          0.00
            1877              4.00       3.00         50.00
Ownership:  1876-1884 C.HERB.STOKES
            Comment 1882-1884 SUSPENDED
Management: Chief Agent 1878-1879 PETER WILLIAMS; 1880-1884
            C.HERB.STOKES
Employment:                 Underground    Surface       Total
            1877                6             1            7
            1878                9                          9
            1879-1880           2                          2


YNYS TUDOR                    TALIESIN                          0261

Production: Lead No detailed return
Ownership:  1880-1881 TUDOR MINING CO.; 1882 ROBT.B.STEEL; 1883 YNYS
            TUDOR MINING CO.
            Comment 1883 SUSPENDED
Management: Manager 1881 JAS.NANCARROW
            Chief Agent 1880-1883 EVAN THOMAS
            Secretary 1880-1881 ROBT.B.STEEL
Employment:                 Underground    Surface       Total
            1880                7                          7
            1881                8                          8
            1882                2                          2


YNYSHIR                       GLANDOVEY              SN 680955 0262

Ownership:  1882 GEO.PADDOCK
            Comment 1882 SUSPENDED
Management: Chief Agent 1882 GEO.PADDOCK
Employment:                 Underground    Surface       Total
            1882                2             1            3


YSTRAD EINION                 GLANDOVEY                         0263

Production: Lead & Silver    Ore(tons) Lead(tons) Silver(ozs)   Value(£)
            1891              5.00       3.50        0.00         37.00
            1892              4.00       3.00       79.00         27.00
            Zinc            Ore(tons) Metal(tons)    Value(£)
            1891             10.00       2.00         15.00
            Copper          Ore(tons) Metal(tons)    Value(£)
            1891              5.00       0.25          7.00
            1896             20.00       4.50        130.00
            1897             20.00       4.50        150.00
Ownership:  1881 ADAM MASON; 1882 ADAM MASON,T.MASON & W.SHAW; 1883-1894
            YSTRAD EINION MINING CO.; 1895-1896 ADAM MASON & W.SHAW;
            1897-1903 ADAM MASON & CO.
            Comment 1902-1903 NOT WORKED
Management: Chief Agent 1881 ADAM MASON; 1882-1890 THOS.THOMPSON;
            1896-1902 DAVID WILLIAMS
            Secretary 1892-1894 ADAM MASON
Employment:                 Underground    Surface       Total
            1882                9             2           11
            1883                7             1            8
            1884                2             1            3
            1885                4                          4
            1886                3             1            4
            1887                5                          5
            1888                6                          6

| | Underground | Surface | Total |
|---|---|---|---|
| 1889 | 8 | 1 | 9 |
| 1890 | 6 | 3 | 9 |
| 1891 | 6 | 6 | 12 |
| 1892–1894 | 2 | | 2 |
| 1895 | 4 | | 4 |
| 1896 | 8 | | 8 |
| 1897–1899 | 2 | 1 | 3 |
| 1900 | 10 | | 10 |
| 1901 | 1 | 1 | 2 |

YSTUMTUEN                       PONTERWYD                         SN 735788 0264

Production: Lead & Silver

| | Ore(tons) | Lead(tons) | Silver(ozs) | Value(£) |
|---|---|---|---|---|
| 1875 | 102.00 | 73.00 | 292.00 | 0.00 |
| 1876 | 175.00 | 131.20 | 525.00 | 2303.50 |
| 1877 | 115.00 | 86.00 | 344.00 | 1437.50 |
| 1878 | 31.60 | 24.50 | 25.00 | 300.20 |
| 1879 | 8.30 | 6.20 | 0.00 | 74.90 |
| 1880 | 5.00 | 3.70 | 0.00 | 48.20 |
| 1881 | 4.50 | 3.30 | 0.00 | 42.70 |
| 1882 | 4.00 | 3.20 | 0.00 | 32.00 |
| 1888–1895 No detailed return | | | | |
| 1901 | 10.00 | 7.00 | 41.00 | 62.00 |
| 1903 | 82.00 | 62.00 | 0.00 | 492.00 |
| 1904 | 45.00 | 34.00 | 0.00 | 292.00 |
| 1905 | 46.00 | 35.00 | 0.00 | 350.00 |
| 1906 | 27.00 | 21.00 | 0.00 | 272.00 |
| 1907 | 25.00 | 19.00 | 0.00 | 280.00 |
| 1908 | 15.00 | 11.00 | 45.00 | 106.00 |
| 1909 | 18.00 | 14.00 | 54.00 | 119.00 |
| 1910 | 35.00 | 27.00 | 105.00 | 230.00 |
| 1911 | 27.00 | 21.00 | 0.00 | 157.00 |
| 1912 | 29.00 | 22.00 | 0.00 | 286.00 |
| 1913 | 12.00 | 9.00 | 43.00 | 110.00 |

Comment 1888–1895 SEE PENRHIW; 1901 INC TYNYFRON

Zinc

| | Ore(tons) | Metal(tons) | Value(£) |
|---|---|---|---|
| 1879 | 11.60 | 0.00 | 39.40 |
| 1880 | 15.20 | 0.00 | 48.50 |
| 1881 | 3.00 | 1.40 | 9.80 |
| 1882 | 3.00 | 1.40 | 6.00 |
| 1888–1894 No detailed return | | | |
| 1896 | No detailed return | | |
| 1901 | 68.00 | 25.00 | 204.00 |
| 1903 | 1069.00 | 400.00 | 5107.00 |
| 1904 | 1267.00 | 454.00 | 5728.00 |
| 1905 | 1537.00 | 527.00 | 10259.00 |
| 1906 | 1134.00 | 380.00 | 5231.00 |
| 1907 | 992.00 | 340.00 | 4556.00 |
| 1908 | 991.00 | 317.00 | 2519.00 |
| 1909 | 527.00 | 173.00 | 2386.00 |
| 1910 | 652.00 | 213.00 | 2627.00 |
| 1911 | 669.00 | 209.00 | 2791.00 |
| 1912 | 429.00 | 134.00 | 1585.00 |
| 1913 | 382.00 | 119.00 | 1356.00 |

Comment 1888–1894 SEE PENRHIW; 1896 SEE PENRHIW; 1901
INC.TYNYFRON

Ownership: 1876–1881 YSTUMTUEN LEAD MINING CO.LTD.; 1882–1883 GEO.GREEN;
1900–1913 RHEIDOL MINING CO.LTD.
Comment 1876 YSTUMLUEN; 1883 SUSPENDED; 1886–1899 SEE
PENRHIW
Management: Chief Agent 1876 AND.WILLIAMS; 1877–1883 ROBT.UREN; 1900–1902

F.DE BAL; 1903–1913 HY.NOTTINGHAM
Secretary 1879–1881 GEO.GREEN (S)

Employment:

| | Underground | Surface | Total |
|---|---|---|---|
| 1877 | 15 | 10 | 25 |
| 1878 | 6 | 6 | 12 |
| 1879–1882 | 4 | | 4 |
| 1886–1895 | | | |
| 1900 | 12 | 12 | 24 |
| 1901 | 36 | 40 | 76 |
| 1902 | 39 | 18 | 57 |
| 1903–1904 | | | |
| 1905 | 18 | 3 | 21 |
| 1906 | 78 | 23 | 101 |
| 1907–1908 | | | |
| 1909 | 23 | 18 | 41 |
| 1910 | 31 | 16 | 47 |
| 1911 | 33 | 17 | 50 |
| 1912 | 30 | 15 | 45 |
| 1913 | 20 | 11 | 31 |

Comment 1886–1895 SEE PENRHIW; 1903–1904 SEE TYNYFRON;
1907–1908 SEE TYNYFRON


YSTWYTH             CWMYSTWYTH            0265

Production: Lead No detailed return
Ownership: 1879–1881 YSTWYTH LEAD MINING CO.; 1882–1884 YSTWYTH LEAD
MINING CO.LTD.
Comment 1884 STOPPED APR.1884
Management: Chief Agent 1879–1880 DAVID WILLIAMS; 1881 DAVID WILLIAMS &
JOHN KITTO & SON; 1882–1884 JOHN KITTO & SON

Employment:

| | Underground | Surface | Total |
|---|---|---|---|
| 1880 | 20 | 3 | 23 |
| 1881 | 20 | 4 | 24 |
| 1882 | 11 | 3 | 14 |
| 1883 | 9 | 2 | 11 |
| 1884 | 6 | | 6 |


SUNDRIES                                                  0266

Production:

| Lead & Silver | Ore(tons) | Lead(tons) | Silver(ozs) | Value(£) |
|---|---|---|---|---|
| 1867 | 30.00 | 22.50 | 0.00 | 0.00 |
| 1868 | 95.00 | 60.00 | 300.00 | 0.00 |
| 1869 | 30.00 | 20.00 | 100.00 | 0.00 |
| 1870 | 50.00 | 30.00 | 0.00 | 0.00 |
| 1872 | 20.00 | 15.00 | 0.00 | 0.00 |
| 1873 | 124.00 | 95.00 | 460.00 | 0.00 |
| 1874 | 150.00 | 105.00 | 525.00 | 0.00 |
| 1879 | 150.00 | 100.00 | 500.00 | 1545.00 |
| 1880 | 95.00 | 70.50 | 350.00 | 1073.50 |

Comment 1879–1880 SMALL LOTS

| Zinc | Ore(tons) | Metal(tons) | Value(£) |
|---|---|---|---|
| 1868 | 47.00 | 0.00 | 117.50 |
| 1871 | 16.00 | 0.00 | 60.00 |
| 1874 | 30.00 | 0.00 | 75.00 |
| 1877 | 22.00 | 0.00 | 82.00 |

Was formed in 1979 to bring
together people who are
interested in any aspect of
Welsh Mines, including their
history, preservation and
mineralogy


If you would like to join: please contact:

Dr David Roe
Welsh Mines Society
29 Somers Road,
Worcester

MINING FACSIMILIES. 41 Windsor Walk,South Anston,
                    SHEFFIELD S31 7EL.

                    ORDER FORM

Now available:
    LEAD & ZINC ORES OF DURHAM,YORKSHIRE AND DERBYSHIRE WITH
    NOTES ON THE ISLE OF MAN. R.G.Carruthers & A.Strahan. 1923.
    114 pp.,2 plates.,6 figs. ISBN 0 948079 01 0.        £8.50 net
                                                          + 42p p.& p.


    LEAD & ZINC ORES IN THE PRE-CARBONIFEROUS ROCKS OF WEST
    SHROPSHIRE AND NORTH WALES.B.Smith & H.Dewey. 1922.
    95pp.,13 figs. ISBN  0 948079 04 5.                  £8.50 net
                                                          + p.& p.

▶ LEAD & ZINC ORES OF NORTHUMBERLAND & ALSTON MOOR.1923.
   S.Smith. 110 pp.,15 plates.
   This volume deals with the geology,history and individual mines
   of this important and interesting area and has been out of print
   for many years.Chapters include:Geological relations of the
   lodes,history of mining,conditions and methods of mining,lead
   and zinc prices;detailed descriptions of the mines north of the
   Roman Wall,the Lower Tyne Area,The Derwent Valley,The Allendales,
   the Nent and South Tyne Valleys and the upper South Tyne.
                                                       £10.65 net
                                                          + p.& p.

▶ LEAD AND ZINC:THE MINING DISTRICT OF NORTH CARDIGANSHIRE
   AND WEST MONTGOMERYSHIRE. O.T.Jones.1922.
   207pp.,27 plates.,4 figs.,coloured geological/mining map.
   This very scarce book (a photocopy recently changed hands for
   £15 !)is regarded as one of the most important works on this
   ancient and fascinating mining area in Mid Wales.Its large size
   (207 pages)allied to the inclusion of many maps and plans and
   replete with the fine full-colour fold-out geological/mining
   map as a frontispiece (approx 19"x 17") will unfortunately make
   this an expensive reprint.However,like others in the series,it
   will be limited to 250 copies thus making it a collector's item
   in its own right. The price will be £19.95 net + p.& P.

▶ To be published subject to viability of demand.
All titles are presented in an attractive hard-wearing laminated binding.